KU-794-629

LEEDS BECKETT UNIVERSITY
Leeds Metropolitan University

17 0113896 0

Creative Destruction

Creative Destruction

A Six-Stage Process for Transforming the Organization

RICHARD L. NOLAN
Harvard Business School

and

DAVID C. CROSON
*Harvard Business School and
Wharton School of Business,
University of Pennsylvania*

HARVARD BUSINESS SCHOOL PRESS
Boston, Massachusetts

LEEDS METROPOLITAN
UNIVERSITY LIBRARY
1701138960
B125V
259177 12.7.95
658.406 NoL
1-3 JUL 1995 £22.50

Copyright © 1995 by Richard L. Nolan and David C. Croson
All rights reserved
Printed in the United States of America
99 98 97 96 95   5 4 3 2 1

Library of Congress Cataloging-in-Publication Data
Nolan, Richard L.
    Creative destruction : a six-stage process for transforming
the organization / Richard L. Nolan and David C. Croson.
        p.   cm.
    Includes index.
    ISBN 0-87584-498-7 (acid free paper)
    1. Organizational change.   2. Information technology.
3. Industrial management.   I. Croson, David C.   II. Title.
HD58.8.N64   1995
658.4'063—dc20   94-39671
                                                          CIP

The paper used in this publication meets the requirements of
the American National Standard for Permanence of Paper for
Printed Library Materials Z39.49–1984.

Contents

Preface

We have experienced an incredible learning journey through researching and writing this book. Although we met as teacher and student in the MBA classroom at the Harvard Business School, our roles have reversed and rereversed so many times in the course of research that a mutually complementary collegial learning team has emerged. This manuscript, which blends years of practical experience with the insights and explanations from economic theory, is the result of our persistent effort to understand what, exactly, "business transformation" is and how to best manage it.

Our work has its roots in original research conducted at the Harvard Business School by Professors Neil C. Churchill (now at Babson College), James L. McKenney, F. Warren McFarlan, and Richard L. Nolan in the 1970s; an outcome of the research was the Stages Theory of computer growth. This theory about the organizational learning of computers in business was basic to the dozen *Harvard Business Review* articles authored or coauthored by the Harvard Business School research team on the various aspects of managing computers. These articles provided advice to general managers on choosing leadership for the Information Systems (IS) function, strategic IS planning, implementing database and minicomputer setups, applying computer-based modeling techniques, considering how to intelligently charge for internal computer services, forming executive steering committees, and anticipating emerging issues associated with information technology such as personal privacy.

This research also provided the intellectual foundation for the launch of consulting firm Nolan, Norton & Co., cofounded by Richard L. Nolan and David P. Norton, Doctor of Business Administration (Harvard), 1972. Nolan, Norton & Co. assisted general managers in developing information systems and strategic plans and was merged into KPMG Peat Marwick in

1987. In 1991, Nolan rejoined the Harvard Business School faculty to continue his research on managing information technology in complex organizations. The "stages" advocated in this manuscript represent a 1990s return to the original Stages Theory spirit of organizational learning, and bear only a superficial resemblance to the benchmarking Stages used in Nolan, Norton & Co. practice.

Upon Nolan's return to the faculty, Professors McFarlan and Nolan conducted a seminar on business transformation with a group of CEOs. At this seminar, McFarlan and Nolan stated strong views, carefully listened to by the CEO audience, and were appropriately challenged with emotion and vigor. Of high interest was Nolan's conclusion that most firms could immediately downsize their work forces by 50 percent with no impact on revenue. Nolan's evidence on his position, however, was sketchy. David Croson, then a student in Harvard University's Ph.D. program in business economics, suggested that a theoretical explanation might be provided for Nolan's assertion that "half size was right size"—or, at least, that "full size was wrong size." The theoretical explanation was based upon the hypothesis that slack had built up in the organization during implementation of computers, but this slack had not been fully converted to real economic benefits due to incompleted downsizing. Over the ensuing summer months, we collected case data and built a simulation model to explore the theoretical process of building up organizational slack and releasing it through downsizing, whereby drastically fewer workers could maintain previous revenue levels.

During this investigation, we expanded our research team to include Katherine Seger Weber, HBS research associate and casewriter for the MBA first-year course "Information, Organization, and Control," for which Nolan served as course head. Matthew MacKay, an undergraduate economics and history major at Harvard University, worked with the research team during the summer of 1992, making important contributions to the business history of organizational change and industrial economy management principles. In fall 1992, this team had produced a research base for assessing the role of information technology in business transformation. Several of our colleagues at Harvard, as well as at other universities, provided valuable comments and constructive criticism at this point.

By spring 1993, our research had progressed to the point where we could hypothesize (and argue convincingly) that the generic organization structure of the information economy is some type of information technology (IT)-enabled network. Accordingly, we extended our investigation to specify the economic foundations of the IT-enabled network.

It was then that we gained the confidence to directly confront the major issue of business transformation: the formulation of a coherent set of management principles for the IT-enabled network of the information economy. Today's practices still hearken back to the management principles of the industrial economy and are, as a group, far from appropriate for the coming information economy. We believe that our new set of 20 management principles provides a sound foundation for executives to build information economy IT-enabled networks with the strength and structures necessary for the fast-paced, sophisticated competition seen in the 1990s and beyond.

Our learning journey was exciting, though exhausting, and well worth the commitment of time and effort. It was also worth, we hope, the time that we extracted from the busy schedules of our colleagues and practicing executives, who were so generous with it.

In this book, then, we propose a new set of management principles that must be understood, critically refined, and adopted by management. Of course, in the spirit of a customer-driven orientation, our readers must be the final arbiters of the importance of our contribution with respect to the effective implementation of these principles through our proposed six-stage implementation process.

Acknowledgments

Having tried to credit as equitably as possible those numerous individuals who have helped us in this effort, we apologize for any inadvertent omissions. If there were a way to make all the people on this list part owners of this project, we would gratefully do so.

Our deepest thanks goes to our spouses, Pamela M. Nolan and Rachel T.A. Croson, without whose support we would never have gotten past the drafting stage. We are also grateful to Katherine Seger Weber, who put in many hours on this project (often on short notice) and generated reviews and questions of extraordinary depth; Sean P. Nolan, for his anecdotes on life at Microsoft and the analogies between IT and living systems; Matthew MacKay, for his insights on business history and the evolution of control systems; Steve Bradley, Jim Cash, John L. King, F. Warren McFarlan, Nitin Nohria, Nick Palmer, and Len Schlesinger for their critical reviews in the early stages; and Bruce McHenry for volunteering to test the new management principles through a survey of 400 computer firms.

For extraordinary support through the entire process, we would like to thank Carol Franco of the Harvard Business School Press, Mary Kennedy, Professor F. Warren McFarlan in his role as senior associate dean and director of research, and Dean John McArthur. We are also very grateful to John Simon for developmental editing and to Julie Hogenboom for her expert copyediting.

And, finally, for their contributions to the professional literature, some of whom are quoted specifically in the manuscript, and their stimulating intellectual discourse, which cannot be so captured, we want to thank Harvard Professors Lynda M. Applegate, Chris Argyris, Christopher A. Bartlett, Stephen P. Bradley, James I. Cash, Richard E. Caves, Robert G. Eccles, David A. Garvin, Robert H. Hayes, Michael C. Jensen, Robert S. Kaplan, Gary Loveman, Anita McGahan, James L. McKenney, D. Quinn Mills, Donna B. Stoddard, John J. Sviokla, and Karen Hopper Wruck; MIT Professor Erik Brynjolfsson; Mr. Bruce McHenry; Dartmouth Professor Daniel Bryan Quinn; IBM Director of Executive Education Stephan H. Haeckel; Florida Atlantic Professor Stephen Zeff; and Harvard Business School doctoral candidates Christopher Marshall and Hossam Golal.

Creative Destruction

Chapter One

The Need for Organizational Transformation

WHAT'S GOING on here? This is the question that CEOs most frequently and fervently ask behind closed doors. Margins are tighter and the risk of any misstep plunging a promising year of performance into the red is much higher than ever before. Operational slack to hide mistakes has thinned or vanished altogether. Tried and proven management practices are breaking down faster than coherent new practices are emerging. Size, once a competitive advantage and barrier to entry, has become a liability as new entrants, who seem to be competing by a different set of rules, forgo the huge investments needed to achieve economies of scale. Viewed not so long ago as a crutch for weaker firms, the outsourcing of activities such as logistics and information technology is today called a strategic alliance, a competitive weapon used by well-managed, stronger firms. Job creation over the past 30 years, on balance, has been by newer companies with fewer than 100 employees, not by the corporate giants widely characterized today as lumbering dinosaurs.

With everything they thought they knew about managing a business being challenged, many CEOs are—or should be—questioning their ability to sustain their enterprises into the twenty-first century. The many businesses that disappeared during the 1980s and 1990s will surely be joined by more. Within the last few years, CEOs of such household-name companies as General Motors, Westinghouse, Sears, and IBM have been asked to step down by their boards of directors. But the bigger story is the transformation of major firms like Motorola, General Mills, General Electric, PepsiCo, ABB (Asea, Brown Boveri), and AT&T, as well as the creation of new major companies in previously non-existent industries like FedEx, ADP (Automatic Data Processing), and Microsoft.

To be answered, the disarmingly simple question "What's going on here?" must be broken down into more specific questions:

Why is the business environment now so volatile and seemingly contradictory?

Why is it so hard to make effective and lasting changes to my organization to cope with the new business environment?

So what should I do?

"Why Is the Business Environment Now So Volatile and Seemingly Contradictory?"

The answer to this first question is that we are in the throes of an epic economic transformation, which is placing extraordinary demands on today's executives requiring:

- Mastery of new information technologies (we will often use the abbreviated form, "IT") of computing and networking, equivalent in power and pervasiveness to the steam engine technology of the industrial economy
- Mastery of new organizational structures, such as the IT-enabled network organization, that leverage information technology as successfully as the M-form (multidivisional) functional hierarchy leveraged industrial economy technology
- Mastery of managing a new dominant sector of employment, *professional entrepreneurs*, freed up by revolutionary productivity gains in industrial activity

The transition from industrial to what is being characterized as an information economy is neither the first, nor likely to be the last, transformation to bring about radical changes in the rules of economic and business activity. The United States' transformation from an agrarian to an industrial economy, precipitated by the invention and refinement of the steam engine, occurred more than a century ago.[1] Figure 1-1 highlights the revolutionary productivity gains in food production—in excess of 1,000 percent—that resulted from this earlier transformation. The 4 percent of the labor force directly involved in agriculture in 1945 produced more than 50 percent of the U.S. labor force so engaged in 1845. Also shown, for comparison, is a parallel transformation, a shrinking of the labor force directly involved

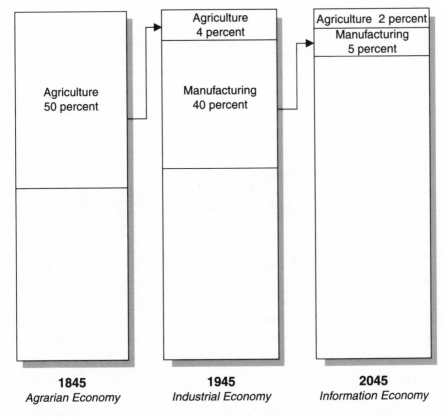

Figure 1-1. *U.S. Workforce Distribution in Agrarian, Industrial, and Information Economies*
Source: *Making Things Better: Competing in Manufacturing* (Washington, D.C.:
Office of Technology Assessment, 1991.).

in manufacturing in the industrial economy from 40 percent to less than 5 percent in the information economy.[2]

In the former economic transformation, productivity gains accrued to the union of new organization and new technology as family farms were consolidated into agribusinesses and animal power was supplanted by machine power. The farm labor force was displaced or redeployed for the most part, into industrial activity such as steel making, automobile manufacturing, and appliance manufacturing. Industrial activity demanded not only new structures for organizing, but also new principles for managing resources. Similarly, information activity demands not only new structures for organizing but also new principles for managing resources. We are very close to being a full-fledged information economy, and the necessity for new management principles is now making itself apparent to the discerning CEO. New technology or new structures alone are not enough.

"Why Is It So Hard to Make Effective and Lasting Changes to My Organization to Cope with the New Business Environment?"

Organizational inertia undermines all but the most aggressive, long-term, CEO-led transformation campaigns. The CEO's first responsibility in organizational transformation is to recognize organizational inertia for the enormous barrier that it is and take aggressive actions to eliminate its sources. There are four main sources of organizational inertia that need to be confronted.

1. Business as usual. Traditional annual planning commences with a request for sales forecasts from business units. These are reviewed by corporate staff to ensure that the aggregate total is sufficiently ambitious to generate respectable performance for the coming year. With sales forecasts approved, each functional area is asked to prepare expense and capital budgets based on a set of projected activities derived from the sales forecasts.

Excessive revenue gains are as dangerous as revenue shortfalls. Revenue "spikes," associated with significant change in some aspect of the total organization-market relationship, imply risk, which is the antithesis of careful planning. Managers, evaluated for promotion on the basis of operating performance, want at all costs to avoid risk, as one severe fluctuation could wipe out years of careful planning and incremental improvements.

The traditional accounting framework translates sales forecasts into numbers of workers and salespeople, materials requirements, and other measurable performance goals. Linearity is the order of the day; if it takes 5 salespeople to generate revenues of $500,000, it must require 10 salespeople to generate revenues of $1 million. Managers know that these approximations are unrealistic, but the available forecasting technology limits use of more sophisticated techniques. Hiring is perceived to be a necessary precursor to growth. Consequently, steady growth in revenues translates into steady growth in employment, with a flat or downward trend in revenue per employee.

Once locked in, annual sales forecasts and budgets are converted to monthly budgets. New targets are established and execution plans implemented to meet them on the first day of the fiscal year, and continue throughout the 12 months of the fiscal year. The accounting department—a divisionalized staff function—monitors monthly progress toward targets. Even today, the folklore has it that managers who do not meet their budgets are "taken out behind the shed and shot." Daily stories in *The Wall Street Journal* about senior executives replaced for failing to meet financial performance objectives reinforce for middle managers the importance of meeting budgets and targets.

Financial audits by the "big six" public accounting firms ensure uniformity of fiscal-year measurement and reporting of financial performance. The impact of a "clean" audit opinion and the power of the big six's collective monopoly on providing credible audit opinions should not be underestimated. Although continuous audits are required by law for only a few firms, an up-to-date audit has become the equivalent of a résumé for any company seeking expansion possibilities or capital. Banks require audited financial statements to approve even the safest working capital requests.

Cost stability among competitors is further reinforced by common compensation and performance measurement infrastructures. The ubiquity of the famous Hay Point compensation system,[3] for example, provides a common basis for evaluating jobs and compensating workers, giving rise to a tacit pricing system in the labor market for top and middle management. Labor unions are responsible for similar uniformity in production worker wages. Similar costs lead to similar prices for products and services.

Planning factors[4] institutionalized in return on investment (ROI) methods ensure steady growth in capital budgets so long as revenues continue their "northeastward march" in the annual report.[5]

Such planning considerations are purely internal; the customer is not recognized except as a component of a sales forecast. Top executives tune the functional hierarchy to the firm's market environment via the relative allocation of decision-making authority between corporate and divisional units (i.e., centralization and decentralization, respectively). Centralizing decision making tends to improve efficiency by squeezing out slack through tighter control; decentralizing decision making facilitates more effective responses to unique market conditions.

External strategic planning emphasizes control of suppliers and distributors through vertical integration and the exercise of market power. Firms with steady growth and high profit margins want to ensure against raw material shortages shutting down scarce productive capacity, or retail blockages causing finished product to accumulate in warehouses, preventing completion of the normal cycle back into cash. Vertical integration complements mergers and acquisitions, and traditional forms of horizontal integration, as a common approach to growth.

Does this sound familiar? As the sustaining force behind the status quo, hierarchy represents the starting point for any organizational transformation. Because restructuring is risky and potentially very costly, organizational inertia will foster continued tacit acceptance of the functional hierarchy. Hierarchy doesn't have to justify itself; the burden of proof of a superior organizational form falls on the challenger.

If this description characterizes your firm, as it does most, you have a major challenge in initiating a transformation campaign.

2. IT that locks in "business as usual." Spreadsheets can help in modernizing paperwork, but can be dangerous in that they can just as easily be used to preserve the status quo. The ease of applying new technology to old principles has a well-documented history. Over a period of three decades, during which they have assimilated three distinctive forms of IT into various management functions, firms have experienced three S-shaped learning curves, each characterized by a particular target market focus and application paradigm (see Figure 1-2).[6]

During what has been termed the data processing (DP) era (1960–1980), the focus was on automating manual transaction processing systems; during the microcomputer era (1980–1995), on leveraging professional workers (e.g., engineers, financial analysts, and managers) by employing computers to access, analyze, and present data. Both of these application orientations—automating, and what has been termed "informating"—had an internal focus.[7]

The emerging network era (from about 1990, overlapping with the micro era) is a consequence of the fusing of computer and telecommunications technology.[8] Interfirm integration of these technologies allows for a new firm structure termed the IT-enabled network, more suited to competition in the global marketplace.

IT has slowly and relentlessly penetrated every nook and cranny of organizations. In some cases, it has completely subsumed procedures once done by employees (e.g., payroll). In others, IT has changed procedures

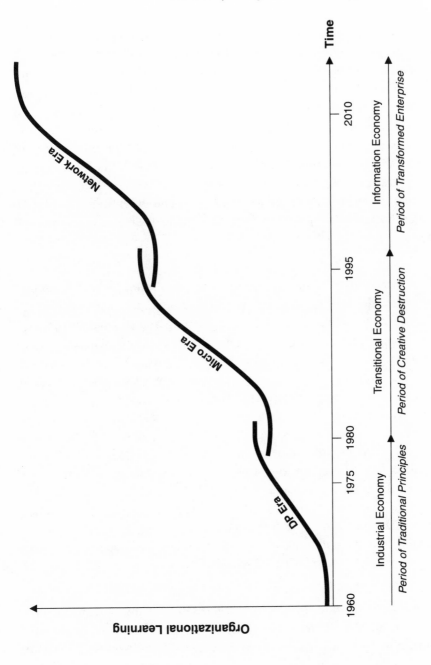

Figure 1-2. Three S-shaped-Curve Eras of Organizational Learning

that involved both employees and information technology (e.g., new product design and customer account maintenance).

For many organizations the software embedded in their computer applications—some of it developed internally, a great deal purchased from outside firms—has become a prerequisite to opening the doors to do business. Seldom does this software exhibit a coherent architecture and rarely is it part of an overall management strategy.[9] Yet any change in organizational operations or structure is contingent on an IT reengineering effort. Restructuring the IT architecture is a major barrier to transformation of older firms, and can engender frustrations and expenses from failed IT projects that are likely to devolve into a major source of organizational inertia.

3. Not evolving into an IT-enabled organizational form. The process through which new technologies enable new organizational forms is both iterative and cumulative. It is both a learning and discovery process as greater experience with IT is accumulated. The evolution of organizational forms at the firm level eventually transforms organization structures at the industry level.[10] Widespread adoption of new network-based forms of organization has altered the structural environment of competition. Smaller firms in the computer industry are now more agile than fragile; the rate of infant mortality among high-tech start-ups pales in comparison to geriatric decay in larger, older firms. This environment is *not* business as usual, and to manage it as such leads to a vicious cycle of cost-cutting just to stay alive. Yet our research suggests that many senior executives lack an understanding of the interaction between available technology and appropriate organizational form. The result is perpetual setbacks from hanging onto the traditional organization too long and not actively managing toward the more efficient IT-enabled network.

4. Workers are not going to fire themselves. Another main driver of inertia is so obvious that it is likely to be missed. It is common for a transformed firm to require 30 to 50 percent fewer workers to produce the same level of output. Workers are not ignorant of this and will fight to hold on as long as they can. Employees who have not signed on as partners in transformation will creatively undermine the best-laid plans and most well-thought out rationales. To assume otherwise is naive.

Understanding that we are in the midst of a fundamental economic transition is important for proceeding to identifying the needs of the senior management team in mastering new aspects of managing technology, organization, and workers. Understanding the incredible barrier of organizational inertia and its main sources is important for realizing that conventional change approaches will not work.[11] Surviving the economic transition and overcoming organizational inertia provide the context for answering the question, "So what should I do?"

"So What Should I Do?"

You should make a newly transformed organizational structure the target of revolutionary change, and manage a process of doable change to make the new IT-enabled organization a reality. This process requires senior management to acquire an understanding of management principles and the change process that is deeper than what has been required up to now.

Management Principles

Management principles are the foundation on which senior management establishes the policies and procedures for operating the organization. They serve as rules of thumb, incorporating existing wisdom so that each new problem doesn't have to be analyzed from scratch. Often these policies and procedures are referred to by inference as management practices, which are the specific implementation of these rules of thumb. The set of management principles for the functional hierarchies of the industrial economy was established so long ago that today's managers generally implement these management practices by default, without thinking about whether a practice is consistent with the underlying management principles specific to their own organization. Nevertheless, senior management discovers and rediscovers the problem of conflict between principles and practice as their firms struggle with survival. Downsizing, for instance, necessitates communication patterns across organization boundaries, which violates traditional communication principles; quality initiatives necessitate teamwork, which violates traditional authority, performance measurement, and compensation principles. After a while, so many management practices are in conflict with one another that exceptions to policies become the rule and further growth becomes stagnation.

The confusion will worsen until a new set of management principles is expressly redefined for relevance and coherence. Our approach is to identify an accepted set of management principles of the industrial economy organization, describe a new set for the information economy organization, and specify a creative destruction process for managing the transformation from the old set to the new. Just knowing where you are and where you're going is not enough; you need to know how to get there, too.

Economic theory underlies these sets of management principles, although most managers need not worry about the theoretical framework. In the industrial economy, classical economic theory emphasized optimizing outputs from scarce resources while moving toward equilibrium. Scarce resources included men, materials, and money (the 3 Ms) and sometimes was broadened to KLEM (Capital, Labor, Energy, and Materials). The resulting economic models and frameworks largely relegate the entrepreneur and technology to "external forces" to be dealt with as exceptions.

Equilibrium-oriented economics is of little use to CEOs who have endured more than a decade of disequilibrium. Entrepreneurs opportunistically shift resources from areas of low to areas of higher productivity. Success in the 1990s relies on mobilizing organizations to accomplish such resource shifts. Hence, professional entrepreneur is a more appropriate characterization of the successful manager of the 1990s than professional bureaucrat, a term sometimes applied to the traditional manager promoted from within and oriented toward maintaining and improving, rather than changing, the existing order of operations.

Economist Joseph Schumpeter postulated, in sharp contrast to the classical economists' notions of optimization and equilibrium, that the norm is not equilibrium but dynamic disequilibrium. Entrepreneurial activity and technological change is not the exception but the rule. Dynamic disequilibrium is caused by entrepreneurs engaged in a process of creative destruction as they dismantle the old order of economic activity (technological, organizational, and managerial) and simultaneously invent and build a new one.[12] Disequilibrium and creative destruction provide a much sounder foundation for understanding what is happening to business today.

Although he did not realize it, cross-disciplinary scholar Max Weber complemented Schumpeter's research by formally defining hierarchical principles for organizing work.[13] The common objective of industrial economy functional hierarchies is the mass production of goods and services for profit. The hierarchy evolved to maximize the competitive leverage of prevailing energy-oriented technologies and labor markets, giving rise to a cost structure characterized by massive economies of scale and fungible workers.[14] Accordingly, industry concentration was relatively high even at broad levels; a small number of competitors inhabited any given product market by virtue of minimum efficient size requirements. Entry and exit were slow, restricted by large capital investments. Clearly delineated boundaries separated employees and resources inside from customers and markets outside the organization.

In this industrial economy environment, General Motors' CEO Alfred Sloan was instrumental in devising management structures that put into practice Weber's notions of bureaucracy in business;[15] DuPont was the first major organization to practice "divisionalization."[16] Peter Drucker, long-time consultant to General Motors and influenced by Schumpeter and Weber, developed and documented the practical principles of hierarchical management.[17] Exhibit 1-1 is a summary of these industrial economy management principles, the organizational results of which—a formal functional hierarchy—are familiar to all.[18]

General Electric, to relax the strict functional organization that prevailed within divisions, subsequently introduced the concept of strategic business units, or SBUs.[19] Divisionalization and SBUs, while generally conforming to the principles of functional organization, make concessions to decentralization in task allocation: they break the organization into centralized functions to be carried out by the corporate office and decentralized functions to be carried out by operating units.

Today, the workings of the functional hierarchy are still embedded in various ways in all but the least formal organizations, providing a sameness in the way that they operate. A big problem, for example, is that the heart of the functional hierarchy beats only once per year, its rhythm institutionalized in the planning process and annual budget cycle whose frequencies are dictated by the fiscal year, an artificial construct imposed by tax law and accounting, and one that is becoming increasingly supplanted by the faster pace of real-time computer technology.

Such modern information technologies are resulting in the mining of raw information to the point that the world's recorded knowledge base is doubling every seven years. As a result, emerging economic theory is expanding the collection of key resources to include information and ideas. Information and ideas as resources have different characteristics than the more traditional scarce resources of materials or labor. For example, infor-

Hierarchy principle: The organization is structured into a three-tiered hierarchy: top management over middle management, and middle management over production workers.

Functional principle: Tasks are organized into fixed functions of line and staff, based upon type of expertise. Line tasks directly relate to making or selling, and staff tasks support these activities.

Centralization/decentralization principle: Organizations are divided internally into a corporate group and divisions—the M-form. Centralized shared activities are carried out by the corporate group and decentralized operations are carried out by the divisions.

Leadership principle: Senior management's role is to set strategy, and explicitly design organization structures and control systems for implementing this strategy.

Strategic-orientation principle: Organization is driven by the physical activities required to produce or distribute the product or service.

Task principle: Tasks are carried out within functions, which are designed for self-sufficiency, minimizing the required communications among tasks and functions. Maximum task independence is the result.

Cycle time principle: The cycle time for making major resource allocation decisions is the fiscal year. Budgeting and financial decision making is driven by the accounting cycle.

Worker-class principle: Workers are divided into categories of white-collar workers, who design the way work is to be carried out, and blue-collar workers, who execute or carry out the actual work.

Information principle: Information flows follow the "chain of command" (the authority sequence in the hierarchy) based upon "need-to-know."

Communication principle: Communications are formal and paper based.

Supervision principle: Supervision is based upon direct observation of workers, and accountability is based on supervisory responsibilities.

Reward principle: Pay is based on responsibility, loyalty, and seniority as reflected by position in the hierarchy.

Span-of-control principle: Span of control of a manager is 6 to 10 subordinates as limited by ability to directly observe and supervise workers.

Exhibit 1-1. Industrial Economy Management Principles

mation is not consumed with use. In fact, the value of the information resource may be increased with use, such as information about a more efficient way to produce a product in a plant for a firm with multiple plants, or access to a cheaper interest rate for a firm with a healthy appetite for capital.

The creation of knowledge is as vital to the modern business enterprise as the creation of capital. The knowledge-creation process—comprising observation, analysis, and learning—is depicted in Figure 1-3. Advances in IT have enabled companies to harness the benefits of information as never before, to achieve new levels of production, and to conduct business in ways that were previously impossible.

In manufacturing, advanced IT enables immediate, unfiltered communication with the shop floor, effectively slicing through layers of hierarchy and action-impeding red tape. This facilitates more timely execution, and instant demand projection and order confirmation systems that govern the loading and dispatch of trucks and railroad cars; coupled with dynamic

Figure 1-3. Knowledge Creation

direction and redirection of goods in transit, advanced information technology holds the potential to eliminate altogether the need for intermediate storage facilities.

In services, the difference is even more pronounced. Former Citibank chairman Walter Wriston's observation that "information about money has become more valuable than money itself" is instructive. What Wriston was suggesting is that success in the financial arena today relies on precise knowledge of the whereabouts of money and favorable investment opportunities worldwide, not a massive capital base.[20] The new barrier to entry excludes slow firms rather than small ones.

Unsalvageable, Salvageable, and New Principles

For some old management principles, alas, there is simply no place in the information economy. Others can continue to be useful if radically rethought with respect to the changing character of work. Finally, some entirely new principles must be creatively constructed and assimilated.

The transition that organizations must face is a well-structured and gradual one, consisting of six stages; the transition that executives must face is a fuzzy and sudden one, not a piecemeal process of changing one principle to another twenty times but a holistic process of moving from one set of principles to another. An "unsalvageable" principle means one that is in the old set, but not the new; a "salvageable" principle means one that is in both sets, and a "new" principle means one that is in the new set but not the old. The divisions among unsalvageable, salvageable, and new in the proposed set of information economy management principles focus on forming the IT-enabled network organization from the functional hierarchy.[21]

Mainstay principles of hierarchical design that must be cast away are the three-tier structure, and the arrangement of an organization into a corporate group and divisions, along with functions and departments. To attempt to salvage these principles will only hinder organizational evolution. Organizations that control and channel information solely through hierarchical structures cannot compete in the information-rich global marketplace. Such firms, hopelessly hobbled by a structural design that prevents them from exploiting the myriad possibilities available from external databases and other accumulations of information, enter the information economy at a distinct competitive disadvantage.

While the hierarchical design as a viable organizational form may not be completely dead, hierarchy as the default organizational form is not only moribund but festering.

To replace the set of industrial economy principles in Exhibit 1-1, we propose the set of 20 management principles shown in Exhibit 1-2, half salvaged and half new, that we believe to be essential to survival in the information economy.[22]

In developing these 20 management principles, we started with an inventory of industrial economy practices characteristic of the M-form functional hierarchy. We then derived 13 management principles that underlie the management practices shown in Figure 1-2. From this starting point, we reviewed contemporary management literature and case studies of successful firms and developed a second inventory of management practices—some similar to industrial economy practices, some entirely different. From this second list, we derived the 20 management principles for effective information economy firms.

We also used simulation modeling to test the coherence and completeness of the new management principles in situations like downsizing, where objectives are clear-cut and measurement is relatively straightforward. Finally, we collaborated with two MIT researchers, Erik Brynjolfsson and Bruce McHenry, in an empirical test of the patterns of adoption of the proposed management principles as well as the elimination of obsolete hierarchical management principles.[23] For this test, our group chose to survey firms in the computer industry on the grounds that there are many young firms in this industry, competition is fierce, and the firms typically operate with a global scope.

An analysis of the survey results of the 400 firms showed a clear distinction in performance between firms that comprehensively adopted the new management principles and those that clung to industrial economy management principles, which were typically the older firms.

All 20 information economy management principles positively correlated with financial performance. One other principle, "The company has a strong mission statement, which executives are held accountable for upholding," was not directly included in our proposed set of twenty information economy management principles, but also strongly separated industrial economy from information economy firms. Its significance in the survey underlines the importance of having a clear shared organizational

1. Leadership principle: Senior management formulates and coordinates the firm's vision, and plays a central role in defining projects.

2. Span-of-control principle: Span of control is variable, and limited by resource availability, not by supervisors' capacity to monitor workers.

3. Supervision principle: Supervision is indirect, through results assessment, versus direct worker observation.

4. Reward principle: Rewards are performance-based, not position-based.

5. Worker-class principle: All employees are treated as a uniclass of knowledge workers, versus the two-class system of white-/blue-collar workers.

6. Value creation principle: All activities of the firm must be justified by their role in maximizing customer value.

7. Information principle: All organization members have open access to all information, instead of restricting the flow based on "need-to-know."

8. Coordination principle: Firm activities are made purposeful and efficient through extensive flows of information, which enable workers to anticipate and expediently correct problems using informed discretion.

9. Dynamic balancing principle: The firm's surplus is monitored in real time, and equitably distributed to stakeholders based on current information.

10. Task principle: Work is organized into projects, and carried out by team members assigned to these projects based upon their expertise necessary to accomplish the project goals.

11. Architect principle: Senior management shapes the firm's structure through the design and redesign of infrastructures necessary for the operation of self-designed teams.

12. Strategic orientation principle: The strategic orientation of the firm is serving customers' needs, versus manufacturing the product or service.

13. Team principle: Teams are formed by leaders offering compensation packages intended to attract knowledge workers with the expertise needed to achieve project objectives.

14. Communication principle: Communication is swift, spontaneous, and point-to-point, unlike paper memos and formal face-to-face meetings.

15. Authority principle: Authority for resource allocation is continuously changing and is awarded to workers who are the most effective decision makers.

16. Cycle time principle: Resource allocation decisions are made in real time instead of on the fiscal year cycle.

17. Control principle: Control is made efficient through extensive performance feedback information, and self-interest-based reward systems which act to motivate workers to maintain high levels of performance.

Exhibit 1-2. Information Economy Management Principles

Exhibit 1-2. (Continued)

---

18. Conflict resolution principle: Conflict between the firm and customers, employees, shareholders, or suppliers is expediently mediated by senior managers; use of third party mediation is the exception.

19. Opportunity principle: Activity is oriented toward fast-changing global market opportunities rather than overcoming organizational inertia.

20. Boundary principle: Organization boundaries are organic—continuously expanding and contracting—as various network relationships are added and subtracted from the firm.

Shaded entries designate principles salvaged from the industrial economy; unshaded entries designate new management principles.

vision, which we have advocated as a prerequisite to successful transformation, and also underscores the idea that the set of information economy management principles is still evolving.

The Process of Creative Destruction

Creative destruction, generally speaking, is the process of adopting new ideas and abandoning the corresponding older ones.[24] In the context of organizational transformation, we use the term to refer to the sequence of events attending the shift between coherent sets of management principles, technologies, and organization. This change should be implemented as a conscious decision before it is required. When a new electronic technology becomes cost-effective, the technology it replaces becomes a curious artifact. So should it be with organizational technology; old organizational structures should not be permitted to disintegrate from cumulative strain, but should be shed while still functioning.[25]

The process of creative destruction involves adding, eliminating, and redeploying employees at many different levels and causes flux in the interfaces between hierarchical levels while traditional authority-based relationships give way to the influences of market-based elements. Even when the starting and ending points are relatively clear, the process does not proceed like traditional change. Broad, comprehensive control processes are required to maintain profitable day-to-day operations in the face of the organizational instability while the firm moves toward the IT-enabled network organization. Consequently, the transition from one set of management principles to another usually takes the form of a series of discrete, "chunks" of improvements over time. A company must keep a firm grip on its established core resources even as it reevaluates their appropriateness. Little will be gained from a new plan without the employees and resources needed to implement it.

New management principles often conflict with existing practice and thus temporarily produce negative side effects for other operations.[26] The dissonance likely to result from this hybrid set of principles cloaks the transition and makes it look like a negative progress. This confusion, a sign of impending success, is the sign of the chrysalis; many firms, however, misinterpreting it, choose to give up at this stage.

As a well-managed sequence of preliminary changes in practice, transformation initiatives may appear to be merely a series of incremental improvements. It is OK—and desirable—that organizational change proceed at a measured pace. But there is also a radical element to transformation: acceptance of new management principles must occur "all at once" at the launch of the initiative. Changes in practice are thus evolutionary, changes in principles revolutionary.

Overcoming Organizational Inertia

A treacherous inclination can arise: inertia causes resistance to casting off obsolete principles, changing salvageable ones, and adopting badly needed new ones. Understanding inherent biases toward the status quo is the first step toward overcoming this inertia before crisis takes place. Mistaking transformation for incremental change is safe; mistaking incremental change for transformation, perilous.

In assessing present circumstances, we see parallels with what Alfred Sloan likely experienced when he took the reins of General Motors in the 1920s. The new management principles for the industrial economy were evident in practice in a number of organizations, but required an integrator such as Sloan to demonstrate the phenomenal economic impact of their collective and comprehensive practice. Sloan's contributions documenting this challenge seventy years ago are still useful today.

The new challenge is vividly described by the following metaphor, used by one CEO to dramatize the magnitude of the transformation challenge that he faced:

> Creative destruction is like undertaking the complete rebuilding of the *Mayflower* into the *Queen Elizabeth II* during the voyage from

Plymouth, England, to Plymouth, Massachusetts, without disrupting the full and normal complement of services to passengers.

The Six-Stage Process of Transforming the Organization

The white-water raft trip of transformation necessarily begins with the existing organizational structure. For older, larger firms, this is generally the institutionalized M-form functional hierarchy. Most firms surviving today are in the process of transformation, whether they realize it or not, having employed IT to slim their classical pyramid shape to a diamond and embellished communications to support an informal shadow network that floats over their formal hierarchy. (We will talk more about shadow networks in Chapter 3.)

Firms founded in the 1970s and 1980s tend to assume the form of advanced IT-enabled organizations more easily, having had the advantage of a slowly emerging body of management knowledge, principles, and techniques that enabled them to exploit the increasingly sophisticated information technology that was becoming available to them. Even so, management theory has not kept pace with information technology, with the result that managers in newer firms continue to rely on traditional accounting, auditing, planning, and budgeting techniques even as they explore new techniques. Their experimentation with business process reengineering, activity-based costing, networks, strategic alliances, and other structures is very much a part of the process of creative destruction.

We fully expect the process of creative destruction to span 50 years or more. Whether one pegs the beginning at the debut of computers in business in the early 1960s or the first wave of corporate downsizing in the 1970s, it has already been going on for 20 or 30 years, and we expect it to continue through the beginning of the next century. Management's tendency to treat elements of transformation—improved quality, reduced cycle time, and customer orientation, for example—as episodic changes, has obscured the view of the broader process and hindered development of the coherent architecture of infrastructures upon which new, IT-enabled organizational forms must rest.

We have engaged more than one hundred CEOs of older, larger, firms in discussions of the creative destruction process of transformation. Although they seem to readily grasp the key concepts of transformation, their efforts to act on this understanding in their own organizations are consistently thwarted by organizational inertia. Many have survived by reacting to the information economy's new ways of competing and doing business. But over time organizational inertia builds an immunity that renders reaction ineffective. Ultimately, CEOs are replaced and large organizations are chopped up into smaller, more manageable units, overcoming inertia.

Our consulting experience and research have identified a six-stage approach for actively managing transformation while minimizing organizational stress during the process.[27] In our framework, an organization first downsizes (Stage 1), then works to effectively master and integrate the art of dynamic balance (Stage 2), by distributing the free cash flow of the firm (partially generated by previous downsizing) to its stakeholders in a real-time equitable manner according to up-to-date information. Thus a base of new economics has resulted from creation of surplus and the ability to act on real-time information to distribute it. The firm subsequently mounts a market access program (Stage 3) to gain new customers, becomes customer-driven (Stage 4) to satisfy existing customers, pursues a market foreclosure program (Stage 5) to prevent "poaching" of its best customers by rival firms, and, ultimately, pursues global scope (Stage 6) to expand its opportunities. The endpoint of the transformation cycle is a new dominant form of organization for work. Inevitably, through this process, the M-form functional hierarchy of the industrial economy is supplanted by the IT-enabled network of the information economy. To reach the IT-enabled network, however, management must methodically overcome organizational inertia, the main barrier to transformation.

Chapter Two

The Six Stages of Creative Destruction

THE GENESIS of our six-stage process for business transformation occurred in an executive presentation in Japan. Nolan was invited to join Alvin Toffler, author of *Future Shock, Power Shift,* and other books on the future, to address and discuss with 100 Japanese CEOs the broad subject of the emerging information economy and business transformation. In advance, Nolan was asked to address

- the role of IT in business transformation
- the specific characteristics of the transformed organization
- the "here-to-there" path of transformation

All three topics were addressed with the aid of the data-loaded composite overhead transparency reproduced as Figure 2-1. First, the context of business transformation was described as the economic transition from the industrial economy to the information economy, involving massive labor-segment shifts. The dominant labor segment was farm work in the agrarian economy, factory work in the industrial economy, and now is in the process of changing to what we call *knowledge* work in the information economy. (A version of Figure 1-1 was used to make this point.)

Second, it was explained that the role of technology is not to cause the economic transition, but rather to enable it. The dominant technologies have changed from hand tools, to energy-driven machinery, to the computer. The IT S-curves of Figure 1-2, describing three eras of organizational learning about each new dominant technology were overlaid on the time line to show the 30-year discovery process of assimilating computers into organizations.

Third, a final overlay of a set of 15 arrows staggered along the time line was used to depict the creative destruction of the structural form of

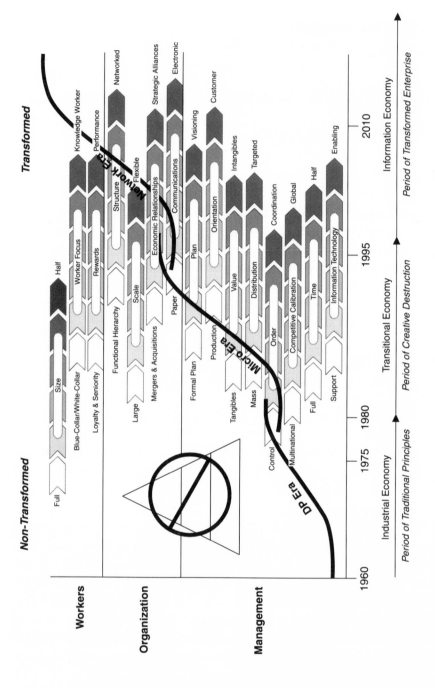

Figure 2-1. Business Transformation: Framework for 1988 Presentation to Japanese CEOs.

organization, described as the journey from functional hierarchy to the emerging IT-enabled network. While crude at best, these 15 arrows helped make the point that the functional hierarchy was an obsolete organizational form, inferior at leveraging the potential of information technology, and that a new form was required. The technique of contrasting the attributes of the functional hierarchy with the IT-enabled network form for each characteristic proved helpful in defining the form of new organization required. For example, the discussion about the worker focus in the industrial economy as a two-class system of blue-collar/white-collar workers in which the white-collar workers designed the way that work should be conducted, and the blue-collar workers simply executed the work, was seen as obviously obsolete, given the arrival of the then-modern concepts of Total Quality Management (TQM) and the continuously learning organization. The notion of a uniclass of "knowledge workers" is a more valid and workable notion of the role of the worker and is more consistent with the desirable new management practices. We use the term knowledge worker to mean one who contributes value by adding or interpreting information.

Taken together, the attributes on the right side of the figure define the operational characteristics of a transformed IT-enabled organization. The process of business transformation was described as creative destruction of the attributes of organizational characteristic on the left side (the functional hierarchy) and transformation into the attributes on the right side (the IT-enabled network organization). The staggering of the arrows along the time line indicates that not all organizational characteristics can be creatively destroyed simultaneously, although the sequence presented in this book was not yet in evidence.

The Japanese CEOs agreed with the arguments about the obsolescence of the functional hierarchy and the emergence of a new form of organization that could be described as the IT-enabled network. The proposed process of business transformation, on the other hand, caused some difficulty. One of the CEOs summed up the group's overall concerns about the business transformation process. He drew two circles on the diagram reproduced in Figure 2-1. The first circle horizontally encompassed the organizational characteristic of worker focus. He then challenged that the process of business transformation was best undertaken by isolating a particular characteristic and trying to manage a complete change from a functional hierarchy attribute to an IT-enabled network attribute for that single characteristic. As an alternative, he suggested that a more effective process might be to incrementally manage a process of change involving multiple organizational characteristics simultaneously evolving to some new level. He illustrated this concept with a vertical circle intersecting several of the organizational characteristics.

This CEO's insight turned out to be vital in arriving at a refined process of business transformation that minimizes organizational stress. The way change is typically brought about in the functional hierarchy model is to hold all organizational characteristics constant except for the one to be changed. This approach minimizes risk of loss of control, and allows the established functional hierarchy model to be fine-tuned and thus made more efficient. The strength of the overall hierarchical paradigm prevented things from getting out of control while change was undertaken. In the information economy, however, the functional hierarchy structure can no longer serve as a stabilizing framework; it is obsolescing so rapidly that it will destabilize the organization during the change process rather than stabilize it. Thus, the change process must embrace both the notion of steadily moving away from the functional hierarchy toward a new model, as well as the idea of making a specific fine-tuning change. To do so, simultaneous incremental change of multiple organizational characteristics is required, a gradual "morphing" of the functional hierarchy into the IT-enabled network.

Our proposed six stages for transforming the enterprise reflect such a sequence of major mutations of the functional hierarchy into the IT-enabled network. They constitute a normative guide to arriving at a new form, a new performance potential, and a new set of management principles for institutionalizing desirable work patterns. One dramatic performance goal is the increase in revenue-generating ability per employee, from approximately $50,000 in revenue per worker to 10 or 20 times that, a potential revenue of $1,000,000 per worker. In the last economic transition, we observed over a 10-fold increase in farm work productivity, and expect no less a productivity increase in factory work.

Assuming $50,000 in revenue per worker as the standard for effective performance of an organization appropriately structured for the industrial economy, that is, the precomputer organization of the late 1950s or early 1960s, we can proceed through a series of programs of creative destruction. The first set aims at achieving a "right-sized" organization capable of delivering the same revenue with only half the headcount; the second round aims at achieving a customer-driven orientation and the potential to realize $500,000 in revenue per worker. The third stage of creative destruction separates revenue from headcount entirely. Apple Computer, following an aggressive shift from a production orientation, reached this second level in 1987. Unfortunately, Apple was unable to stay the course, and responded to increased demand in a rather traditional way—adding workers—because "their spreadsheets made them do it." As a result, they fell back to $400,000 in revenue per worker in 1988, and have been struggling ever since to create "The New Enterprise."[1]

Transformation is a long-term process, and achieving one stage in the process is no guarantee that the next stage will be achieved. It is also a risky venture. Some practitioners estimate that 70 percent of comprehensive reengineering efforts (most of which are started as some form of business transformation) fail.[2] Most of these failures are unnecessary, brought about by errors in planning or execution made by overburdened managers trying to do their best in a difficult situation.[3] Management attention is both limited and costly, and its quality declines with increased demand for it. Managers trying to do everything at once get nothing done at all.

It is to ease the burden on management that we have broken up the transformation sequence into six sequential stages, each involving the launch of several initiatives tied to the creative destruction of management principles. Such a structured approach makes the transformation process a surgery, not a butchery, with the goal of maximizing the patient's chances of survival, not getting the meat fastest.

Stage One: Downsize!

To align a firm's structure for carrying out work so that the information technology that it has assimilated over the years can be leveraged, a firm must be prepared to downsize forcibly and painfully. A commitment to eliminate upward of 50 percent of the workforce while maintaining current revenue levels, with no excuses accepted for failure, forces an organization to relax restrictive management principles and practices associated with the functional hierarchy. (Firms that have achieved a similar effect—doubling revenues while holding the number of workers constant—are a distinct minority among non-transformed firms.) This shock works much better to overcome organizational inertia than would a series of 10 percent cuts; inertia dissolves immediately.

Before it can downsize and still maintain revenue, however, an organization must achieve a critical mass of underutilized technology-based automation. The logical first target of downsizing is the part of the workforce involved in the routine and clerical work that has been automated. But in practice automation is seldom complete, leading to confusion about how to downsize efficiently. Firms that downsized in the mid-1970s tended to do so in an arbitrary manner that yielded productivity improvements on the order of 10 percent. Had they reorganized with perfect foresight to match the new technology, these firms might have realized productivity gains in excess of 50 percent or more. The 1990s have seen organizations begin to complete this arrested downsizing, reducing their headcount by half while maintaining previous revenue levels, and thereby forcing remaining employees to integrate available information technology into day-to-day work routines.

An organization's viability is at extreme risk during and immediately following a downsizing initiative. The workers remaining cannot possibly do the same volume of work using the old business processes; they must adopt new ones quickly. The dread of sudden vulnerability after persistent comfort leads many firms to lose their resolve and back off from further downsizing after a 10 percent improvement, with the result that transformation momentum is lost, performance continues to slide, or new top leadership is brought in to get back on track.

When approximately 30 percent of the workforce has been redeployed or eliminated, it becomes crystal clear to those who remain that the downsizing initiative has passed the point of no return. The organization begins to operate in a manner that reinforces, rather than opposes, the transformation initiative. Employees, interested in being on the winning side, contribute by rethinking and redesigning work based on their particular expertise. Firms can feel confident in funding focused development programs for workers surviving downsizing and offer assurances that downsizing is over.

Stage Two: Seek Dynamic Balance

A promise of future security and training allows the benefits of downsizing to be shared with surviving workers. After all, surviving the downsizing stage for the remaining workers means that they have learned how to perform work with substantially fewer coworkers, by tapping into new sources of information on how to become more productive, and sharing this new information with the firm; reciprocity from senior management is called for. Further, after downsizing, the discovery is usually made that a great deal of untapped valuable information exists both inside and outside the firm, and that this information is accessible and much cheaper than originally thought. It is critical to assure remaining workers that cooperation is rewarded; this assurance comes in the form of shared gains from their cooperation.

In many cases, a large portion of this information resource would be inaccessible without information technology, which has gained importance at least equal to that of the traditional labor, materials, and money resources of the industrial economy. Information was clearly important in the industrial economy, but more expensive to obtain, process, and communicate. Industrial economy management practices such as "need-to-know" access and "chain of command" reporting significantly restricted the flow of information as a way of reducing the cost of its transmission and control. Continuing these restrictions on the flow of information severely impedes realization of the increased worker productivity potential. Even more importantly, trying to hide information about costs can lead to dysfunctional effects by either overpaying or underpaying for the factors of production; overpaid factors happily siphon off profits, underpaid factors sullenly seek other employment. Management is much better advised to assume under the current environment that "everyone knows everything now" and pay the right amount.

What this means is that management's stewardship of the firm's resources is known with lightning speed by shareholders, employees, and customers. It is therefore incumbent on managers to dynamically balance the interests of these three key stakeholder groups. To fail to do so risks disruption of transformation efforts through labor unrest, shareholder action, or customer defection—all risks that can be avoided if the right balance is maintained. Reports of transformation efforts suspended due to retaliatory actions of slighted stakeholders appear daily in the business press; reports of disgruntled customers are usually kept secret, but are no less devastating.[4]

Shareholders demand a fair return for at-risk capital and know which companies are their best bets. Moreover, we believe that investors are significantly better informed about the calculus of the short- and long-term than many managers who carp on the pressures to sustain short-term performance might think.

Worker demands for timely payment, roughly proportional to value added, are caught in the upheavals of the economic transition. Recent engineering graduates are better equipped to contribute, and extract, value in the information economy than are engineers trained for industrial economy work, whose wages are being lowered despite their seniority to reflect the lesser value of their contributions as engineers. Though casting aside these workers' valuable experience and knowledge would be myopic, these assets must be used in new roles.

Intensifying competition among expanding sources, and widespread availability of competing quotes, gives customers more choices for securing products and services for what they "should cost." Customers' expectations of maximal value for their money transcend nationalistic feelings and product loyalty; many customers apparently feel that patronizing a foreign competitor (or an alternative long-distance carrier, or a new credit card) serves as a wake-up call for domestic sources or traditional providers, and that it is their duty to provide such a shock.

Because IT enables customers to find out quickly when prices and their cost determinants change, management that does not respond quickly stands to either pay too much or lose valuable resources on a continual basis. Firms that are slow to incorporate a new computer technology that increases fuel economy, for example, will lose not only customers but also key workers to competitors or entrepreneurs.

More complete information also facilitates a better balance between short- and long-term success. If suspicions that firms would be milked in the short term by new leveraged buyout shareholders had come true, for example, such firms would have been inclined to shy away from such longer-term investments as information technology. Yet informal surveys of CIOs revealed that IT was among the most favorably received investment proposals in firms that had experienced leveraged buyouts, probably for its effect on leveraging return on equity.[5] There's a lesson here: with tight controls put in place for some outside reason (such as high leverage), IT investment pays off dramatically.

The volume, accuracy, and timeliness of information are vastly different than what they were even five years ago, with the trend continuing toward cheap, perfect information in real time. It is extraordinarily important that management fully comprehend this new reality, and act on it. The days of relying on holding back information to create strategic advantage in bargaining are over; advantage now comes from revealing that you are informed.

Stage Three: Develop a Market-Access Strategy

Having gotten the new production economics in place and stabilized stakeholder interests, the transforming business enterprise has averted the first crisis; its attentions must then turn to responding to the market environment that will characterize its future. The industrial economy was a "make and sell" environment, in which companies mastered mass production and mass distribution to satisfy pent-up demand for their products and services. To attract and retain customers in the information economy, which is oversupplied with traditional undifferentiated products and services, businesses must offer something new. Manufacturing firms are likely to focus on quality improvements; service firms are likely to improve their responsiveness. Accordingly, automobile manufacturers have targeted improved quality, and Wall Street financial services firms are offering speedier responsiveness by reducing the cycle time for introducing new and innovative products. Consider, for example, financing tools devised for companies with poor credit ratings. Anyone can jack up the interest rate, but it takes innovation to weed out the good risks from the bad. Innovative financial instruments such as asset-backed commercial paper, credit swaps, inverse floaters, down-and-out options, and synthetic securities today amount to a $45 billion market.[6]

The general pattern notwithstanding, whether it is best for manufacturing and services firms to pursue market access through quality initiatives or cycle time improvement depends on internal capabilities and the external competitive environment. What is important is that whichever path is taken, management must be prepared to dismantle rigid, task-based department structures, promote continuous learning, enhance problem-solving skills, and implement project-based teams as the dominant form for doing work. Opportunities for market access have been terrifically broadened by information technology, to the extent that entire books have been written about the technology itself as an offensive weapon,[7] but little has been written on its organizational implementation as a competitive tool.

Stage Four: Become Customer Driven

The midpoint milestone in the transformation process is the institutionalization of a fundamental shift from an inward-focused "make and sell" orientation to an outward-looking "sense and respond" orientation. This is a nontrivial reorientation that relies on understanding, tracking, and responding with unprecedented speed to customer needs and wants for innovative products and services. The requisite organizational change involves a concomitant shift in leadership orientation; bosses must become intrapreneurs and project managers, not supervisors. The customer-driven firm views tasks not as hurdles to be surmounted centrally, but as problems or cases to be resolved locally by teams.[8] Executives must give up on the idea that processes can be redesigned centrally, instead giving broad discretion to teams and team leaders to carry out the particulars.

Stage Five: Develop a Market-Foreclosure Strategy

Successful downsizing and market-access programs (both quality and cycle time) create a temporary investment pool, what we term a *customer dowry*. To achieve long-term stability, it is imperative that this pool be expediently and effectively reinvested in a market-foreclosure program, which defends existing customers from competitors.

Ford stands out as a manufacturing firm that succeeded in market access only to fail in market foreclosure. Ford's introduction of its Taurus/Sable midsize cars in late 1985 represented a five-year, $3 billion investment. The highly engineered cars closed quality gaps with Japanese competitors and were, at their introduction, stylish trendsetters. Market response, in 1986, rendered Ford more profitable than General Motors for the first time since the introduction of the Model T, as Ford's market share in the United States jumped from 14 percent in 1985 to 38 percent by 1991. Ford was well-positioned to re-invest its profits in dramatically expanding its engineering effort to target new customer-oriented features. Instead of investing to take advantage of this disequilibrium to solidify its relationship with its newly found customers, however, Ford invested in an industrial economy "business as usual" mentality and fell off the transformation trajectory. Management capped capital investment at 5 percent of total revenue, diversified into the financial and defense sectors, and spent $2.6 billion to buy Jaguar. When the Ford lines appeared with minor cosmetic changes in 1992, showrooms were full of competitors' Taurus/Sable copies.[9] Ford's market share has begun to shrink back to its normal level.

Competing on the basis of information is harder on the defensive side. But although defensive strategy receives little attention in the management literature, it is successful and consistent defense, not flashy offense, that ensures continued profitability.[10] Having captured customers' attention, a firm must prevent competitors from distracting them by imitating its movements. Market foreclosure, the heart of defensive strategy, aims at restricting other firms' market access. It is an investment with invisible payback—if it is successful, business as usual will prevail—but crucial nonetheless.

Stage Six: Pursue Global Scope

A firm achieves global scope, the end objective of the transformation process, when it consolidates its market-foreclosure advantage in its existing markets enough to start thinking about entering new markets. At this point, the identity of the firm as a decision-making body is completely divorced from that of the corresponding basket of resources, because the cache of firm resources has shifted from a static organization-bound ownership-based hierarchy to a dynamic, market- and alliance-based network. The new organization, characterized by a fundamental decoupling of revenues from employees, can generate $1 million or more per remaining employee. Such an organization does not have hard, fixed boundaries, but it is more organic as a result of having dense strategic alliances and partnerships, and a flexible responsiveness to customers in innovative ways in real time.[11]

The business enterprise being, by definition, a dynamic organism, the process of organizational change does not end when global scope is achieved. Just as the functional hierarchy evolved over time, giving rise to a knowledge base rich in management theory and practice, so the global IT-enabled network will evolve as a form, going through multiple market-access/foreclosure loops and engendering a new set of management principles and success factors. Over time, all organizations will experience the globalizing impact of information technology and network organization structures.

Managerial Vision and the Transformation Process

Transformation begins at the top, with the CEO and the senior management team adopting new management principle #1.

> **The New Set of Management Principles**
>
> 1. Leadership principle: Senior management formulates and coordinates the firm's vision, and plays a central role in defining projects.

Management's first challenge is to understand what must be done. Its second challenge is to formulate and share with the enterprise a vision of transformation. Management's traditional role as strategy provider is insufficient, as strategy and vision are fundamentally different in the transformation process. Strategy bespeaks road maps, action programs, and long-range plans—cold, sterile, and analytical images that represent a planned sequence of 10 percent changes. Vision, on the other hand, brings about personal involvement. It involves pride, passion, and commitment. Vision represents a shift in principles that can yield gains on the order of 1,000 percent.

President John F. Kennedy's vision of putting a man on the moon by the end of the decade exhibits five important qualities that can guide assessment of the visions of contemporary CEOs:

1. It was inspiring: it signaled conquest of the "final frontier" and symbolic superiority over the "enemy."

2. The vision could be understood by and mandated local actions on the part of the visionary's constituency; the American people signed on to the objective, not by rushing out to enroll as astronauts-in-training, but by encouraging engineering and science curricula in education.

3. The vision was measurable: Americans glued to their television sets in 1968 witnessed one of their own walking on the moon.

4. The vision was achievable in the specified time frame. Kennedy's bold, but, in retrospect, doable deadline of 1970 permitted both tactical and strategic choices to be made in a time frame to which people could relate.

5. The vision mandated a radical, not incremental, change in the status quo; putting a manned science station on Antarctica would hardly have evoked the same response!

An organization relies on its CEO for both vision and the charismatic leadership needed to preserve the vision throughout the chaotic transformation process. The CEO must, by example and day-to-day inspiration, articulate the steps that will result in the realization of the vision. Information economy CEOs derive their mandates from their inspirational abilities, not their technical expertise; they often charge teams of specialists to suggest innovative methods of taking the requisite steps.

The task of constant innovation is problematic for CEOs who have become accustomed to one particular view of the world. Research suggests that it is difficult, to say the least, to change an entrenched CEO mindset.[12] Many CEOs, caught flat-footed by the need to downsize their organizations in light of the initial impact of computers and subsequent automation of work, and failing to understand the implications of the transition from an industrial to an information economy, have responded with incrementalism. They have downsized by 10 percent to relieve the symptoms of competitive pressure, were surprised when they had to downsize by another 10 percent, and were amazed when they had to downsize by yet another 10 percent. Treating the symptoms rather than the underlying affliction has revealed that they did not know what was going on or, worse, that they elected to conceal their confusion from their employees. Such CEOs have lost credibility and, consequently, the ability to inspire and lead their organizations. Kodak, after five years of firing senior managers and enduring continual incremental reorganizations, finally recruited a CEO from the outside.[13] A similar story can be told of IBM.

Business Process Redesign

During the 1990s, managerial vision has come to encompass what is called "business process redesign," the notion that analysis and redefinition of fundamental business processes is the only route to significant improvements in efficiency and effectiveness. Examples of successful business process redesign include IBM Credit, which multiplied tenfold the volume of quotes for purchasing leased computers that could be prepared in a given period of time while reducing the time to prepare individual quotes from seven days to one, and Mutual Benefit Life, a large insurance company that halved its costs of policy underwriting and issuance by reconciling the respective processes with newly available technology.[14]

Business process redesign, to its credit, shifts management's attention away from traditional hierarchical functions such as marketing, manufacturing, and purchasing, toward more generic business processes—a major improvement in focus. Practitioners' interpretations of the number of processes required to define a business effectively vary widely, ranging from two—managing the product line and the order cycle[15]—to several dozen. IBM has defined its business with 18 business processes, Xerox with 14.

We believe that business process redesign is an important, albeit incomplete and potentially distracting, step towards creative destruction of the hierarchy. Significant among its shortcomings is that the approach is silent on the unique merits of the network organization, implying that hierarchy can be fine-tuned to enable an organization to compete in the information economy. We are convinced that fine-tuning is not sufficient. Moreover, business process redesign does not explicitly address the dichotomy between the stabilizing function of organizational infrastructure and the flexibility and responsiveness afforded by networks. We believe recognition of this dichotomy to be essential to a complete practical theory of organizational design or redesign. Finally, business process redesign does not specify endpoints or overall objectives beyond "order of magnitude improvements." Even experienced practitioners find such questions as "Why is this possible now, but not before?," "What is driving this improvement?," and "Where are the limits to improvement?" confusing if not impossible to address.

Practitioners of business process redesign advocate replacing industrial economy practices with new practices: a good start, but one that stops short of the mark. To bring lasting improvement to management practices requires the practices to be built upon a solid foundation of coherent management principles consistent with the competitive environment of the information economy.

Infrastructures of the IT-enabled Network

In contrast to the functional hierarchy, the IT-enabled network is constantly changing, driven by a keen responsiveness to customer needs. To achieve this responsiveness, information technology plays a major role in connecting professionals to one another and keeping a high output and low cycle time information flow coming their way. The actual work of the firm is accomplished by self-designed teams of these professional knowledge workers who in effect subcontract tasks from the executives.

Essential to the functioning of the self-designed teams is a set of infrastructures, also organized in a network form, which the teams draw upon for resources and coordination. Figure 2-2 shows the IT-enabled network consisting of two main parts: self-designed teams and a firm infrastructure. The firm infrastructure, in turn, is made up of seven individual infrastructures:[16]

1. Information technology infrastructure: for providing the network of communications, and ensuring that high output and low cycle time prevail

2. Shared knowledge and database infrastructure: for providing knowledge assets to knowledge workers and ensuring that communications can have substantive content

3. Human asset infrastructure: for providing the list of knowledge workers available to the firm, and ensuring that information and queries go to the right place whether inside or outside the formal organization

4. Project tasking infrastructure: for providing the structure for organizing and coordinating the activities of the firm, and ensuring that the needed work is clearly identified

5. Performance management infrastructure: for providing incentives and evaluations necessary for maximum effectiveness and efficiency, and ensuring that team members who provide high value added get appropriate recognition and compensation

6. Resource allocation infrastructure: for providing optimum use and management of resources, and ensuring that these resources aren't caught up in "empire building" but rather are available for suddenly arisen opportunities

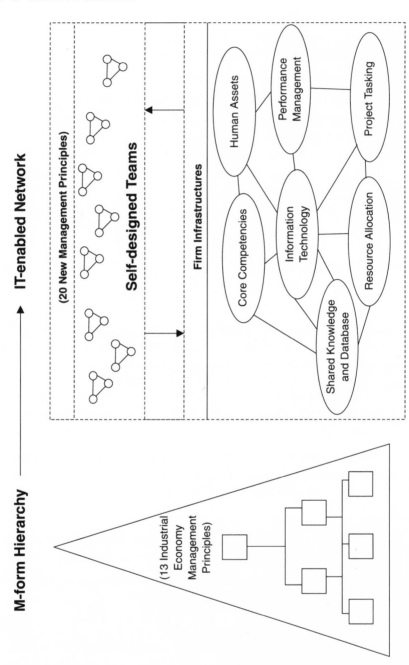

Figure 2-2. Transformation from the M-form to the IT-enabled Network Organization

7. Core competencies infrastructure: for providing development and management of the unique capabilities of the firm, and ensuring that these competencies aren't lured away by competitors, leaving a large hole in the organization's knowledge base

The firm's seven-part infrastructure requires senior management design and a level of investment similar in magnitude to the investment required to build the mass production and mass distribution infrastructures of the functional hierarchies of the industrial economy. During the six-stage creative destruction process of the functional hierarchy, the seven infrastructures evolve to form the foundation of the IT-enabled network.

In the chapters that follow, we examine the six stages in the transformation process with specific reference to the management principles affected by each. We review first the creative destruction of affected industrial economy management principles, both unsalvageable and salvageable. We then consider the creative construction of necessary information economy management principles. Over the course of the six stages, unsalvageable management principles are sloughed off and salvageable management principles redefined as and accumulated with emerging information economy management principles. In the end, as the industrial economy abandoned agrarian management principles, so we forsake the set of management principles of the industrial economy in favor of a set of information economy management principles compatible with the IT-enabled network organization form. Taken together the new management principles provide the foundation to design an IT-enabled network and tailor a set of coherent management practices required to effectively compete in the information economy.

Chapter Three

Stage One: Downsize!

TRANSFORMATION didn't start with the computer's introduction. The computer's debut into business was a non-event of the 1960s and remained so for more than a decade. Because mechanical punch-card equipment of the period looked much like any other capital-based technology designed to automate production, business organizations were inclined to treat IT as a specialized form of capital rather than a new factor of production. This constrained view of its functionality severely limited IT's role in the hierarchy. Computers were first applied to the automation of low-level, routine work of the accounting departments responsible for their management. Over time, as more knowledge of their potential business use accumulated, computers became more pervasive, penetrating purchasing, controlling inventory, entering orders, and controlling manufacturing processes. A critical mass of capability and experience was reached in the mid-1970s, which signaled the need for a different response from management.

To convert productivity gains realized at lower levels of the hierarchy into bottom-line profitability, management needed to identify and eliminate assets, employees, and divisions that automation had rendered either obsolete or underutilized. Because organizational structures and ways of doing work had remained fairly stable throughout the first decade of computer use, a tremendous amount of slack had built up before the first wave of downsizing broke and transformation began in earnest.

Targeting Organizational Slack during the Data Processing Era

Project proposals evaluated primarily by means of capital expenditure analysis based on ROI (return on investment) were justified on the basis of expected cost savings. But although many of these projects achieved operating and administrative efficiencies, automation was seldom complete. An unwelcome surprise awaited management seeking to trim slack personnel: managers could not fire part of a person. Because individuals who continued to perform crucial steps in partially automated processes could not be eliminated, many underutilized people kept their full-time jobs, depressing short-term efficiency and affecting the accuracy of performance statistics. Only partial IT productivity gains could be counted in justifying the equipment costs. Even worse for future efficiency, retaining inefficient workers reinforced middle management's incentive to withhold its knowledge and effort in automating crucial tasks, teaching them that holding back paid off. When managers approved a potentially cost-saving investment, but continually failed to collect the potential savings, the generated benefit went to workers, not shareholders; jobs got easier all around—the investment begat inefficiency.

Implementation problems were rooted in the approach used to gather information. Newly trained systems analysts frequently engaged prospective automation customers with words like: "I'd like you to tell me what you do so I can build a computer system to automate your job." It took little imagination to correlate the analyst's success with unemployment, so employees frequently withheld information on subtle, but crucial portions of their jobs. Efficiency experts generated inefficiency.

Of course, many tasks were simply not amenable to full automation given the technology of the day. For these, it would have been necessary to restructure the work to isolate the parts that could be automated. Such restructuring did not occur because neither analysts nor employees were authorized to initiate organizational changes. The organizational hierarchy interfered. Organization begat inefficiency.

These obstacles, obvious in hindsight, were not so obvious at the time. Business school academics questioned whether investments in computers really paid off. Cries for more rigor in post-audit management of computer projects echoed throughout the literature, with measurement held up as the principal problem.[1] As had been the case with technologies such as the gas turbine engine and urban electrification, the benefits of computers—networking ability, improved accuracy, and decision-making and strategic information management assistance—were not fully grasped at the outset, but rather discovered only through accumulated experience.[2]

Taking Up Slack at the Bottom: From Pyramid to Diamond

Early-1970s management technologies such as rudimentary statistical process control, automated accounting systems, and operations-research principles could do little more than point to the build-up of slack. Efficiency studies that combined early 20th-century "scientific management" principles with detailed data processing reports further documented it. Moored in hierarchical inertia and lacking any guiding methodology, management arbitrarily "combed" large numbers of workers from lower levels of the hierarchy. Although this was a step in the right direction, blindly eliminating jobs without taking account of the organizational reverberations of doing so proved short-sighted.

Shareholders favored downsizing to recover substantial computer investments, but were unwilling to sacrifice hard-won market share or profitability to this end. Firms that strove to maintain revenues looked little changed to outsiders; they exhibited a lower cost structure but offered the same products at the same prices.

Lower cost structure seemed a compelling strategic reason to downsize quickly, as the first company to achieve new economies could set the tone for future competition. But downsizing as a strategic tool suffered from a fatal flaw: it could not be kept secret. Downsized firms were forced to look "lean and mean" just when they wanted to look meek and unassuming.[3] Any downsizing move sent an unmistakable signal to competitors that the newly svelte firm would use vigorous price competition to punish any attempts to disrupt cozy oligopolistic markets. Even though this implied threat acted as a continuing deterrent to any firm's firing the first shot in a price war, downsizing as a strategic weapon suffered from being too readily emulated. Second-movers had an easy time of it, indeed, often easier, the first-mover having borne the brunt of unfavorable public opinion.

Once a company eliminated significant slack, competitors were practically forced to follow suit to remain cost-competitive. This incentive, coupled with the generic nature of traditional methods of formulating the appropriate reaction, precipitated a sustained period of widespread downsizing in nearly every industry with little overall gain to shareholders. In the wake of this dramatic resizing, managers adopted a new set of economic rules of thumb for determining appropriate levels of economic activity per worker. Although traditional management approaches could not provide precise measures, the new economics could be summarized as higher expectations for certain critical operating ratios.[4] These operating ratios required employees to work harder. The customers got all the benefits.

A study of the historical evolution of the shapes and structures of thirty companies from 1960 to 1980 revealed a striking trend: the traditional pyramid shape of the functional hierarchy was, as a consequence of the sudden slimming of its bottom layers, being molded into a diamond shape and being reduced in area, if not height. In addition, network communications could be seen evolving in the middle of the diamond (see Figure 3-1).[5] This reshaping appeared to be an entirely natural consequence of deploying automated machinery to replace direct labor in manufacturing and clerical tasks. Indeed, the image of the "lights-out factory" with no workers at all became the symbol of automation carried to its logical extreme.

But further reflection reveals that this period of downsizing, the early result of computer automation, is not the only change automation might have brought about in hierarchical structure. If fewer direct workers were involved in a given manufacturing activity, fewer indirect workers should have been needed to coordinate the activity. The adoption of automation should have had an indirect effect on middle levels of the hierarchy as managerial levels not directly in contact with the new technology became somewhat unnecessary as well.[6] But although logical targets for elimination, these middle levels were left intact by the 1970s downsizing movement; potential gains were judged insufficient to cover the costs of further restructuring. It was a case of the good being the enemy of the best; satisfied with progress at the bottom, the downsizing movement spared middle levels.

Belt-tightening at the waist is only now occurring, more than three decades after Leavitt and Whisler suggested that technology would reduce middle-management responsibilities.[7] Whereas line-level workers had a motive for impeding automation, mid-level managers had both motive and method; decision-making authority with respect to technology rested in part with them. But perhaps more important, middle management still served a purpose in the diamond-shaped organization. Shop floor IT increased the amount of information flowing up, and middle management's interpretation and evaluation of this information was critical to the overall production process. Not until another form of coordinative technology

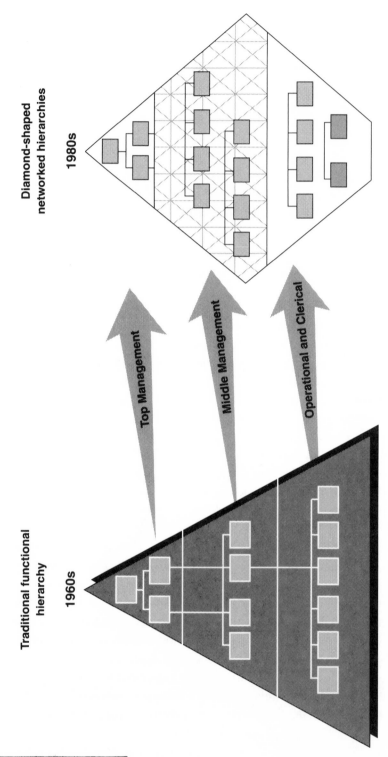

Figure 3-1. Downsizing the Hierarchy

LEEDS METROPOLITAN
UNIVERSITY
LIBRARY

performed this interpretive function could the middle levels of the hierarchy be removed. Only when microcomputer and networking technologies created a bridge between line-level employees and top management with which both could comfortably interact could organizations seriously address their bulging midriff.

Building the Information Technology (IT) Infrastructure

The story of the development of most firms' IT infrastructures begins in the early 1960s. After a few years of IT investments, the IT infrastructure took shape, although the idea that a planned architecture might be important was still far in the future. Through time and three eras of technological growth, as illustrated in Figure 1-2, IT infrastructures have become so important that business literally stops if something in the IT infrastructure breaks down.

The first IT infrastructures were designed to support the predominant functional hierarchies used by businesses. Systems used sequential files and accessed hierarchical databases, which paralleled the organization structure of the time: sequential chains of communication and hierarchical lines of authority. Increased use of computers led to discoveries and learning, accompanied by a growing suspicion (usually unwise to voice) that IT could enable more efficient business processes than those institutionalized in the functional hierarchy. Personal computers and growing use of E-mail began to make possible shadow networks, which not only permitted decisions to be made faster, but also tapped the knowledge of more people, thus improving the quality of decisions. Today these shadow networks are finally being formalized to completely replace the traditional functional hierarchy.

However, apart from a few rare exceptions found in relatively new firms, the existing IT infrastructures of most firms have evolved over three decades not as a result of careful planning, but more as a discovery and learning process, a charitable way to describe a lot of trial and error in search of the perfect infrastructure. The IT infrastructures typical of medium-to-large companies represent investments of hundreds of millions of dollars; they are the product of at least three major approaches to building IT systems and capabilities (automation, informating, and reengineering), and of a whirlwind of new generations of technologies (including computers, telecommunications and software). Some of them work, others don't.

Many senior managers are just now realizing that their IT infrastructures are strategic to business transformation and are not only weak, but are like foundations of sand: impossible to build upon. Exhibit 3-1 charts the evolution of IT infrastructures for typical firms. The infrastructures consist of millions of lines of software code, and parallel the three eras of

---

Automating

- DP Era (1960–1980)
- Operational level systems were automated, primarily with COBOL
- Standard packages emerged for Payroll and General Ledger, and initiated purchases of application software
- Applications portfolio consists of millions of lines of code with typically 50 percent purchased from outside

---

Informating

- Micro Era (1980–1995)
- User-oriented software purchased consists of wordprocessing, spreadsheets, graphics, and CAD/CAM
- User tasks leveraged through direct use of microcomputers and purchased software
- Purchased user software consists of millions of lines of code, almost 100 percent purchased from other companies

Embedding

- Micro Era (1980–1995)
- Specialized code embedded in products and services to enhance functionality
- Thousands of lines of code developed both by specialized internal programmers and outside contract programmers; mixed, and highly variable combination of internally developed and purchased software

---

Networking

- Network Era (1990–   )
- User-oriented software purchased for E-mail, database sharing, file transfer, and groupware for work teams.
- Millions of lines of code; almost 100 percent purchased from and maintained by outside software firms

---

Exhibit 3-1. Evolution of IT Infrastructure

growth in the computer industry: the DP era, the micro era, and the network era. During the micro era, microcomputers were used both to inform workers in the firm, as well as to create "smart" products and services as they were embedded in products like automobiles, and credit cards (i.e., smart cards) to provide enhanced informational services. In the network era of today, computers are becoming more and more specialized for networking and databases; individually used computers of the micro era are now more likely to be linked together.

Retracing the Evolutionary Steps in the Growth of an IT Infrastructure

The first step for a transforming firm in reforming its architecture (both technology and organizational) is to comprehensively retrace the evolution of the development of its IT infrastructure, as a basis for redesign and reengineering.

Automating. Prior to the Industrial Revolution, productivity-enhancing innovations in hand- and animal-operated tools had largely complemented and magnified the effects of human effort. The subsequent displacement of human energy by first steam and, later, electric power marked the first *substitution* of technology for human expense in the basic provision of effort. Human involvement at a different level remained integral, however, until fully automated machinery substituted mechanical feedback mechanisms for the human decision-making element. The complete automation of routine work relegated human intervention to times of crisis rather than business as usual.

Automation of low-level information-processing jobs is described by the first information technology S-curve. (see Figure 1-2). Displacement of information workers during the data processing era was dramatic, albeit less immediate. We estimate that between 1960 and 1980 more than twelve million actual and potential information-handling jobs were automated by data-processing equipment.[8]

Informating. Automation of routine factory work and information transfer was commonplace by the late 1970s, bringing about a slight but significant change in the hierarchical management framework, and a simultaneous redefinition of supervisory responsibilities. A new market for information technology emerged in the middle of the organization as information flows from the factory floor—or its productive equivalent—increased.

Because DP-era technology increased in cost roughly proportional to the square of the difficulty of automating a task, its adoption had stopped abruptly at the middle level. In the face of the steep cost/complexity curve for technology, hierarchical organizations were inclined to stick with traditional pencil-and-paper systems for the majority of middle management tasks. In an effort to seed a market at the hierarchy's middle level, innovative computer companies placed stand-alone, desktop computers on the desks of middle managers that possessed a fraction of the information processing power centralized in mainframe computers.

Knowledge-intensive tasks of higher-level workers were not so easily replaced by automation as lower-level tasks were. Consequently, what came to be called the micro era revolved around the deployment of a servant technology devoted to expediting information processing tasks and making information easier to collect and evaluate by higher-level workers. This technology informed rather than automated; that is, it enhanced the managers' ability to apply their particular knowledge and judgment.

The informating paradigm leverages existing human resources. Rapid and considerable expansion of line-level supervisory reporting discouraged task specialization, the hallmark of the functional hierarchy, freeing mid-level, professional information workers to concentrate on evaluation and interpretation—the precise areas to which their skills brought the most benefit. Partially in response to the sharing of benefits from this technology between line and mid-level workers (an idea we will revisit in the next chapter), opposition to this sort of computer investment was considerably reduced over the automation-intensive DP era.

Embedding. Continuously falling prices and increasing capability have made personal computing technology ubiquitous not only within organizations, but also in the products they sell and services they deliver. By our last count, some thirteen microprocessors in a Ford automobile were doing everything from regulating fuel consumption to monitoring vital vehicle functions. Microprocessors tell the owner when a car is due for service, and also download information for repair workers, expediting the service process. Problems with a car are documented and corrected quickly, before they become serious, and targeted preventive maintenance ensures that few problems will be encountered during the interval between service check-ups. An internal local area network (LAN) is being developed to support communication with other networks, both internal (within the car) and external, connecting the car with outside networks such as the Global Positioning System satellite network. (The Global Positioning System satellite network enables computers on earth to detect signals from satellites and calculate an object's latitude and longitude.)

In a similar vein, financial institutions are developing "smart cards," credit card-sized microcomputers that record customers' banking activities in real time and provide on-demand personal financial summaries via ATMs.[9]

Networking. The last S-curve in Figure 1-2 represents the linking of DP- and micro-era technologies to yield comprehensive network-based information systems, represented by the networking box in Exhibit 3-1. Acting first as terminals (a DP-era function) and second as processors (a micro-era function), personal computers in today's networking environment act as the "clients" in the so-called "client-server" structure. This important technical architecture consists of "server" computers providing interconnection and data services to "client" computers directly used by workers. The emerging network era takes its name from the electronic linkage technologies that are enabling it. Internal networks link multiple locations of a firm; external networks link firms with customers and suppliers. The network era fosters dramatic extension of organizational presence into new areas. As obstacles to the integration—because of information processing and interpretation incompatibility of hardware as well as incompatibility of data formats and software—are swept away in the network era, we can expect a union of these long-divided tasks, as the reengineering approach focuses on exploiting the potential of IT by redesigning functional hierarchy-oriented business processes.

The Interaction of Information Technology and Organizational Structure

Viewed from the perspective of its impact on organizational structure, information technology falls into three basic classes. The first, as we have seen, is infrastructure-building. The mainframe computers and software that automated much routine work at lower levels of the organization constituted the first electronic information infrastructure for large hierarchical firms. Although class I technology did not directly alter the structure of organizations, the eventual distribution of data collection for centralized computing laid the foundations for the network organization.

Although data could be moved around using class I technologies, it was not very useful in its raw form. The second class focuses on distributing this information in forms useful to decision makers. Class II information technologies include database software and software with on-line capability; early functional networking technologies that, in combination, facilitated functional integration of routine transaction processing. Commercial banks, for example, used class II technology to automate the activity surrounding their core business—demand-deposit and savings accounts.[10] In-bank teller terminals were interfaced to centralized databases via class II networking technologies. Mainframes, databases, and on-line terminals in combination yielded on-line teller systems, which subsequently evolved into the automated teller machines (ATMs) that have fully automated demand-deposit and saving transactions. The resulting cross-functional integration within banking organizations forced bank managers to think in terms of networks rather than functional hierarchies, a change in managerial perspective that was to give financial institutions a considerable lead in adopting network structures.

Class III information technologies extend networking across organizational boundaries. In banking, for example, class III technologies have been deployed to support automatic personal bill paying, loan and credit card application, and marketing of third-party providers' services via ATM.

A similar pattern of class-by-class progression of IT use can be observed in the retail grocery industry. Class I technology automated routine functions such as inventory, sending hand-determined orders via electronic data interchange (EDI), billing, and accounts payable and receivable. Class II technology, in the form of data gathering through point-of-sale (POS) checkout scanning systems, supported on-line store inventory, instantaneous updating, and daily profit and loss reporting from store to store. Class III technology made possible the linking of hand-held computers with POS scanners via telephone networks for real-time exchange of information, and enabled warehouses to process store orders, create pick lists and invoices, and ship goods the same day, thereby greatly reducing in-process inventories of perishable goods.[11]

In both of these examples, we observe the difficulty of sorting out the effects on middle management of two opposing forces of information.

Increased information flows from line-level activities at once exert greater demands on the information-conveyance structure and result in the transfer of the functions of mid-level employees to a technological liaison. The traditional functions of mid-level employees now include acting on the new technologically produced information and also require new technological assistance to process effectively. Each technological advance enables management to add value to the product or service being provided, but few force management to do so.

The second force results in direct use of the technology by customers. Bank customers, for example, can access their personal financial summaries at any time. Supermarket customers experience fewer stockouts and enjoy fresher fruits and dairy products. Both of these conditions affect what middle managers do and the number of managers needed to do the work.

The technology was not installed specifically to benefit customers but by permitting some of its benefit to spill over to customers a firm can create competitive advantage. Checkout scanners speed the flow of shoppers through a supermarket while collecting immense quantities of data about customers' purchasing habits; customers are "paid" for providing this information with shorter checkout times. But it is competitive pressure and not the capabilities of technology that encourage banks and grocery chains to provide these benefits.

It is simple to see that fewer mid-level employees will be needed to achieve a given level of value added as each one's capacity to add value increases. Yet the net effect of information technology development on mid-level employment is both ambiguous in theory and difficult to assess in practice, as value added is not held constant but constantly increases; the higher-capacity mid-level employees each become more valuable to the firm, suggesting that more should be employed. The relatively low levels of increased value passed through to customers and shareholders suggests that organizations, in general, have not eliminated as many unproductive resources as they might. Existing hierarchical organizations can likely look forward to continued downsizing as networking technology clears the organizational learning hurdle.

The Persistence of Old Management Principles and Assumptions

Automation at lower levels of the hierarchy entailed no significant corresponding change in the managerial principles that governed the coordination of tasks. The technology of the day, although sufficient to automate routine shop floor and back office tasks, was no substitute for the constant application of personal judgment, middle management's purview.

Within the limits of useability (early microcomputers were closer to baby mainframes than to the user-friendly systems available today), microcomputers expanded the locations at which the analysis that supported top-level decisions could occur. Microcomputer technology was introduced under a set of what proved to be inappropriate assumptions carried forward from the previous technology; middle managers had little experience with and even less use for programming, and found character- and command-oriented interfaces with microcomputers intimidating. Individual and organizational complaints about the technology enticed venture-capital firms to fund promising innovations that would better attune applications to managers' needs and make interaction with the devices more intuitive. Companies such as Lotus and Apple shaped the new technology into a form that could get its foot in the door. But it took three to five years before the assimilation of microcomputers yielded improvements in task efficiency.[12]

Organizations that assumed that productivity gains would accrue to a one-time purchase of microcomputer hardware were likely to omit user training and support for maintenance and hardware-configuration updates from their plans. Unfavorable user experiences set microcomputer initiatives back in such organizations by a year or two, giving competitors who mounted more thorough implementations a head start and perhaps a foothold. Although the "bad" learning experiences contributed to the organizational learning process, they did little for customer relations. Customers wanted timely delivery of a product or service, not the excuse that "the computer was down." New businesses unburdened by a hierarchical heritage of fighting changes in routine did not suffer the three-to-five-year learning lag. These start-ups began to attract customers away from the more established companies. In some industries like financial services, new leaders emerged and the previous leaders are still struggling to catch up.

Their reduced supervisory and coordination responsibilities effectively offset by growing demands for information analysis and the need to shorten lags in organizational learning, middle-level managers attempted to hold their ground. But neither expanded information flows nor middle-level analysis inherently created value. A glut of information and insufficient direction in its use spawned "analysis paralysis." Middle managers with microcomputers analyzed budget results ninety-six ways with no positive, and sometimes even a negative, impact on the business.

To ignore the information being pumped fast and furiously from below impeded organizational learning, giving rise to a self-fulfilling prophecy: if top management does not expect information from lower levels to be used, middle managers will neither use it nor pass it along to top management. The result was that top managers had no more and no less information than they did when they presided over bloated pyramid-shaped hierarchies. Worse, many top managers did not notice what they were missing.

What was needed was to evaluate both potential benefits and processing costs of information generated by the lower levels of the hierarchy. Analysis of previously unavailable data on product or service performance and customer needs often yielded innovative insights into how to manufacture more efficiently or deliver a service more effectively. When such analysis was appropriately performed at the middle levels, a value-creation role emerged for middle managers that has led to their more appropriate designation as knowledge workers.

Changing Functions at the Middle Level of the Hierarchy

Under enormous pressure from shareholders and corporate raiders to eliminate slack resources, managers had few alternatives. Apart from dramatic revenue growth, the only way to bring about the needed reduction was to *flatten* the hierarchy. The mid-1970s "combing" downsizing that had eliminated perhaps 20 percent of the bottom levels of organizational hierarchies had left the middle and upper levels unaffected. The organization was thinner but no flatter.

A hierarchy is flattened by substituting some form of technological liaison for one or more of its levels. To subsume middle management levels, a technological liaison must be capable of (1) interpreting, evaluating, and summarizing for the level above information from the level below, and (2) expanding, operationalizing, and communicating directives from the level above to the level below; in other words, assuming the information-transmission function of middle management, but not its form.[13]

Even operating under management principles of the functional hierarchy, networked microcomputer technology and shared databases rendered obsolete the old managers-and-memos organizational communication structure by providing a common platform for exchanging data among hierarchical levels. Shop floor data, including comments and supervisory reports automatically captured by manufacturing systems, could be processed by manufacturing engineers' specialized applications, which, in turn, could make productivity data available to accountants. In the traditional hierarchical framework, communication would have followed the chain of command; lateral communication was frowned upon and diagonal communication unheard of. Networking technology gave rise to the emergence of informal "shadow networks" that gradually usurped formal responsibility for resource coordination from the traditional command-and-control structure. These shadow networks seemed to float on top of the hierarchy, and were used to communicate across functions to expediently accomplish tasks that would take too long if executed through the formal hierarchy.

The experience of Digital Equipment Corporation (DEC) is an instructive case study of how the shadow network works.[14] DEC's formal functional hierarchy, documented with organizational charts, was used as the basis for management control. DEC also used an explicit information network to allocate capital to new products and services, which acted as a shadow network. This network, supported by an extensive worldwide e-mail network, was headed by an executive with responsibility for allocating new product-development capital and who relied on both personal and electronic networks to carry out the task.

While the shadow network seemed to be effective, operating the two organizational structures simultaneously became, in comparison with even its initially high expense, increasingly inefficient and confusing. Although there are arguably many causes of DEC's business performance problems in the 1990s, one important issue was the effective transition from the formal functional hierarchy to the formal IT-enabled network. DEC seemed to get stuck in the middle of the transition for far too long.

In mid-1994, DEC announced another in a series of downsizing moves.[15] This downsizing involved a restructuring in which 20,000 workers were cut from its workforce of 85,000. Fifteen thousand of these workers were cut from sales, marketing, manufacturing, and engineering of the 35,000-person Computer Systems Division workforce. The general manager of the Computer Systems Division reported that the reengineered "hierarchical management of the Computer Systems Division represents a rejection of Digital's past matrix management in which every action had to be approved by people in several different operations."[16]

The DEC situation is all too familiar: historically successful companies become complacent with respect to a new kind of competition in the information economy. They then find themselves under attack by fierce competition from new companies that have more efficient cost structures and are a lot faster in the marketplace. The company begins first to lose market share, then profits turn to losses, creating a crisis. Downsizing follows—a 10 percent solution. Rather than moving forward in business transformation, however, the company goes "back to basics," regressing to what had worked in the past. DEC began with an enviably flexible situation: a hybrid hierarchy/IT-enabled network structure. Rather than forging ahead to formalize the network, however, DEC chose to shore up the hierarchy, and gain efficiency by dismantling the network.

We strongly suspect that this approach of waiting for the crises and then "winging it" will not succeed in the long term. The lesson is first not to fall behind your competition, but if it happens, don't clamp down and regress to industrial economy management principles and structures, which will make the situation even worse. Move forward.

Downsizing, as it became more pervasive, began to be called right-sizing to counter the negative connotation of job loss due to inadequate revenue growth and, by extension, lack of management vision. The latter term is better reserved for dynamic long-term plans for firm size. Management's search for the "right-sized" organization had tended towards "up-sizing" throughout much of the industrial economy era during which economies of scale prevailed.[17] The downsizing of the mid-1990's is but an eddy in the eternal process of adjusting organization size to technological imperatives. The downsizing of the 1970s, like the upsizing that preceded it, was also a management response to new technology. Just as cost-effective mass production and distribution technologies had suggested the need for vertical integration, so automation technologies are summoning systematic downsizing, essentially a form of horizontal *dis*integration.

Dissolution of the Functional Hierarchy

Built-up benefits from automation technology ignited the first major changes to the functional hierarchy. When business after business showed that it was possible to reduce production employees without adversely affecting volume, the hunt began in earnest in almost every other firm for ways to do the same. But the benefits of eliminating indirect workers failed to enter the decision-making process. Too many managers considered automation-spurred downsizing an end in itself rather than part of a larger process needing continuing management attention.

Indirect benefits arising from the interaction between technology and organization were ignored. Only automation investments justified on the basis of direct labor savings were undertaken. Eliminating a supervisory level and the resulting simplification of the hierarchy were not seized upon. The lesson for today's firm is that the broad effects of introducing new technology—indirect benefits or costs that result from altering one portion of a complete system—are too important to be ignored. Indeed, the indirect savings can often make up the bulk of cost savings from IT investments. Don't skimp on thinning out extra layers of management if implementing some new IT system has unexpectedly made this possible.

High initial capital investments associated with electronic networking technology, user training, and organizational restructuring, are more than offset by the savings in salaries and benefits realized by eliminating a level of the hierarchy. Although traditional accounting principles do not recognize their capital value, efficient organizational technologies afford shareholders real economic benefits. The equity market recognizes what the outmoded accounting frameworks miss: organizations that implement technology-supported downsizing have higher earnings expectations, which increase their market value.[18]

The fact that networking technology has threatened chaos in complex organizations ruled by the accounting and budgeting functions explains in large part the delay in adopting IT-enabled network principles, and suggests that although the costs of organizational distress were appropriately included in cost/benefit calculations, benefits were omitted or understated. The inclination to estimate benefits conservatively variously reflects shareholder pressure for consistent results, poorly-designed executive compensation schemes that use earnings-improvement targets, and simple fear of the unknown. Although many organizations that delayed adoption of networking were affected adversely, the internal transformation of the hierarchy was not slowed.

As automation became an integral component of manufacturing, job requirements were substantially redefined. Those whose jobs survived automation were expected, in addition to being responsible for routine tasks, to contribute their individual expertise to the design and creation of innovative knowledge-based tasks that would improve productivity. It is ironic that the industrial economy's emphasis on efficient production served to dampen this long-term innovation and learning process; the short-term focus on costs effectively crowded out innovations that would have yielded indirect cost savings. In any event, it fell to the employees most threatened by automation—middle managers—to define the new set of management principles required to formalize the adoption of the network organization. It's no wonder that the process was so slow.

Quantifying and Managing the Benefits of IT

Information and industrial technology are perhaps most readily distinguished by the ability to quantify benefits. Used successfully, most industrial technology yields tangible productivity benefits, while most information technology yields intangible productivity benefits. Even in the earliest internal sites where IT-automation was used, productivity gains, although identifiable, were not always immediately quantifiable. Despite measurement difficulties, however, investment in technology can yield substantive economic gains. The difficulty in quantifying such gains does not mean investment should be reduced, but that more sophisticated tools should be developed to measure these benefits. The reason new technologies often do not appear productive is that two very different methods exist for measuring productivity, only one of which is usually measured: a change in the input requirements for a given productive capacity, versus changing the rules about how inputs must be mixed. The first conforms more to conventional cost/benefit methods than the second application, and thus is more frequently adopted.

For an illustration of the first application, consider a firm that sells widgets. The technological recipe for widget production calls for two hours of a highly skilled trades person's time, two two-by-fours, and two wood screws. A new experimental technology halves these requirements. This scaling-down improvement is easily grasped and the calculation of its benefits straightforward; the value of the new technology is the cost savings from the ingredients it eliminates: one hour of time, one two-by-four, and one wood screw. No calculation is necessary; this new recipe saves money. The type of technology will likely be adopted immediately.

To illustrate the second type of application, suppose that a new longer procedure, say three hours, for producing the widget would eliminate one two-by-four. Whether this type of technology is worthwhile depends on the relative prices of wood and labor. Even if the two-by-four is more valuable, management still has to analyze this type of change to determine whether it's worthwhile to adopt. If the cost of an hour of labor exceeds that of a two-by-four, management is unlikely to adopt the technology, though it might keep it on the shelf as a hedge against a run-up in the price of wood.

Even these simple illustrations suggest that rule-changing technology is less likely than scaling-down technology to garner investment for the simple reason that benefits that are more obvious are more likely to be pursued. Only when relative costs change are firms inclined to look a little harder, to undertake the more complex calculations that are likely to make rule-changing technologies suddenly look attractive.

Indeed, the fact that information technology is designed to assist the coordination and control of a firm's resources, rather than act as a substitute for them means that resulting economic gains from technological improvement will, unless a realistic baseline is constructed, remain unmeasurable. An appropriate baseline would not represent the status quo, but instead would be a best estimate of the business outcome if the technology were *not* implemented. That is to say, the true consequences of technological investment must be measured from a hypothetical "no-investment" baseline rather than based on historical firm performance.

In the industrial economy, technological improvement took the form of incremental or dramatic alterations to existing production processes. Frederick Taylor's philosophy of scientific management formalized analysis of production processes, rendering the status quo measurable and quantifiable as a realistic alternative to investment in technological innovation. In this framework, technological investment is advisable only if its net present value is positive when net cash flows are discounted at the appropriate cost of capital. Cost-saving investments are particularly easy to evaluate, as the present high-cost state is known and the future low-cost state easily defined.

But although they have been pouring capital investment dollars into information technology for more than thirty years, managers continue to rely heavily on investment evaluation principles rooted in the industrial economy. The benefits of information technology, unlike those of industrial technology, do not take the form of incremental cost-savings cash flows that drop straight to the bottom line, but tend instead to contribute to the revenue side of the profit equation.

Many MIS industry observers have questioned whether benefits are commensurate with investment in IT, and a number of respected academic economists have been unable to provide a definitive answer.[19] Moreover, such benefits as have been identified have tended to accrue almost exclusively to customers, employees, and suppliers and only rarely to shareholders. Although this initial distribution is not necessarily critical, that shareholders tend to benefit only indirectly suggests that management must implement some control process to recapture a portion of identifiable benefits to justify their original investment.[20]

We believe the benefits of IT have been appropriated by layers of hierarchical management, divided haphazardly, and reduced by conflict among suppliers, employees, and customers. This suggests that management's first mandate ought to be to develop and deploy concrete methods for measuring IT benefits and restructure the firm to facilitate their appropriate distribution.

Over time, IT has changed fundamentally the way that work is done or not done in organizations, necessitating the development of a coherently designed framework or IT architecture. Effective IT management at the senior executive level requires a basic understanding of how IT works in the organization, a vision of a transformed organization, and a global perspective on change. The senior executive's vision of transformation—the product of a deep-seated and abiding commitment to rethinking the nature of work in the organization from the first principles of efficiency, quality, and customer satisfaction—lays the groundwork for this architecture; technical experts do the rest. The acid test in today's fiercely competitive environment is whether any technology used in a business will be directly useful.

Creative Destruction of Management Principles through Downsizing

Downsizing gets the economics right in terms of appropriately leveraging IT, which has been invested in for a long period but not fully exploited. To successfully downsize requires (1) creative destruction of one unsalvageable management principle, the rigid three-tier structure, (2) creative destruction through completely rethinking the attributes and interpretation of four salvageable industrial economy management principles—span of control, worker focus, compensation, and role of supervision, and (3) creative construction of a new information economy management principle: value creation.

> **Unsalvageable Principle**
>
> Hierarchy principle: The organization is structured into a three-tiered hierarchy: top management over middle management, and middle management over production workers.

Downsizing reduces workers to a number insufficient to accomplish the current level of work in the manner institutionalized by the old corporate structure and middle management levels. Under episodic initiatives like "radical decentralization," the power of the upper levels of the three-tier hierarchy is reduced, providing a necessarily supportive environment for restructuring work. These initiatives to flatten the hierarchy spearhead the destruction, and, ultimately, the obsolescence, of the three-tier hierarchy. Making the traditional hierarchy truly obsolete, however, is a long-term process dependent on the organization's success in creating new IT-enabled network structures.

Building the Performance Management Infrastructure

> **The New Set of Management Principles**
>
> 2. Span-of-control principle: Span of control is variable, and limited by resource availability, not by supervisors' capacity to monitor workers.

The industrial economy version of this principle holds that no supervisor can effectively manage more than six to ten subordinates. Consequently, hierarchy accumulates levels to accommodate growth in numbers of products and workers. The traditional management literature treats span of control as an organizational property that ought not be tampered with. Early economic literature treats it as an exogenous constant largely unaffected by management actions.[21] The institutionalized notion that control deteriorates markedly whenever a supervisor is responsible for more than "eight, plus or minus two" subordinates has its roots in the size of military squads: eight soldiers under the command of a squad leader.

Widespread adoption of electronic networking and the concomitant breakdown of traditional authority-based relationships demonstrated conclusively that span of control was, in part, a function of monitoring and communications technology. To become an organizational choice instead of a constraint dictated by tradition, span of control must be considered in light of existing performance measurement and reward structures. Although prevailing management principles make it appear so, information technology does not necessarily increase the optimal span of control. Rather, it changes the essence of control from direct supervision to indirect coordination. Although this shift increases the maximum possible span of control, the result is often, counterintuitively perhaps, a vastly lower optimal supervisor/worker ratio.

When salvaging an industrial economy management principle such as span of control, it is important to guard against an incremental change trap. For example, many companies have expanded span of control from one manager for 6 to 10 subordinates to one manager for 25 to 30 subordinates. The result is typically confusion that forces the adoption of some sort of indirect control to help frazzled supervisors exert even minimal leverage over their charges.

A transformational change (i.e., a 10 $\times$ return on investment, or 1000 percent) reflects a fundamental redefinition of the principle. For example, one might abandon the idea of a "correct" span of control entirely. Reduce supervisors by, say, 50 percent, but reassign 100 percent of responsibilities horizontally so that no supervisor bears any responsibility for former subordinates. Consider a 10:3 team-based approach. A 10:3 team might comprise ten knowledge workers who formerly performed line-based tasks and three who formerly performed staff-based tasks. If value creation can proceed apace with a high level of vertical communication, the 10:3 approach will create close-knit teams. But if vertical communication introduces time lags, value is destroyed rather than created by intensive staff-line interaction.

We advocate a pragmatic rather than dogmatic view of span of control. Other models that offer consistent views of a static environment consider neither dynamic technological change nor repeated interaction.[22] Indirect control techniques such as incentive alignment and automatic monitoring (as through pay-for-performance contracts), properly applied, can theoretically expand the possible span of control indefinitely, but maintenance of such a performance measurement infrastructure becomes so time- and effort-intensive as to limit the efficient span of control. The elusiveness of effective performance measurement systems can offset the ease of collecting data, leaving management no better informed.

The New Set of Management Principles

3. Supervision principle: Supervision is indirect, through results assessment, versus direct worker observation.

The principle of supervision in the industrial economy relies heavily on the direct observation of workers. The crisis-control nature of intervention in the information economy demands a job classification devoted to supervision, but of a different sort than the overseeing of manual labor required in the industrial economy.[23] In the era of human-powered machinery, a supervisor's principal task was to pressure potential shirkers to maintain peak output. Monitoring technology was limited to a supervisor's watchful eye. The central responsibility of the supervisor of an automated activity is to identify and remedy developing problems with the production system before they disrupt the work flow; problems will be automatically flagged by negative feedback loops. In the information economy, in the office as well as on the shop floor, supervision is concerned with responding to exceptions. Direct monitoring has been replaced by indirect information gathering, analysis, and control systems.

The New Set of Management Principles

4. Reward principle: Rewards are performance-based, not position-based.

Anchored in the functional hierarchy, the industrial economy interpretation of the principle of compensation and rewards placed great weight on a worker's relative position, quantified by cumbersome measures such as budget size and number of people directly or indirectly supervised. The Hay Point System, for example, explicitly equated organizational importance and contributive capability with hierarchical rank. In the industrial economy, compensation and rewards were based on contributions required for mass production and mass distribution. Blue-collar workers were compensated for meticulously following procedures and meeting production quotas: white-collar workers were compensated on the basis of their contribution to disruption-free and flawless mass production and mass distribution. These practices became highly consistent and uniform among companies.

The transition to the information economy has had a significant impact on how value is created. Mass production and mass distribution are no longer a big deal; knowledge about these techniques has been widely disseminated over the years and can be implemented by any company or country that puts its mind to it. The value that customers are willing to pay for today depends more on intangibles such as service. These intangibles rely on new technologies, innovation, and new knowledge.

Companies that employ equity-based compensation systems oriented toward pay for performance/contribution, such as Microsoft does, are attracting the most competent and promising workers of the information economy. Microsoft's policy of attaching small, frequent bonuses, such as baseball tickets, to a generous overall stock option package and a modest salary, as a reward for performance, applied knowledge, and exceedingly demanding team performance, is much more in tune with the requirements of the information economy than the highly acclaimed Hay Point System of the industrial economy.

Building the Human Assets Infrastructure

The New Set of Management Principles

5. Worker-class principle: All employees are treated as a uniclass of knowledge workers, versus the two-class system of white-/blue-collar workers.

A firm that has eliminated a significant number of workers (20 to 30 percent) is in a vulnerable position with respect to developing more productive ways to do its work. The productivity problem can be addressed in part by the build-up of the IT resource, but it cannot be solved unless the underlying industrial economy attribute of the blue-collar/white-collar dichotomy is challenged.

The traditional management model classifies workers largely on the basis of formal education. So-called "white-collar" workers who have generally attained a higher level of formal education are typically assigned job responsibilities that relate to designing the way work should be done and monitored. White-collar workers are certified by earning a degree and presumed to remain competent through on-the-job experience. Blue-collar workers are not expected to have completed, or even attended, college, and are employed to carry out the work assignments conceived by white-collar workers. Training of blue-collar workers, who have often been considered fungible, has been largely through superficial, hurried, on-the-job coaching. A ready labor supply has assumed to be waiting for any help wanted newspaper ad that offers the going wage.

Downsizing mandates that work be done in different, more productive ways. Creative destruction of the blue-collar/white-collar dichotomy is a prerequisite—the difficulty of which should not be underestimated. In many companies, the white-collar/blue-collar management principle has provided the foundation for a workers' "pecking order." For example, in a very successful aerospace company, workers were required to wear color-coded badges. Orange badges designated upper management; yellow badges, engineers; blue badges, non-technical white-collar workers such as accountants; and red badges, assembly line workers. The worker pecking order was reinforced by differences in parking privileges, dining rooms, and who had to punch the time clock and who did not. All but orange- and yellow-badge wearers had to punch in and out. This very successful company was experiencing the largest backlog in its history, while also experiencing the possibility of losses because of its existing cost structure. Again, many issues are involved in understanding this paradoxical situation, but one clear-cut area for improvement is the worker focus principle.

Eliminating the policies and procedures institutionalizing the white-collar/blue-collar management principle is an essential early step in creative destruction of the old dichotomy and movement toward a more appropriate management principle based on a uniclass of knowledge workers. The principle will be further attacked as the human assets infrastructure is extended.

The New Set of Management Principles

6. Value-creation principle: All activities of the firm must be justified by their role in maximizing customer value.

The value-creation principle mandates that all activities be viewed in their capacity for creating economic value to the customer. This new management principle is dictated by the deficiency of, and derived from industrial economy principles related to, production orientation, the blue-collar/white-collar distinction, and the role of supervision.

Consistent production initiatives must target customer needs. Spit-and-polish consistency for its own sake must be rejected as a goal and consistent quality initiatives curtailed when they fail to produce customer value. At a higher level, customer-satisfaction initiatives must be curtailed when they fail to produce long-term shareholder value.

Periodic review is insufficient to measure employees' ability to create value in the downsized organization. Value creation is ultimately judged as a noisy combination of short-term profit and the value of investments in customers, suppliers, and knowledge workers. The distinction between line and staff—or managerial and nonmanagerial—becomes a distinction between performers and non-performers, the former aggressively sought, the latter shunned, by would-be team leaders.

Just as general managers have moved (or need to move) beyond the balance sheet and income statement as methods of evaluating firm performance, so team leaders need better tools than traditional performance evaluation with which to benchmark individual performance. Managers need to formulate and apply some hybrid measure of stakeholder approval of human-capital investments. The dimensions that matter are best evaluated by employees themselves.[24] To forestall future problems, the supervisory review should be instigated as a diagnostic benchmark by the reviewee.

Why couldn't value creation be implemented in the industrial economy? Value creation was impossible to measure. Mechanisms for collecting employee performance data and comparing it against established benchmarks in a timely manner simply did not exist in the industrial economy. Traditional benchmarks of employee performance were often artificially generated from managers' idealized expectations, and tended to reflect "what we expect you to make happen" rather than "what actually happens." Such objective benchmarks as did exist relied, of necessity, because of the time and effort consumed by collection, compilation, and interpretation, on data that were seriously dated. Moreover, the data lost their relevance whenever the nature of the value-creation process changed, whether through technical improvements, workforce turnover and experience, or product-design changes.

All the computers in the world could not improve the accuracy of managers' accounting-based models of reality in the absence of documented principles describing how the new network was supposed to operate. Innovative accounting techniques such as activity-based costing (ABC) followed mainframe and microcomputer technology into management control systems, providing a basic accountability-based framework for the new network.[25] The lag between innovations in computer hardware and innovations in accounting techniques largely explains the bulk of the organizational slack created during this period.

Availing themselves of on-line information technology, today's managers can feed the results of efficiency studies back to employees almost immediately. Rising expectations and other trends can be identified month-to-month rather than in the wake of annual productivity studies. By making expectations clear and defending them with data, managers can safely claim the shareholders' slice of surplus without bogging down the value-creation process.

It is notable that the new management principle of value creation is being directly related to the notion of a "high-performance workplace." The U.S. Labor Department describes a high-performance workplace as one that provides workers the necessary "information, skills, incentives, and responsibility to make decisions essential for innovation, quality improvement, and rapid response to change."[26] A study commissioned by the California Public Employees Retirement System, a system which includes an $80 billion pension fund, showed a direct performance connection between workplace practices and corporate performance.[27]

Don't Do It All at Once: An Implementation Lesson from the Downsizing Stage

An important implementation lesson from the downsizing stage is that although multiple management principles must be simultaneously addressed in a particular stage, not all of them must be. Further, each management principle involved must be altered gradually to make accomplishment of the downsizing objectives and their associated performance improvements possible.

For example, the downsizing stage directly involves six management principles that collectively enable the organization to achieve a new economics with respect to the ratio of number of workers per unit of output—broadly, a constant output with 20 to 30 percent fewer workers. To accomplish this improvement, the following management principles are altered to support downsizing:

Management Principle	Transition that Supports Downsizing
1. Three-tier hierarchy	Delayered
2. Span-of-control	Fixed to variable
3. Workers	White-/Blue-collar to Uniclass
4. Supervision	Direct to indirect
5. Reward	Position-based to performance-based
6. Value Creation	Background to direct focus

Each of the management principles will continue to evolve to new levels throughout the transformation process as learning progresses. However, these evolving new levels not only take time, but are dependent upon a holistic process of continued mutual fine-tuning among all the management principles. This continuous adjustment process has always been the art of management, an art that changes media but not message in the information economy.

The Significance of Downsizing in the Transformation Process

Downsizing is essential to the new economics enabled by IT, but it is not sufficient for survival. Senior management must understand the big picture with respect to transformation. CEOs not up to the challenge who do not step aside jeopardize the very viability of the firms they head.

Transformation is a messy process. The day-to-day reality of creatively destroying institutionalized management principles and inventing new ones, eliminating unneeded workers and hiring needed ones, and making decisions and then having to backtrack is perpetual chaos.[28] Even the most confident CEO will have misgivings. It is in an attempt to help executives cope with the inevitable chaos that we have subdivided the recommended path of transformation practice into six discernible stages. Although the new set of information economy management principles should be adopted all at once, changing the organization all at once would lead only to a violent change of corporate leadership, if not total business collapse.

Downsizing is a traumatic shock that signals major changes in the revenue per employee (RPE) economics of the firm, form of organization, and value-added process. This first stage of transformation is an opportunity to communicate new realities and set future expectations that CEOs dismiss at their peril. Downsizing is an occasion for explicitly reassessing management principles. Manifestations of obsolete principles—the three-tier structure, corporate/divisions structure, functions/departments structure—clearly cannot be discarded in one fell swoop, but it must at least be understood that these industrial economy principles are not salvageable over the long term. Other industrial economy principles need to be confirmed as salvageable, with some of these radically redefined during downsizing. Finally, executives must continue the process of adopting the new management principles of the information economy, already begun by the adoption of the leadership principle at the onset of transformation.

Downsizing is the most important initiative in transformation because it upsets the apple cart, igniting change. It alone can overcome the inertia of old industrial economy management principles and the accompanying perception that "business as usual" is still competitive behavior. Moreover, downsizing initiates a larger campaign that senior management must manage and sustain in nontraditional ways. Understanding downsizing is crucial to the management team's success and to understanding change patterns important in subsequent stages of the transformation process.

While the adjustment of headcount to revenue can theoretically also be accomplished by revenue growth, relying on such growth is usually only wishful thinking. The right size is more frequently achieved by a major cut in the size of the workforce during a short period of time. This sudden shock contributes to overcoming organizational inertia, and consequently, is more likely to launch a company onto a long-term campaign of successful business transformation where old management principles are discarded, or radically changed, and new management principles are simultaneously implemented. Nevertheless, the downsizing stage should not be executed as a hard-nosed expression of management's toughness; it should be promulgated and viewed as a first step toward making the firm globally competitive, and as an important signal that senior management is providing the leadership necessary to make this promise a reality. An organization must be the right size before it can proceed.

Chapter Four

Stage Two:
Seek Dynamic Balance

INDUSTRIAL history offers little evidence of managerial anticipation of any aspects of technological change until they become threatening to the firm. Even as the cost-effectiveness of information technology continues to accelerate, planning techniques for anticipating future technological developments are only now being devised.

In hindsight, we believe that the impact of technology on organizational structure can and should be somewhat foreseen. Much of the trauma from downsizing occurs because it is sudden and unanticipated. Being forced to react to sudden shocks is unpleasant to management's three key constituencies: shareholders, who prefer steady growth to roller coaster earnings; employees, who prefer continuous employment to an overtime/layoff cycle; and customers, who prefer consistent product quality.

In less intensely competitive times, organizational slack served as a "shock absorber"; indeed, organizational theorists advocated deliberate tolerance of such slack.[1] The only substitute to emerge for this comfortable layer of slack is flexibility, which requires cooperation from all stakeholders. Given that the slack has been squeezed out through downsizing in Stage One, management must learn in Stage Two to distribute the benefits from this slack and achieve this flexibility before transformation can proceed. Distributing this surplus in the right proportions results in dynamic balance, a state in which all stakeholders work together harmoniously for the greater long-term viability of the firm. Learning these techniques is crucial not only to stabilizing the downsized firm, but to achieving high quality, fast cycle time, customer orientation, and global scope. Even after the firm has fully transformed, holding the firm in dynamic balance will continue to be a primary responsibility of professional managers.

The Hidden Value of Flexibility: Continuous Renegotiation

Investment in flexibility is both crucial to achieving dynamic balance and enabled by it; flexibility enables managers to reduce the organizational trauma brought about by the emergence of radically new technologies without being forced to maintain existing technologies at the leading (or "bleeding") edge. Such investment yields no immediate measurable benefits, but instead pays off in the future as technological change marches inexorably on.

The rigidity of traditional contracts can be replaced with flexible continuous renegotiation among managers (as shareholders' agents), employees, suppliers, and customers. Continuously renegotiating agreements works surprisingly well when each side remembers past behavior and understands that Machiavellian behavior will be punished in the future. It enables decisions to be put off until the ideal moment, and allows for a "make it up as you go" strategy, which maximizes the value of knowledge without unduly restricting future choice. Insisting on contracts of arbitrarily short duration permits unexpected events to be accommodated and avoids having contracts become locked into unfavorable terms for long.

Frequent renegotiation is not without its problems. Direct costs—parchment, attorney time, and frustrating hours spent at the bargaining table—can be high, and the specter of opportunistic behavior—the deliberate exploitation of a superior position for short-term gain, the damage to a future relationship not withstanding—is likely to burden renegotiation with indirect costs. These costs arise from keeping sensitive information secret, ensuring that one's partners are not cheating on the agreement, and needing to post a bond (at one's own expense) committing not to defraud one's partner, no matter how attractive it may seem to do so.[2] The relatively small empirical economic literature on optimal contract length suggests that this indirect cost can be substantial.[3] Any one-time contracting activity thus makes a painful tradeoff between nebulous costs of foregone flexibility and obvious direct and indirect costs of recontracting.

Information technology, in combination with appropriate firm design, offers a startlingly direct method of addressing the inherent problem with frequent renegotiation. Contract-writing and enforcement technology and the strategic relationship between contracting parties are factors in assessing the tradeoffs between flexibility and renegotiation costs. If we change the technology, we can potentially have it both ways—greater flexibility for the same contracting costs or lower costs for the same level of flexibility.[4] To get something for nothing, however, managers must improve their ability to make binding commitments, both internally with employees and externally with customers and strategic partners.

Ideally, a manager working in a continuous-renegotiation environment would use today's projections to delineate a strategic plan for the future and tailor contractual arrangements, formal and informal, with employees, suppliers, and customers to this theoretically optimal path. If this new method of coming to agreement were truly costless, managers would be able to write many short-term contracts and increase flexibility for a given cost level without bound.

But we have so far showed only that improved technology can address the direct costs of contracting; to implement short-term contracts without incurring the potentially devastating costs of opportunistic behavior, all partners must be provided with a very good reason not to take advantage of their situation. Reputation is the least costly method of enforcing informal contracts; parties that expect to interact again are unlikely to disrupt a cozy arrangement (in effect, forfeiting the "bond" of their good reputation) for the sake of a relatively small, one-time gain.[5] Insisting that each contracting party invest in the success of the contract is another way to discourage opportunism. A combination of the two would suggest that both partners in a strategic alliance might insist on media scrutiny; knowing that a cheating partner would be immediately exposed would give both partners incentive to cooperate fully.

Interestingly enough, lower contracting costs foster the establishment of reputation even as they depend on its establishment to create benefits. The more often two parties interact, the less likely each is to "take the money and run" rather than uphold the agreement each day. The cheaper it is to interact, the more often they will do so. Reputation and cheap contracting thus bolster one another.[6]

The Demands on Executives of Seeking a Dynamic Balance

The introduction of information technology caught many organizations by surprise. They were ill-prepared to quantify and capture the benefits derived from its implementation. The transition from pyramid to diamond-shaped hierarchies is incomplete in these surprised firms due to the lag between the availability of technology and management's understanding of its impacts. Today more than ever, however, management operates in a fish bowl. A CEO slow to pick up on a new idea or technology will likely read about it in the business press, by which time key stakeholders will likely already have acted. Employee confidence in company leadership will have been shaken, customers will have shifted to a competitive product or service, and shareholders will have moved their investments elsewhere.

This new management mandate to immediately act on information is a result of the information explosion, which continues to build momentum, fueled by the trend of 30 percent annual cost/performance increases in computer technology with no end in sight. Management needs to operate as if everyone knows everything, immediately.

To operate in this manner requires mastery in implementation of information resource management to make sure that all stakeholders receive an equitable share of benefits from transformation. New information about events needs to be captured as the events happen. Then the information needs to be swiftly analyzed and acted upon in a way that dynamically balances the interests of the firm's key stakeholders: shareholders, employees, and customers, such that none becomes disgruntled. To not do so disrupts a delicate balance of equity among the stakeholders causing them to undertake actions unfavorable to the long-run health of the firm.

Management's balancing challenge is particularly evident in attempting to capture the benefits derived from IT, which are substantially different from those derived from earlier technologies. Management's traditional tool for identifying and capturing benefits or slack, the audit, is too crude and imprecise. To be identified and harvested, a sufficient amount of surplus must be present; small quantities evade the traditional audit. Like economic order quantity (EOQ)-based inventory monitoring, these traditional control techniques set off "alarm bells" only when certain critical levels are exceeded.

But surplus from IT investments and downsizing is perceptible and accessible to other interest groups well before it builds up to the critical levels that will attract the attention of internal or external auditors. Employees who have daily access to these benefits need await neither an audit nor an invitation to appropriate the benefits. Those who have control make all the difference. If management controls distribution of short-term surplus among the three stakeholder groups—employees, shareholders, and customers—shareholder value can be increased without unduly angering customers and employees. If management loses control, short-term shareholder value can still be increased, but the pitched battle for the remaining surplus will likely consume longer-term shareholder benefits.

The problem is neither the opportunistic self-interest exhibited by those who consume the surplus (whether in money, time, or satisfaction), nor the ignorance of those charged with managing its production and consumption. The intrinsic organizational failure is the coincident combination of natural opportunism and management ignorance.[7] Management's and employees' incentives are not always aligned in the short or long terms, although they are far from opposed. If they were aligned, employees could reveal and accept accountability for the consumption of benefits without fear of retribution. Management could concentrate on coordinating resources, without worrying about keeping a close eye on employees' actions, leaving the distribution of benefits to employee agents who value long-term mutual gain. Alone, opportunism fosters eyes-open bargaining between management and employees. Accountability can be assured by basing performance compensation on either actions or results. Ideal incentive-compensation systems promote productivity investments and mutual gain by playing on employees' self-interest.

Management's Predicament: Where Should the Benefits Go?

The value that can be extracted from organizational slack is a slippery fish; if not landed immediately, it will get away. Without a concerted management effort to transform slack resources into increased shareholder value, organizations tend to mysteriously reabsorb the slack, a phenomenon that lends credence to Parkinson's Law: "Work expands to fill the time available for its completion."

Management's raison d'être, as the agent of shareholders, is to maximize long-term shareholder welfare. To do this, they must allocate resources with an eye toward both short-term efficiency and short-term equity. By distributing short-term cash flow among employees, suppliers, customers, and shareholders in the form of higher wages, orders for more product, lower prices, and retained earnings, management strengthens long-term relationships among its stakeholders. Sophisticated shareholders do not want all of today's benefits *today*; most stakeholders recognize that they stand to capture more of tomorrow's unrealized surplus by trading some portion of the dividend derived from the elimination of slack for long-term cooperation, customer loyalty, or an improved strategic position.[8] Managers who bemoan shareholders' short-term perspective often miss this point; shareholders want near-term stock appreciation, true, but this appreciation can come either from short- or long-term plans if the long-term plans are clearly and credibly communicated.

Because gains derived from control are much more easily quantified than those derived from flexibility, industrial economy managers concerned with justifying their decisions to auditors frequently leaned toward excessive control and short-term payoffs. Ideally, though, the tradeoff between control and flexibility should be based not on audit-reported accounting benefits, but on more nebulous market benefits. The latter are tougher to measure because there is no dollar amount associated with increased customer satisfaction; value is determined by uncertain future rewards, and these assets cannot be quantified in any reasonable way.

Systematic application of experience-based judgment, the hallmark of the general manager, breaks down when the effects of radical change are overly complex. All that can be done is to observe the (equity) value of the firm to the best-informed parties before and after the change in policy; if the value improves, the benefits are real. This measurement technique favors equity value-based compensation for decision makers, for whom wiser decisions will generate greater rewards. Information generated by their "best estimates" can be captured and put to work, on the team level as well as on the firm level.

Excessive control tends to induce rigidity and the inability to exploit favorable but unexpected circumstances;[9] it depends on renegotiation being undesirable. Hierarchies are particularly resistant to renegotiation, even to one-time renegotiations to accommodate mutually beneficial "side deals."[10] The happy medium is to design an organization that is capable of adapting to unforeseen circumstances on a continuous basis. A flexible environment, in which promised benefits of future cooperative interaction encourage all parties to keep tabs on their own behavior, diminishes the threat of any set of stakeholders being too greedy by demonstrating that present cooperation begets future cooperation—an indirect control mechanism.[11] Removing the incentive to grab the whole pie through a concern for one's own future reputation allows the design of the agreements between management and stakeholders to incorporate flexibility without having to either specify every last contingency or fear being taken advantage of.

An appropriately "equitable" distribution arrangement not only bespeaks good corporate citizenship, but also maximizes long-run shareholder wealth.[12] Efficiency and equity must temper one another lest customers be encouraged to defect or shareholders to search for better returns.

How Much Is Enough?

The assimilation of IT by organizations that have not yet downsized has generally been fragmented and haphazardly planned. Yet in hindsight, it is evident that as early as the mid-1970's, sufficient IT existed in most firms to support existing revenue levels with 20 to 30 percent fewer workers. What was missing was a way to accomplish this downsizing without depleting all the surplus in the process.

The downsizing stage of transformation not only overcomes organizational inertia, but demonstrates the importance of the interaction of IT and organization structure in making higher levels of activity per worker possible. Realizing this, many firms today monitor revenue per employee as a benchmark for the effectiveness of their firm's IT infrastructure. To reduce the trauma of downsizing for those workers remaining, the IT inventory taken at this stage must ensure that a viable infrastructure exists that is sufficient to maintain a firm's current level of output (e.g., revenue) with considerably fewer but more secure workers.

Five Conjectures about Surplus Distribution

Although there is no single right way to divide today's surplus after downsizing, we offer five conjectures about the distribution relative to market structure. Three represent industry characteristics that are, for the most part, beyond management's control; two are the crux of management's dilemma.

1. The more competitive the output market is, the larger the customers' portion of surplus and the more managerial effort will be expended to minimize employees' and suppliers' portions. This is a relatively undesirable situation for managers, who will constantly be fighting against similarly desperate competitors rather than innovating to improve mutual value. Not surprisingly, such situations encourage over-control.

2. The more regulated the environment, the larger employees' and suppliers' portions will be. Regulated environments such as electric utilities seek to provide a limited fixed rate of return to shareholders. When (and if) technological innovation occurs, any surplus generated is likely to be consumed internally rather than rebated to customers if stringent controls are not imposed.

3. The more competitive the supplier markets are, the larger the shareholders' portion. This situation represents a payoff to shareholders through exploitation of a superior strategic market position. Conversely, this is where supplier power can cost shareholders, as surplus from production is appropriated by input suppliers.

4. The more closely distribution of surplus parallels the bargaining power of the various factions, the larger the aggregate long-term gains for all. Because conflict among stakeholder factions can destroy surplus, some amount of cooperation is warranted, whether motivated by mutual trust and bonhomie or the sure knowledge that Machiavellian tactics will be amply repaid in future encounters. The surest method of getting ahead is to get along—a lesson not adequately learned by some industrial economy firms. Distributing short-term surplus according to short-term power is essentially an effort to avoid an inefficient "holdup" by power holders and has nothing to do with a desire for equity per se, only a desire to get on with transformation. Managers must recognize that pacifying power holders in the short term (and recovering from them in the long term) prevents a costly loss of momentum. Instances in which cooperation is mutually desirable encourage more long-term cooperation than instances in which individual maximization is best. If all crucial members get an equal share of surplus (i.e., in proportion to their equal shares of power), such cooperation is virtually guaranteed.[13]

5. The smaller the shareholders' portion, the less capital will be available to create future surplus. Because capital markets are highly competitive in relation to output markets, doling out today's cash favors employees or customers at the risk of forgoing capital and the opportunities for innovation that it might find. Top management's dilemma stems from its own role as an information-gathering, decision-making, and reporting mechanism for shareholders. Top management further compresses and transmits to shareholders information that was compressed and transmitted to it by middle management. But shareholders, insofar as they lack industry-specific experience, are not in a position to issue the kinds of visionary directives or offer the sort of fruitful commentary that top management routinely provides to middle management. They can only invest in managements (and elect directors) they trust and avoid those they don't.

Improving Management's Information Position through Information Gathering: Extending the Information Technology Infrastructure

Management that accurately estimates the magnitude of surplus generated by downsizing, that observes and understands the process of creating it, and that demands accountability for its consumption, has at its disposal a tremendously powerful competitive tool. Carrying out these activities is tantamount to a continuous audit process with a very accurate tolerance. The auditing of IT benefits must be a continuous process if management is to actively direct their distribution; even a perfect traditional post-audit will not suffice. Post-audit procedures, no matter how improved, cannot reveal more than that the benefits had indeed been created, but consumed by other stakeholders—employees, customers, and suppliers—before management got around to distributing them properly. Such a perfect post-audit would point out that management had been woefully slow in claiming shareholders' share of these benefits. By continuously auditing, however, management can make dynamic decisions about the distribution of benefits before it is too late.[14]

With this task firmly, perhaps too firmly, in mind, MIS experts during the DP and micro eras concentrated on the collection and transmission upward of information. This concentration has even drawn fire from some control theorists, who suggest that less time and energy should have been spent moving information to decision makers and more emphasis placed on giving decision-making power to knowledge holders.[15]

The role of reporting structures in the firm must be revised from being shareholder tools for disciplining management, to management tools for administering the distribution of surplus. Because decisions pertaining to the amount of IT investment and the role of reporting structures are inextricably linked, the short-term conflict-of-interest problem among stakeholders must be solved by reputation in a long-term relationship if an efficient level of IT investment is to occur. For information transfer to improve decision making, performance incentives for those who route information to decision makers must be aligned with the incentives of the firm's shareholders. Alignment can be achieved by replacing opportunistic agents with docile machinery—a substitution-based automation approach—or by applying direct incentive compensation to information gatherers—a complementary informating approach. A firm's choice of new organizational technology depends not only on the availability of IT, but also on the potential ability of the firm's decision-making infrastructure to capture and usefully employ the expanded information flows.

In one way or another, IT has influenced all factor and product/service markets. It is important for firms to obtain and incorporate information from these IT-based markets into their decision making. Executive information systems, for example, pipe real-time information to executives on commodity prices and product markets as well as global stock market prices. Most importantly, these markets provide information for a new dynamic of efficient resource utilization demanded by firms' major stakeholders.

Managing Information as a Resource

Early automation of the general ledger made practical both month-by-month budgeting, and monthly closing of the books to assess profit and asset positions. Managers, who viewed accounting as a tool for shareholders to keep tabs on management, reasoned that monthly closing gave shareholders and creditors eight additional reports on which to base assessment of managerial performance while providing little additional management information.

Over time, management discovered that up-to-date accounting data could serve its ends as well. Advanced on-line systems, tools for informing management rather than monitoring its performance, enabled financial institutions such as Morgan Stanley to close its books on a daily basis, worldwide, to assess financial position and risk exposure. Such continuous monitoring made financial hedging strategies feasible that were previously deemed too risky; day-to-day checks enabled prompt action to avert or mitigate potentially disastrous consequences of market fluctuations. Information-leveraged banks could pluck golden apples out of the reach of other banks. If a branch of the apple tree showed signs of weakness, the information-leveraged banks could beat a controlled retreat rather than suffer an ignominious fall.

Spreadsheet software made a significant contribution to speeding up and improving budgetary control. Automated transfer of spreadsheet data to mainframe-based general ledger (GL) systems constituted first-generation electronic data interchange (EDI) and the eventual integration of mainframe GL systems and personal computer spreadsheet software. This allowed departmental budgets to be up- and downloaded freely, as a step toward a universal data format.

As an example of technology in practice, consider the adoption of well-known analysis techniques. In 1972, fewer than 5 percent of organizations used discounted cash-flow to evaluate investment alternatives; by 1992, the number had grown close to 100 percent. These techniques had been known for decades, but organizations had been unable to justify their expense. The extent to which organizations can now afford to employ these techniques attests to the massive decreases in cost brought about by spreadsheet software.

Similarly, banks supplied on-line terminals to client organizations' chief financial officers (CFOs), so an enterprise could update its cash status as well as apply for a credit line extension on the spot, rather than undergo the usual business lunch process. The CFO's organization benefited from more efficient capital management; the bank benefited by locking in the organization as a continuing customer.

Marketing departments adopted on-line order entry systems to speed order processing, and mail-order firms began to encourage customers to order via toll-free (800) telephone numbers, rather than return prepaid reply envelopes. Credit card payment eliminated the uncertainty of returned checks for retailers and offered consumers purchase and price protection. Together, these practices spawned a generation of dedicated catalog shoppers. Card issuers charged a small commission in return for allowing merchants to honor their cards. Some technology-proficient firms established themselves as expert order-takers for many different stores in return for a piece of the action. Mail-order merchants, customers, order-processing firms, and banks all gained from 800-number technology.

Corporate Intelligence

Information flowing through the IT infrastructure is valuable only to the extent that it makes organizational decision making more intelligent.[16]

Even the best information is without economic value if the decision-making process cannot use it. An informed top management group must use the information available to it to configure relevant infrastructures, using indirect controls and information-gathering mechanisms. Lack of an appropriate organization-wide incentive scheme to promote the capture and use of information dooms an organization to realizing little or no measurable benefit from its IT investment. Data becomes information only through evaluation and classification into decision-making aids, which, in turn, are valuable only to the extent that their use improves the speed and consequences of management decision making.

A policy for distributing the value realized from the use of information—easily the most important source of value—is only vaguely defined in most organizations. The network structure's reliance on a knowledge reservoir rather than a set of information pipelines necessarily dilutes ownership of information and, hence, the rights to benefits derived from its use. In the absence of strong intelligence-gathering, employees and customers are likely to claim a disproportionate share of benefits, reflected in frequently disappointing IT-investment results, using traditional measures such as net present value and return on investment.

Application: Monitoring for Mutual Benefit

To distribute information benefits according to value-added, management must monitor organization members' performance, which often means monitoring the workers themselves. Such monitoring is generally and understandably, but unjustifiably, regarded with Orwellian suspicion. Employees, regardless of their work ethic, do not view monitoring favorably. A management group that anticipates a high proportion of slackers will monitor constantly at considerable cost in dollars, effort, and worker uneasiness. Management that minimizes or abandons monitoring in anticipation of a low proportion of slackers is likely to attract slackers in such numbers as to force monitoring's expansion or reinstatement, particularly if management's inclination in this direction is known.

Our experience is that newer monitoring technologies used in voluntary programs and accompanied by suitable rewards can better the lot of non-slackers by affording them an opportunity to differentiate themselves from slackers at no cost to personal integrity. The dilemma is that this monitoring must be both open and voluntarily submitted to, given workers' aversion to concealed monitoring in any form.[17] Whether monitoring of volunteers is done continuously or intermittently but randomly turns out to be irrelevant, a win-win situation that finds management, over time, able to raise the wages of nonslackers without diluting profits by overpaying slackers. To assure sufficient volunteers (slackers tend to select themselves out by virtue of not applying) management can attach a substantial wage premium to monitored jobs.

Voluntary monitoring also creates an additional flow of information from the factory floor into the managerial network and makes targeted pay-for-performance an option. The traditional objections to monitoring might be an issue concerning distribution of the fruits of labor rather than an issue of their creation. Whether traditional hierarchical authority extends to the right to monitor is hotly contested but unresolved, although the courts have recently upheld the right of employers to "listen in" on archived e-mail conversations. Such issues are moot in organizations that introduce monitoring as part of negotiated change in compensation structure rather than through fiat.

What Does the Right Set of Controls Look Like?

The central tradeoff between communal information ownership for short-term efficiency, and largely individual information ownership for long-term efficiency, necessitates a compromise between potential efficiency and the practical distribution of surplus. Two possible solutions to this problem—indirect control and information gathering—lead us to the following proposal:

A dinosaur of the industrial economy, direct control has survived into, but is totally out of context in, the information economy. The "right" set of controls in the IT-enabled network organization will be a combination of indirect control and information gathering, not either alone.

While direct control requires thinking only of shareholders, indirect control requires understanding the objectives of other stakeholders as well. "Stakeholder perspective," the theme of managerial responsibility in a multistakeholder environment, is taught in ethics programs around the world. The moral and ethical responsibilities of managers as individuals who belong to communities, religious organizations, and similar social constructs are hotly debated and beyond the scope of the present discussion. To avoid undue complication, we confine ourselves to a narrowly construed definition of the legal and ethical responsibilities of management as they pertain to the organization of the firm.[18] In this narrow construction, managers' sole responsibility is to represent the shareholders, who provide equity capital in return for claims on the value of the firm left over after satisfying its formal contractual obligations, such as debt and external contracts.[19] The classic predicament of stakeholder analysis—determining how short-term benefits should be channeled among customers, employees, or shareholders to best serve shareholders in the long run—illustrates the formidable intellectual challenge management's job entails.

The Action Plan: How to Create Value through Better Control

The relative positions of shareholders, employees, suppliers, and customers in the surplus-sharing game have changed greatly and unpredictably since the 1950s. We can reasonably anticipate more of the same kind of change.

The manager's task boils down to how to distribute today's surplus to maximize the present value of shareholdings. Figure 4-1 presents a compact road map of surplus-division decisions based on management's best guess as to future bargaining situations.[20]

In this simplified analysis, management has but one decision: where to draw the line between shareholder and employee surplus.[21] The smooth path described in Figure 4-1 is optimal even though it leaves surplus to employees because it maximizes the value of shareholdings (i.e., the present

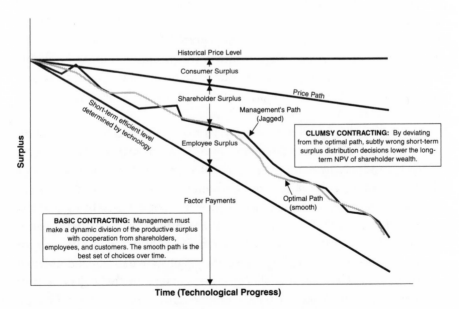

Figure 4-1. Surplus Division Graph

value of dividends plus capital gains) as distinct from short-term share-holder surplus such as dividend payments.[22] A common mistake made by industrial economy managers was to err on the side of overcontrol, grabbing too much shareholder surplus from employees and customers; this wins the battle but loses the war. In distributing some free cash flow to employees in the form of rewards for outstanding performance, a firm in effect pays more than it must for services in the short term in order to make more profit than it otherwise might in the long term. Catering thus to sophisticated shareholders makes the world of Figure 4-1 particularly rosy, and manage-rial results would prove it.

Whereas the smooth curve in Figure 4-1 is composed of a large number of extremely short-term contracts (minute-by-minute wages, for example) the real world looks more like the jagged path, in which the shortness of the contracts management can write is limited by the costs of renegotiation. This limitation makes the curve choppy, reflecting management's best efforts to approximate the smooth path by suddenly lurching from first gear into third.[23] Instead of dividing the pie with a smooth cut, small bits of benefit are left stuck to both sides of the knife.

The smooth path can be more closely approximated by negotiating alliances instead of formal contracts. An alliance is, in this sense, a group of implicit agreements that amiably divide the surplus derived from joint activities to the partners' mutual benefit. The open-endedness of an alliance lessens the threat of all surplus being grabbed today, in contrast with performance under a long-term contract; the promise of future profitable interaction with a strategic partner—and the threat to withhold such gain from cheaters—is usually enough to dissuade a firm from behaving greedily today.

Following the jagged path downward from the smooth path in Figure 4-1 improves short-term shareholder payouts at the expense of long-term value. Consider a dividend policy that calls for an extremely large payout to shareholders in the short run. Although on average this decision to return cash surplus to shareholders is probably correct, it is likely that the last few dollars of the payout are, on the margin, coming at the expense of future flexibility rather than from a current abundance of idle cash. In making the best decisions possible, management systematically makes small errors in short-term surplus allocation that, taken in the aggregate, can dramatically reduce long-term shareholder value.

Also evident in Figure 4-1 is the relationship between shareholders' normal return on investment and the surplus division process. Like employees' time, supplies, warehouse rent, and so on, shareholders' capital needs to be paid its wage (factor payment) before any division of the residual surplus is contemplated. We suspect that the negative productivity associated with IT investments stems not from the inability of such investments to create surplus, but rather from the ex post misallocation of the surplus they do create. Shareholders pay for IT by approving the use of free cash flow for investment rather than dividend distribution.[24] The normal return on shareholders' implicitly invested capital is frequently lost in the maelstrom before shareholders recover even their initial investment. The inability of a traditional post-audit methodology to capture these surpluses is perhaps the most pressing argument for a new continuous-audit paradigm for evaluating the benefits of technological investment.

Dropping the Ball: Real-World Cases of Mismanagement of Slack Resources

Misallocation of benefits can change more than a firm's internal configuration. We offer three cases in which the gradual buildup of organizational slack through ongoing technological progress, combined with misinterpretation of the correct method of realizing and distributing the benefits derived the elimination of that slack, has led to dramatic changes in firm and industry structure.

Too Much to Employees, Too Little to Shareholders: Safeway and the Leveraged Buyout (LBO)

The introduction of electronic scanning devices in the early 1980s dramatically increased the flow of customers through the supermarket check-out process. As revenue capacity per store increased without an accompanying increase in demand, slack in the highly competitive grocery business built up in the form of underutilized stores.[25] Beset by rigid union contracts and poor labor relations, the Safeway chain permitted customers and employees to siphon off the benefits of the slack before they could reach shareholders.[26] Kohlberg Kravis Roberts (KKR), through a leveraged buyout followed by downsizing and divestiture, drastically redistributed Safeway's surplus with the lion's share going to the new shareholders. Without sacrificing revenue, KKR was able to trim the chain in size, selling off many stores, some of which sat on valuable real estate worth much more on the market than under it. The effects of consolidating excess capacity and selling off underutilized real estate—a $2 billion improvement in shareholder value—are illustrated in Figure 4-2.

Safeway's persistent tendency to under-allocate surplus to shareholders precipitated the violent restructuring and change of control. KKR had both the legal opportunity through share ownership and the financial clout through leverage to carry out the redistribution; Safeway employees, acting as a unionized group trying to preserve both hard-won and IT-created

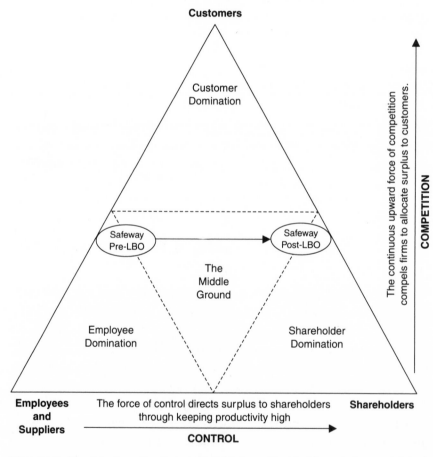

Figure 4-2. *Too Much to Employees, Too Little to Shareholders: Safeway and the LBO*

surplus, ended up with nothing. Greater cooperation might have resulted in a more flexible redistribution that would have reduced trauma all around and left all stakeholder groups better off.

Too Much to Shareholders, Too Little to Customers: The U.S. Auto Industry

Despite their cyclical nature, the U.S. automotive industry's stocks have historically yielded handsome returns. The industry's current competitive difficulties stem, at least partially, from consumer perception that Japanese cars offer better value and from problems encountered in renegotiating labor contracts.

Prior to the 1980s, U.S. automakers, in their quest to maximize shareholder wealth, exploited the lack of market alternatives available to U.S. consumers by keeping prices artificially high for long periods of time. This pricing strategy generated tremendous shareholder surplus over time, mostly at consumers' expense. As labor unions caught on to this excessive profitability and began to demand their "rightful share" of the surplus funneled to shareholders, automakers further squeezed consumers. Eventually the old "no alternatives" paradigm vanished with the influx of safe and stylish Japanese cars. What happened when consumers voted with their wallets is illustrated in Figure 4-3.

Unfortunately for shareholders, the surplus consumed during the good years in dividends, in furnishing plush offices at the executive level and in paying high hourly wages at the line level, was difficult to reclaim. With competitive forces dictating that a larger portion of the surplus be allocated to consumers if they were to be convinced to "buy American," something had to give on the shareholder or labor side.

Too Much to Customers? IBM, Compaq, and "Commoditization"

The personal computer industry offers a series of instructive distribution errors tied to rapid advances in technology. IBM and Compaq seem to have made the same error as the U.S. auto industry in not anticipating market entry by competitors. When Compaq entered the high-end clone market, its strategy was to produce a high-quality, IBM-compatible personal computer at a price somewhat less than IBM's own, with the expectation that IBM, due to its high costs and rigid structure, could not readily retaliate by cutting prices. This strategy worked well for a while, making Compaq the fastest-growing company ever. But Compaq hurt its long-

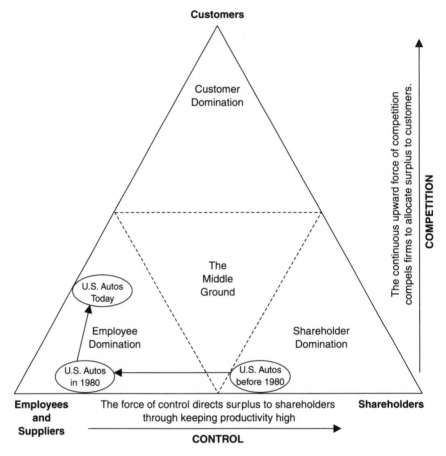

Figure 4-3. Too Much to Shareholders, Too Little to Customers: The US Auto Industry

term prospects by setting its price only marginally below that of IBM, leaving ample room for it to be undercut when widespread dissemination of manufacturing know-how precipitated massive market entry by other clone manufacturers. This scenario is illustrated in Figure 4-4.

The essential difficulty in creating long-term shareholder wealth is that at least part of any gains from technological improvements in manufacturing is eventually frittered away in competition for market share. Creating a truly differentiated product is difficult. Moreover, a significant portion of the surplus was "donated" to Intel as a dominant supplier until the x86 chip market started experiencing turbulence of its own with the entry of new competitors. The prices of IBM and Compaq stock effectively

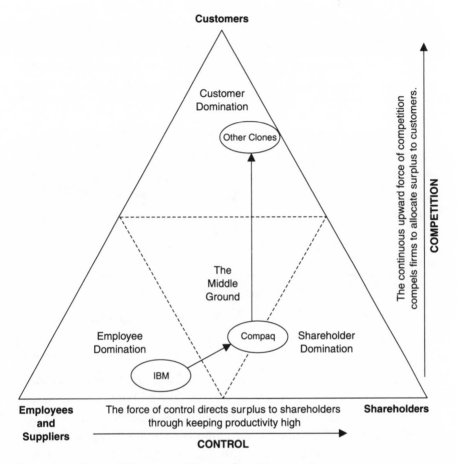

Figure 4-4. Personal Computers: Too Much to Customers?

experienced a bubble based on extraordinary, but inherently unsustainable, earnings. In the final analysis, the surplus generated from manufacturing technology has been largely transferred to those who are just now getting around to purchasing personal computers in the form of low prices. New personal computers used to cost the same as new automobiles; with 486-based PCs now under $800, new computers cost less than new refrigerators.

What can we learn from these real-world examples of surplus misallocation? None of the three industries examined has completed its transformation, that is, reached the middle ground. It is ironic, but not particularly surprising, that the much-maligned U.S. auto industry has progressed the most in its transformation. Having experienced both shareholder and employee disappointments resulting from competitive pressures, the auto industry is making tough shareholder-labor tradeoffs to win more customers. We hope it will bite the bullet and make quality, cycle-time, and customer-oriented improvements at the same time that it addresses costs.

Management Principles Central to Dynamic Balance

Stage Two, seeking dynamic balance, requires the refinement of the rewards principle and the creative construction of three new information-economy management principles: the coordination, information, and dynamic-balancing principles.

Extending the Human Assets Infrastructure

> **The New Set of Management Principles**
>
> 4. Reward principle (revisited): Rewards are performance-based, not position-based.

The emergence of knowledge work as a dominant employee classification makes recruiting and retaining high-value employees while simultaneously discouraging and eliminating low-value employees problematic without a structural change in compensation practices. The information economy version of the rewards principle must encourage self-selection, that is, it must lead high-value workers to want to join, and low-value workers to want to leave.

The limitations of a traditional compensation system become painfully evident when applied to, say, a knowledge worker who is personally responsible for overall customer satisfaction with the product developed by a cross-functional team of outside contractors associated with a long-term strategic alliance partner. A compensation system composed primarily of measurements that equate pay with position is unlikely to reward the levels of performance necessary in less formally structured environments.

The trend for all reward systems must be toward pay for performance. Simply stated, pay-for-performance compensation systems reward the achievement of specific goals rather than the expenditure of effort. Pay for performance often incorporates an equity or profit-sharing component, as well as both individual and team performance incentives tied to quantifiable goals or productivity measures. The implementation of pay-for-performance compensation systems is frequently followed by a simultaneous rise in productivity, compensation level, and profitability. Total compensation is higher, but so is the total profit earned by the firm after accounting for compensation. Shareholders surrender surplus to knowledge workers on a percentage basis in exchange for a larger surplus base for distribution.

Expansion of pay-for-performance systems has become practical with advances in information technology that support shop floor-to-executive suite information sharing and communication. With these advances, the success of pay-for-performance systems may parallel that of activity-based costing. Pay for performance (in effect, activity-based compensation) looks not for cost drivers, but for contribution drivers that measure, in absolute terms, the amount of surplus that knowledge workers contribute to the overall surplus pool.

Extending the Performance Management Infrastructure

Dramatic improvements in monitoring technology over the past twenty years have lent substance to the theoretical measurement techniques we have described. Managers use activity-based costing techniques to monitor and document activities related to the consumption of input resources such as capital, employee time, and raw materials in order to establish the cost basis of output. Pay for performance measures the quantity and value of output, completing the management information cycle on the revenue side.

The ability to benchmark observable and quantifiable performance against industry standards improved greatly with the advent of external databases of productivity information. Using such benchmarks, in conjunction with directly observable information about individual productivity, managers were able to separate individual performance differences within the firm as well as make competitive inferences about their rivals.

Pay for performance is, in a nutshell, the only way to motivate sufficient innovation and intrapreneurship among a firm's employees. Alternative forms of motivation are drastically weakened by the increasing efficiency and tightness of the labor market—particularly in technical fields such as software programming—engendered by the electronic grapevine. Management can get little mileage out of employment insecurity when knowledge workers know that they can readily locate employment elsewhere.

The greatest limitation of pay for performance is senior management error in targeting and assigning weights to the performance attributes to be rewarded. Systematic errors that might destroy a compensation system's credibility are inevitable, but their effects can be contained through benchmarking, pilot programs with volunteers, and continuous and public revision of performance standards. Continuous revision fosters reasoned choice based on information collected about the efficacy of the current system and benchmark comparisons with similar systems in other firms.

Information technology is essential to constant monitoring of the effectiveness of pay-for-performance compensation systems. IT also makes possible isolated experiments with compensation systems, a useful approach when external benchmarks prove unsatisfactory. A sufficiently diverse workforce guarantees that such experiments will find a willing constituency, as knowledge workers with particular skills clamor to demonstrate their superior proficiency. Rewarding highly skilled knowledge workers appropriately reinforces indirect, incentive-based control over the positive inflow of skills into the firm.

A 10% change. Institute a profit-sharing plan across levels of the organization. Share the wealth in good times by paying according to division or overall firm performance.

A 10✕ change. Reward productive performance, not the expenditure of valuable resources. Commit to monitoring and measuring performance based on the creation of economic value to the firm. Compensating workers according to how much of a valuable resource they expend—whether their own time (hourly pay) or others' (Hay Points)—is patently ridiculous from an incentive standpoint. Avoid company-wide profit-sharing plans that do not reflect individual or team achievement or that lead toward dilution due to firm size. Such plans are easy to plan and administer, but have no direct incentive effects, as dilution blurs the connection between effort and reward. Instead, base rewards on performance attributes that are difficult to measure, and be generous in sharing value that would never have been created but for the efforts of knowledge workers. A generous sharing policy, credibly demonstrated, will induce the creation of value all around.

Creating the Shared Knowledge and Databases Infrastructure

The New Set of Management Principles

7. Information Principle: All organization members have open access to all information, instead of restricting the flow based on "need-to-know."

Before computers, information, like raw materials, was managed according to husbandry principles designed to maximize the value of scarce resources. Today, in the age of the $800 mainframe equivalent, information is still managed to maximize the value of a scarce resource, a conception of information seriously dated in view of the capabilities of modern information technology. Information management that continues to focus on scarcity does so to the detriment of distribution.

Information need not be jealously guarded against shortage in the manner of scarce fossil-fuel resources; it need not be paid even its opportunity cost in the manner of capital resources. The "contrived scarcity" of information covers inefficiencies in its distribution within the firm. The cost of obtaining, refining, and distributing units of information is moving ever downward, and much of the value of information is not, as with other resources, truly consumable; information is not used up when employed in production. In this respect, information without a proprietary component is more like capital than raw materials; a large initial investment followed by regular maintenance expenditures provides an ongoing stream of value to the owners of an information store.

This begs the question of defining the value of proprietary information. Consumption of information is generally fully nonrival. Like Thor's goats in Norse mythology, which returned to life each morning after being eaten for dinner, information returns over and over again for further analysis even after being used for a particular decision. Even some confidential information is only partially rival in that, although it is not consumed through use, its value depends on a user's relative position in the queue—in its first use the information is extremely valuable, in each subsequent use only marginally so.

This partial rivalry for use is often confused with the time-based decrease in the value of topical information, but the two are quite different. In the case of so-called insider trading, both the value and confidentiality of the names and characteristics of takeover targets are self-evident. In this case, the tradeoff of information access hovers between releasing the information too late, depriving decision makers of needed knowledge, and releasing it too early, depriving the information gatherers of their deserved rewards. The latter course may be lucrative in the short run, but destroys both the long-term reputation of the investment firm and the incentive to collect proprietary information in the first place.

Confidentiality is also an issue when an organization wants to suppress information that might send an undesired signal. High-cost firms, for example, want to keep detailed cost data from competitors. Such information, although not valuable in the limited rivalry sense, might compromise the firm's competitive position by signaling its vulnerability in a price war. Similarly, proprietary knowledge can be an asset that distinguishes a firm from its competitors. Successful firms, for example, want to keep secret techniques for holding costs down from competitors. That costs are lower may not be confidential, but why they are lower is, if opponents can use the new information to imitate the lower cost structure.

In the special case where the value of information depends on limiting rival use, some organizational security measures are necessary. The same networks that serve so admirably to collect information can be disastrously leaky sieves, distributing sensitive information prematurely if incentives for discretion are not in place.

Information cannot communicate itself; a network member must propagate it for the greater good, or ill, of the organization. Management's task is to prevent outside sources from influencing network members to release information either prematurely or belatedly. Deliberately starving decision makers for information—the industrial economy's "need-to-know" principle—seems to solve the premature revelation problem at low cost, but carries heavy penalties on decision-making effectiveness. Confidentiality can be enforced more economically via indirect controls than by physically restricting access, as physical restriction introduces costs associated with *not* distributing needed information. Information is too important to be managed in a catch-as-catch-can manner.

Ultimately, all information from the mundane to the embarrassing should be made available throughout an organization. Even sensitive information withheld for strategic reasons should eventually be released. Investment banks are among the leading proponents of doing so, holding comprehensive briefings for employees immediately after the public release of proprietary information.

A 10% change. In support of a broad employee equity sharing reward program, put all the firm's financial information into a database accessible to all the firm's employees. Provide seminars and training to help employees interpret cash flow statements, balance sheets, and monthly pro-forma profit and loss statements.

A 10✕ change. Put all the available information about the business, its customers, and its competitors into an online data base, including financial analyst reports. Encourage snooping. Encourage the use of electronic communication for employees to get answers to any question that they might have from the firm's management or technical professionals. Focus the firm on staying ahead of the competition and away from protecting present gains and positions by emphasizing that the big deal is the mastery of continuous learning, not in discovering closeted skeletons.

Creating the Resource Allocation Infrastructure

The New Set of Management Principles

8. Coordination principle: Firm activities are made purposeful and efficient through extensive flows of information, which enable workers to anticipate and expediently correct problems using informed discretion.

Chester Barnard defined "executive work" as the specialized work of maintaining the organization in operation, not of contributing directly to the work of the organization.[27] A CEO's call on a customer, although certainly of value, would not be considered "executive work" by his definition; providing a system of communication, securing essential efforts, and formulating and defining organizational purpose would qualify.[28]

In Barnard's time, the system of communication was determined by the "scheme of organization," that is, the organization chart. Securing essential efforts entailed providing indirect inducements (e.g., material inducements such as higher salaries for higher hierarchical levels, as well as nonmaterial inducements such as prestige and praise) to engender worker loyalty. This gave rise to the "company man" organizational personality.[29] Formulating and defining purpose consisted of delegating assigned responsibility and performing formal strategic planning.

Senior management's responsibility for designing the mechanism used to measure performance and distribute surplus does not conform to any existing hierarchically-motivated management principle. A manager shifts from controlling resources to coordinating them by establishing a distribution policy and then adopting a hands-off attitude toward distribution.

In any laundry list of responsibilities of hierarchical managers, one privilege and duty associated with rank in the hierarchy stands out. The executive, in exercising responsibility for ensuring that the organization serves the long-term interests of its shareholders, is granted authority to use either positive or negative reinforcement. The executive can say either "yes" or "no" to proposals, whereas many subordinates in the chain of command can say only "no" or, alternatively, pass the buck to the next hierarchical level.

The "yes" or "no" decision is a prime example of a control function, since simply withholding approval dooms any proposal. This implicit veto power biases a firm toward inaction, since in order to even have a shot at success a proposal must either pass through all levels of the hierarchy, or somehow be passed to the top through collusion at lower levels.

A 10% change. Turn the organization chart upside-down. Put the customer on top and let customer demands rather than internally issued orders drive top-level decisions. Shift to equity-based reward systems and define purpose as delivering perceived customer value.

A 10✕ change. Make a radical shift in the orientation of executive functions from control to coordination. Prepare senior managers to act as internal consultants—as peer-level knowledge workers who coordinate real-time interactive communication, formulate robust incentive systems that promote self-selection, and maintain a dynamic consensus-based organizational purpose. The role of troubleshooting and ensuring availability of emergency assistance will be shifted to the intrapreneur. The intrapreneurial function in this organization follows the classical Schumpeterian vision of the entrepreneur in the economy: a coordinator who allocates market outcomes rather than a controller responsible for enforcing contract terms.

Creating a New Role for Senior Managers

The New Set of Management Principles:

9. Dynamic balancing principle: The firm's surplus is monitored in real time, and equitably distributed to stakeholders based on current information.

We have described the role of senior managers as that of coaches and referees rather than players or spectators. The overall level of performance of the business world has been improved by the actions of senior management acting in these new roles. In the traditional hierarchy, when senior management was a distant spectator, decisions were weighed annually in the course of the budgeting process. In today's electronic environment, production is weighed against sales, revenues against factor prices, and distribution against global conditions in real time. Decisions are made in seconds by computers operating in picoseconds, applying decision rules generated by years of top-management experience. The challenge for senior managers is to get in sync with the new required cycle time in order to be able to balance firm resources with global opportunities in real time.

The much-ballyhooed "zero-sum-game" conflict of interest between shareholders, employees, and customers occurs only in the short term, when it occurs at all.[30] In the long term, generating shareholder value is rarely at odds with producing meaningful jobs and high-quality products. Indeed, management's rational short-term sacrifices on shareholders' behalf serve to bind the productive partners together for mutual long-term gain. But short-term nimbleness on managers' parts is required, lest other stakeholders make off with the pie before it is cut.

Why couldn't dynamic balance work in the industrial economy? Less was expected of managers when their tools were cruder. Competition in concentrated industries required efficient use of existing technology but not continuous innovation. Balancing constituencies on a year-to-year basis was enough; customers and employees believed that to get immediate satisfaction was unrealistic. In today's competitive environment, rising expectations of both groups demand that management fully exploit knowledge-generating tools in pursuit of sustainable market access. In the information economy, the responsibility of the professional manager is to manage information as a resource with a steady hand, using it to wheel and deal in an informed manner on a daily basis, allowing neither too much surplus to slip through her fingers nor clutching it too tightly.

Chapter Five

Stage Three: Develop a Market-Access Strategy

AFTER OVERSEEING the initial distribution of surplus from downsizing, executives must shift their focus to the new "business as usual": the ongoing creation of customer value. No matter what their initial position, products and services take on commodity-like characteristics over time as more and more firms learn the techniques and processes for producing them. This spreading of knowledge is particularly inevitable in information-intensive businesses that rely on specialized human resources, as underutilized entrepreneurial employees leave to start their own firms or are attracted by competitors, whereas underutilized PCs just sit on the desk.

In the industrial economy, this trend toward commoditization was slowed by the sheer amount of investment required to build mass production and distribution capabilities. Developments in information technology have gradually reduced these barriers even in heavy industries such as steel making, where the large steel mills were attacked first by flexible and modern minimills, and later by even more flexible "micromills," driven by sophisticated process controls that provide precisely engineered custom steel products in small lots.

Firms unable to satisfy new customer demands enter a death spiral. First, they lose market share to the new entrants. Second, this loss of market share leads to less volume over which fixed costs can be spread at the same time that profit margins are squeezed due to increasingly intense price competition. Third, tight cash flow forces the curtailing of investments, sacrificing future profitability for present solvency. Finally, the asset base is eroded by selling assets or through creative accounting, as a last-ditch attempt to show short-term profits. The investment community quickly sees what is going on, and the firm is effectively cut off from the equity and bond markets.

At this point the only means of survival left is for the firm to reattract customers by changing its focus to provide new valuable services that are not yet commodities. We term this tactic *market access;* it is the third stage in the transformation process. For manufacturing firms, market access is achieved through providing consistent quality. For service firms, market access is generally achieved through increased speed in satisfying customer needs.

Market Access through Quality

The past two decades have seen many dominant companies put on the defensive by competitors that learned how to achieve superior levels of quality and used this ability as a strategic weapon to coopt traditionally loyal customers of cost-based firms in promising markets. U.S. managers got an unwelcome wakeup call from consumers and critics who recognized that many imported products—notably, but not exclusively, products manufactured in Japan—were clearly superior in quality to equivalent products manufactured in the United States. The usefulness of quality as a market-access tool is far from over.

Whether there exists an inverse relationship between quality and absolute firm size or not, our experience suggests that it is difficult, if not impossible, for a "wrong-sized" firm to match the superior quality of a "right-sized" competitor. Their commitment to traditional consistency-based quality measures notwithstanding, both General Motors and IBM failed to simultaneously improve quality and cut costs to new competitive levels. Progress in quality improvement was not significant at either company until downsizing initiatives took root.

The reasons for downsizing first are simple: downsizing expands managerial resources and provides a driving mandate for rapid change. It breaks the piggy bank that has been building up by underexploited information technology, releasing an immediate flow of badly-needed cash for the reconstruction process. But this cash had better be used wisely; the piggy bank can be smashed only once. Costs must be kept low, and savings in cash flows from increased efficiency must be used to fund new technology initiatives required for transformation. Employees who remain must find significant motivation to quickly improve the company's operating performance.

Automating Technology Supports Consistency

Since manual labor cannot achieve the near-perfect levels of consistency realized by automation technologies, manufacturing operations that resist technological innovation will be slowly, or not so slowly, squeezed out by competitive pressure. Substitution of automating capital for labor is merely a matter of waiting until the technology achieves the desired price/performance ratio.

Automating routine production processes is key to consistent quality and represents a giant step toward achieving total, customer-driven quality.[1] It permits immediate redirection of human talents to redesigning processes to further improve quality. Through sheer consistency, automation makes possible tremendous leverage of innovative design talents. Innovation inevitably leads to process improvements that take advantage of the increased consistency to make inroads in both quality and production cost. Improvements in quality and reduction in production cost lead, in turn, to further investments in automation. The cycle is self-reinforcing; the more automation, the greater the ability to leverage the skills of designers and engineers.

Why, then, have so many manufacturers resisted automating routine production tasks? Part of the answer lies in the historically haphazard management of the distribution of the gains derived from automation. Traditional compensation schemes were not designed to induce the cooperation and resource pooling necessary to repel contemporary competitive threats.

Moreover, there is in the traditional hierarchical framework an implicit conflict between the interests of management and labor. Indeed, when short-term surplus distribution is considered, workers' losses are shareholders' gains. Clearly, not all workers will benefit—whether in the short run or the long run—from the straight substitution of automating capital for labor. Employees at the lowest skill levels performing the tasks most easily automated will find their jobs eliminated by "soulless machines," leaving them with outmoded skills in the unemployment line. The entirely rational unwillingness of such employees to cooperate in self-elimination poses a formidable barrier to firms that would complete the downsizing process and improve quality through automation. It is to competition that this barrier ultimately falls; employees either accede to automation or the plant is forced to close. At higher skill levels, where employees recognize that they can preserve their jobs by encouraging automation, cooperation is assured.

Market Access through Cycle Time

While manufacturing firms typically choose quality as their market-access vehicle, service firms achieve market access more typically by improving their speed in satisfying customer needs. For example, success in the fashion industry is marked by the time it takes a fashion creation to reach retail outlets, not by its production cost.

The information infrastructure of a leading "quick fashion" retailer provides a direct contrast to the traditional approach of established retailers such as Sears. Fashion experts working for "quick" retailers roam the world looking for the next hot fashion. They take digital color photographs of the fashion candidates, convert the photographs into computer graphics files, and then print full-size versions on real fabric using a color laser printer. Using CAD, they size and cut the fabric for sewing prototype garments from this "one-off" cloth. Finished garments are modeled for groups of fashion experts at the corporate think tank, who make go/no-go decisions on the spot. Elapsed time from photograph to modeling session: only a few hours. Given a "go", a prearranged manufacturing facility (most likely in the Far East and not the company's own) is dedicated to producing the garment run, which is air-freighted to a distribution center from which it is forwarded, in small lot sizes, to hundreds of retail outlets. Sales are closely monitored and additional manufacturing capacity allocated as required.

Sears could get the same merchandise at a similar cost if it wanted; it just couldn't get it as quickly. In the world of fashion, not getting merchandise quickly is as unprofitable as not getting it at all. The advantage in cycle time is clearly a deliberate market-access strategy on the part of leading fashion retailers, and, in fact, defines the way they do business.

Similar links between cycle time strategy and consumer perception can be found in the personal computer industry. Computer manufacturers' version of the "hot fashion" challenge is technological innovation at the component level. When Intel perfects a new microprocessor (as the company does with increasing frequency), cycle time becomes a powerful market access tool. Major computer manufacturers that do not produce (or cannot "scramble" into production) a computer that can use this processor potentially lose the benefits of the innovation. For example, when Intel brought out its 386 chip, Compaq scooped IBM by putting 386-based microcomputers onto store shelves months before IBM could push the product through its cumbersome distribution channels. Since the 386 substantially outperformed its predecessor, the 286, consumers perceived the 386-based Compaq computers to be "zippier" than the 286-based IBM AT. The Intel chip produced the "zip," but Compaq got the customers.

Modularity and upgradeability, two forms of flexibility that can be used to hedge a firm's position with respect to future developments in technology, also have potential as differentiating attributes in the product market. The modularity revolution, in particular, is a product of both consumers' realization that upgrades will eventually be needed, and manufacturer's acquiescence to consumer "pull" over technological "push."

Informating Technology Supports Quick Reactions

An important impact of information technology has been to create vibrant markets where none previously existed, and an exponential increase in the efficiency of markets. There is no better example of this effect than electronic markets, both formal and informal. Many informal markets operate on the Internet, such as the one for used computer equipment. Used computer equipment listed and bid on the network is efficiently cleared by a global marketplace. Used equipment prices quickly reflect product price changes announced by manufacturers, or else are roundly criticized as "rip-offs." As the Internet becomes more open to commercial use, new firms with innovative products and services are able to satisfy global demands with Internet's global distribution by using the "infobahn" as their own wide-area network. As a result, instant $10 to $100 million revenue companies are being born. These companies with innovative products or services are not burdened with the logistical problems of traditional marketing and distribution systems. They use multimedia techniques to describe their products to Internet users via the World Wide Web, as well as e-mail to the other millions of potential buyers from other networks that Internet interconnects with America Online, Delphi, Prodigy, Compuserve, and MCI Mail. If these techniques are foreign to you, your firm is behind.

Context for Consistent Quality and Cycle Time Reduction: Past and Present

Quality programs are not new. Even before quality competition from imports forced managers to take a hard look at quality levels, quality control management was a familiar function in most manufacturing industries. Traditional quality control such as statistical process control emphasized consistency—ensuring that a manufacturing process conformed to specific tolerances over time—rather than any market-based evaluation of quality. This orientation, a logical outgrowth of the scientific-management movement at the turn of the century, was purely cost-driven. Because the embedded value of labor and material could suddenly be lost if a glitch in the manufacturing process forced scrapping of the semi-finished product, prevention of glitches became the paramount goal of production engineers. Small improvements in the consistency of individual components of the line process translated into big improvements in yield for the line as a whole.

A cost-control focus was entirely appropriate for the industrial economy. With immense, pent-up demand for industrial goods, almost anything that could be manufactured could be sold, rendering available manufacturing time and capacity a valuable commodity. But such an exclusive focus on the cost side severely neglected the consumer as a vital stakeholder in the surplus-creation process. The shift from massive production runs to customization and shop-floor innovation redefined cost-control and consistency as useful quality measures rather than as ends in themselves.

The virtue of a consistent, hands-off process is that observation costs are small. Business as usual can be sustained without constant crisis-management troubleshooting. To make the process easy to manage, however, design and manufacturing tolerances must be set conservatively for easy manufacturability rather than to reflect customer preferences. This process might be likened to testing eighth-grade students not on the material taught but on the material they already know; the standard is universally met, but remains low, and the process discourages learning and experimentation. Continuous improvement relative to past performance works as a satisfactory learning measure only when all competitors adhere to the same standards.

Manufacturing firms insulated from intense product-market competition tended to target the smallest acceptable level of quality (see Exhibit 5-1). Quality greater than this threshold represented surplus that might

---

1. Estimate how sensitive consumers are to quality considerations.
2. Estimate cost of improving quality or payoffs from reducing quality levels.
3. Determine the level of quality that will maximize profits.
4. Assign new quality standards to manufacturing engineers.
5. Design a consistent manufacturing procedure that minimizes production cost while meeting minimum acceptable quality standards.
6. Compensate or reward process engineers on the basis of production costs.

Exhibit 5-1. Industrial Economy Steps for Estimating and Enforcing Quality Tolerances

have been retained as profit by the manufacturer and was being passed unnecessarily on to consumers. "Turning down quality" was viewed as an acceptable way to reduce costs, "turning up quality" was laughed at because the attendant costs would mean lower margins without significantly increasing market share.

As early as the late 1960s, when the threat of competition from Japanese automakers was a bad party joke, *Road & Track* magazine was complaining about quality defects in American cars.[2] U.S. automakers during this period clearly were managing for the bottom line, not for long-term customer satisfaction, a strategy that paid off handsomely for shareholders in the short run. General Motors stock, for example, between 1960 and 1980 returned in excess of 20 percent annually. This may not seem like such a great accomplishment until we consider that one dollar invested in GM stock in 1960 would be worth four times as much in 1980 as an equivalent amount invested in U.S. savings bonds.

Justification for this huge premium—the risk of entry—lay in product, not financial, markets. It was late when U.S. managers awoke from their industrial economy reverie and discovered the necessity of competitive benchmarking on quality aspects, but not too late for them to recover and compete in the vast majority of information economy industries.

Organizing for Quality: The Total Quality Orientation

U.S. manufacturing's awakening to aggressive Japanese forays into quality-sensitive U.S. markets was sudden and rude. Japanese industry had traditionally excelled at rubber-stamp manufacturing, achieving perfect consistency through tight process-control guidelines. Product quality, in terms of fitness for use, did not initially match Japanese manufacturers' interest in high production consistency. Up was the only direction for Japanese manufacturing to go from this high-consistency, low-quality position.

New product entries targeted markets in which quality was particularly important and changed the profile of Japanese manufacturing forever. As the new focus of Japanese companies on product quality began to speak for itself in the marketplace, their reputation for poor quality was forgotten. Despite four decades of experience with shoddy Japanese goods, by 1992, nearly all American consumers stated that they would consider purchasing a Japanese car, and more than half believed Japanese automobile quality to be significantly superior to U.S. automobile quality.[3]

With ferociously competitive entrants setting quality standards well above those achieved by tolerance-based manufacturing, U.S. manufacturing's notion of "consistency as quality," as embodied in its traditional functional organization, was suddenly woefully inadequate to sustain competitiveness. Some U.S. firms could not achieve Japanese quality levels at all without major manufacturing-plant reconfigurations, an impossible task in the short run, and even limited quality changes could be realized only at prohibitive cost.

Attention to total quality as a market-foreclosure tool became critical in markets that had not yet been targeted. For firms under attack that had elected to fight, wielding a total quality orientation as a market-access tool became the first step to reclaiming lost market share. Firms that chose not to fight were reduced to lobbying for trade barriers.[4]

A total quality orientation requires a commitment to critical and unrelenting self-examination, a customer focus to guide what needs to be done, the willpower to suggest and effect changes in fundamental processes, and the wisdom to recognize when and where to fight or flee. Total quality derives from customer orientation driving manufacturing process improvements, not the other way around.

Total quality orientation has a place in transformation as a market-access tool. The total quality orientation strives to add the most competitive strength to the product that can be achieved entirely within the manufacturing process. Because consistently low quality is no longer sufficient for market access, achieving parity in consistency is only a first step. Total quality is more than consistency; it encompasses other competitive strengths such as customer service, product innovation, and quick delivery.

Organizing for Improved Cycle Time: Decentralizing Decision-Making Rights

We borrow the term cycle time from the vocabulary of quantitative management of manufacturing processes, in which context cycle time is defined as the elapsed time between inputs entering and a finished product exiting the manufacturing process.[5] Cycle time is thus a negative indicator of process speed: a higher cycle time indicates a slower process, a lower cycle time a faster process. Accordingly, "decreasing cycle time" and "improving cycle time" are synonymous, "increasing cycle time" and "improving cycle time" opposites. Decreasing the cycle time of any given process increases the productive capacity of the process over any given time period.

Bottlenecks and cycle time: targeting and improvement in the information economy. Cycle time is entirely dependent on a system's slowest component, or bottleneck. Two logical approaches to improving cycle time are (1) to attack bottlenecks where they occur, and (2) to redesign the system so that the bottleneck is involved in the process less frequently. Up to a certain point, the first method yields a direct one-for-one improvement in cycle time when the slowest component is made faster. After this point, a new bottleneck will intrude on future improvements, as every system will always have a slowest component. We call this a direct improvement.[6]

The second method forgoes component-level improvement for system-level improvement, redesigning the process to avoid the slow component. The slow part will still be incredibly slow compared to the rest of the system, but its comparably rare use will raise the effective speed of the system. We call this an indirect improvement.

Real-time decision making is a bottleneck in today's organizations. This bottleneck can be attacked in two ways: distributing information faster, or decentralizing decision-making rights to economize on required information transmission.[7] Transmission delay between information gatherers and centralized decision makers represents a direct cost in efforts to decrease response time. Agency costs associated with decentralized decision making can be partially overcome by assigning accountability to the agents. Using CAD/CAM to reduce cost and improve product quality, a direct improvement, created increased cross-functional communication as a byproduct, an indirect improvement.[8] Similarly, on-line customer databases, ostensibly developed to improve customer relations by making historical information immediately available (a direct improvement), put decision-making rights in the hands of contact-level employees (an indirect improvement). Such accountability does not slow the progress of individual decisions and thus does not reverse the cycle time improvement gained by eliminating the transmission delays.

Though maintaining the flow of information occupies the bulk of management attention in the traditional hierarchical organization, the speed of flow also directly affects managerial performance. Electronic mail has accelerated organizational communication. Specifically, it reduced the cycle time of management tasks in much the same way that just-in-time (JIT) reduced cycle time for assembly-line technology; electronic mail took only a few moments to flow through the system before it was accessible—a direct improvement.

Making managers responsible for picking up their E-mail quickly proved another matter. Early implementations of electronic mail as a substitute for memoranda and the telephone represented little more than the automation of paper-based management, emphasizing the mundane transfer of information among normally connected individuals. The medium's speed and unique ability to connect the hitherto unconnected was ignored. Only recently has this communication method favored by technical experts become widely employed by project managers and others. When electronic mail eventually reached a critical mass of internal use, two events occurred almost simultaneously: (1) the medium's capability was expanded to accommodate entire formatted documents, and (2) a vocal and sufficient minority of users began to demand that electronic mail be formally recognized as an acceptable method of intraorganizational communication. Eventually all employees who wished to be "in the loop" felt compelled to adopt electronic mail. The indirect improvement is on the way.

But electronic mail was not to be restricted to intraorganizational communication for long. Continued growth and standardized formats rendered the medium ideal for external communication with suppliers, customers, and competitors. User-friendly interfaces running on personal computers permit even non-technical users to access this medium's full power. International networks, such as Internet and BITNET, further expanded the scope of E-mail and quickly became essential to educational institutions, commercial firms, and government agencies, precipitating an explosion in internal networking among firms eager to tap into such ready resources. Discussions, technical and not-so-technical, from telecommunications to poker strategy, quilting, and favorite recipes were accessible to just about anyone. The indirect improvement may exceed the direct!

Multimedia technologies such as videoconferencing are expanding the bandwidth of electronic communication, enabling face-to-face communication across continents. Only smell, taste, and touch are lacking for total sensory interface. The boundary between reality and virtual reality is being blurred by technologies designed to simulate such common real-world events as negotiation. One investment bank sawed a mahogany table in two, shipped one half to London, and constructed a "virtual bargaining table" through videoconferencing. With participants able literally to look across the table at their partners, the traditional stomach-clenching tension of negotiations was preserved across the transatlantic link.

How can cycle time be improved? Inside every functional hierarchy composed of processes with vastly different cycle times there is a network organization struggling to get out of its shell. Many eventually succeed. But in attempting through strict control techniques to reinforce the hierarchy during the DP era, management poured cement into the cracks in the shell, delaying considerably the network organization's hatching.

Managers who apply old organizational techniques to the management of new technology cheat their firms of a smoother and shorter transformation process. Senior managers today must recognize that applying new organizational principles to the management of new technology yields not a 10 percent improvement, but ten times greater benefits.

Some networks will escape their shells on their own without external help, others will founder before reaching the light of day. Instead of patching the shell, management should carefully damage it: strike a precise but forceful blow by formalizing the shadow network, weakening the external constraints and letting the forces from within do the rest. Patching an already seriously cracked shell will produce only a compromised hierarchy and a smothered core of entrepreneurs.

The strength of weak ties. The cracking of the shell heralds the arrival of the network organization. Network organizations are composed of links of varying strength and character. Networks of weak (informal) ties based on mutual expectations of performance, professional reputation, and the electronic grapevine demonstrate considerable strength in maintaining cooperative behavior inside organizations in the absence of strong (formal) ties such as employment contracts.[9] Microsoft, for example, guards against high employee turnover not with legally enforceable employment contracts, but with an innovation-nurturing atmosphere and tremendous breadth of resources that work to make its employees a tightly-knit group driven by challenging project milestones and rewarded with stock-option incentives. Microsoft's weak ties maintain organizational cohesiveness far more effectively than do many hierarchical organizations' stronger ties.

Traditional notions of organizational size based on revenue or number of employees have little meaning in networks of employees, independent contractors, and specialists. Network structure blurs organizational boundaries, making it difficult to tell who is "inside" and who "outside." The ability to tap into significant external resources owning huge amounts of assets makes actually owning these assets irrelevant, enabling even the smallest networks to take advantage of competitive opportunities as they arise.

Management Principles Central to Achieving Market Access

Pursuing a market-access strategy focuses an organization on gaining customers by providing value that was generally unattainable or unprofitable in the industrial economy. It involves the creative destruction of three industrial economy management principles and the creative construction of two new information economy management principles. Functional organization needs to be discarded and the strategic orientation and task principles need to be fundamentally reinterpreted. In addition, new management principles are needed that will shift senior management's role to that of organizational architect and emphasize reliance on intrapreneurial teams.

Discarding the Functional Organization Form

Unsalvageable Principle:

Functional principle: Tasks are organized into fixed functions of line and staff based upon type of expertise. Line tasks directly relate to making or selling, and staff tasks support these activities.

Within the functional hierarchies of product divisions and corporate activities, work was organized into functions carried out by departments of workers. Manufacturing and marketing, the traditional line functions, were supported by staff functions, traditionally accounting, planning, personnel, purchasing, legal services, and information systems. Line workers were perceived to create value directly, staff workers indirectly (hence, the reference to staff as indirect workers). This is a totally obsolete principle that needs to be scrapped.

A 10% change. Emphasize teamwork. Mandate the organization of teams, drawing on direct and indirect workers to fit skills to needs. Hire additional workers in areas in which current resources are insufficient.

A 10X change. Totally reject functional organization in favor of a team and project-based organization. Let team leaders—your corporate intrapreneurs—select team members; emphasize that they must accept the risk of failure as well as the rewards of success.[10] Accountability and compensation based on incentives will change these intrapreneurs from standardized employees into hundreds of parallel decision makers. Separate nonintrapreneurial employees into two categories: those sought as team members, and those shunned as team members. Encourage the former to join teams and encourage the latter to improve or leave; outsource their tasks. To sustain competitive advantage, the human resources available to teams must be globally competitive. If your own resources—human and otherwise—do not meet the globally competitive standard, contract with outside resources. Your competition surely will.

Cross-functional teams do more than lower production costs; they also foster cross-functional investments, as in the simultaneous improvement of MIS sophistication and underlying processes. Many consultants are forced to recommend million-dollar repairs on complicated MIS systems knowing that $100,000 in shop floor improvements would provide the same level of clarity. Their efforts to improve management's information position are frustrated by functional walls that prevent them from addressing the problem at its shop floor source.

Total integration of functional teams has been problematic for a number of reasons. Functional areas with separate goals and responsibilities carried over from decades of hierarchical organization have never interacted directly before. Although functions have generated information useful to other functions, each required a different format to maximize efficiency.

It did not make sense, for example, to require engineers to go through balance sheets to obtain critical cost information, which was nonetheless necessary to product design.

The introduction of IT smoothed these differences, encouraging cross-functional communication among existing employees and thereby facilitating the transition from functional to project organization. Integrated databases made enormous volumes of centrally stored information universally accessible and individual workstations supported remote processing in individualized formats. The integration of CAD and CAM effectively forced engineering and manufacturing to adopt common standards, databases, and protocols while continuing to allow for the viewing and interpretation of information in idiosyncratic ways.

The gains from functional integration and cooperative data sharing, first evident in CAD breakthroughs, led to the puzzling result that some products could be designed, but not built. This problem was particularly frustrating to a company that was receiving a hammering in the product market; to know that the solution is on the drawing board but cannot be manufactured has irritated, to say the least, many chief operating officers. The considerable capital investment in production technology focused manufacturing managers' energies on cross-functional activities aimed at catching CAM up to CAD. This is an instance of managerial myopia contributing positively to the transformation momentum; management's fixation on past CAD expenditures lit a fire under CAM.

Building the Project Tasking Infrastructure

> **The New Set of Management Principles**
>
> 10. Task principle: Work is organized into projects, and carried out by team members assigned to these projects based upon their expertise necessary to accomplish the project goals.

Functions in a pure hierarchy are joined only indirectly, with common vertical authority stemming from their relationship to the corporate body. Functional independence presumes that organizations are most effective when activities are as mutually exclusive as possible. Responsibility for product safekeeping and value-added progress are defined explicitly by the physical movement of product. This mutual exclusivity of tasks, in enabling effective specialization and focused effort, attempts to take Adam Smith's ideal division of labor to its logical extreme.

Creative destruction of functions calls for an alternative for carrying out tasks. This alternative is projects. Projects are defined at a point in time based upon requirements and resources available. Consequently, project organization of tasks is more flexible and efficient than functional organization.

A 10% change. Rotate employees across tasks to ensure a secure source for all critical skills needed to create value, i.e., cross-train. Keep a roster of who's been cleared to perform which tasks.

A 10× change. Celebrate interdependence. Interdependence is what makes a group an organization rather than just a basket of resources. Create a real-time database of skills and interests and indicate whether these skills are fully utilized in existing jobs. Broadcast the highlights of the findings—for example, that eight people in the firm speak fluent Farsi or that only three CPAs in the corporate office are computer literate. Create a corresponding database of project needs, but let individuals and teams find one another. Enable, do not dictate, these link-ups.

The Changing Nature of Command and Control

> **The New Set of Management Principles**
>
> 11. Architect principle: Senior management shapes the firm's structure through the design and redesign of infrastructures necessary for the operation of self-designed teams.

To allocate decision-making rights to reflect the location of specific knowledge is to split the responsibilities of senior management along the lines of control and command. The command task falls to specialists within the organization who excel in the efficient scheduling of human, capital, and information resources, and setting up incentives to make resources command themselves. Senior management involvement on the command side must be limited to providing for a smooth transition to the new structure.

The control function will become more important once the transformation has run its course. At the core of control theory is the tradeoff between information transfer and agency costs. Locating decision-making rights where specific knowledge resides—and not, by default, at the top of the hierarchy—means bringing about both information transfer and agency costs, the latter being the cost of improper use of decision-making rights.[11] Minimizing these costs by making information more accessible, implementing incentive-compatible compensation systems, making decision makers more accountable for outcomes, and monitoring the overall process, becomes the primary focus of the executive in a network environment. As enforcers of the game rules, executives' control efforts add value by providing credible commitment to formal contracts and informal treaties. Senior management must draw on years of coordination and control work in hierarchical situations to demonstrate unquestionable competence at this new control task.

Command of resources is by definition dispersed among intrapreneurs in the network organization. Since it is hardly a given that senior managers will prove more intrapreneurial than other network members, we predict the rapid demise of the command function of senior managers in the modern corporation. After the organizational transformation, senior managers' time will be spent on building network architectures and facilitating coordination. As internal expert consultants, they will have to justify their value to other network member-users or face the outsourcing of their own function.

The dynamism of the customer-driven marketplace demands that senior managers transmit their organizational learning to other members and develop expertise in leveraging their coordination skills through structure and resource commitment. Traditional executive responsibilities of a more static nature, such as explicit organizational design, will be replaced by dynamic experimentation, prototyping, and "going with what works." In their new role as coaches, senior managers will split the difference between being on-court players and their previous role as spectators.

Changing the nature of supervision need not mean losing control. Supervision has a negative connotation, in which subordinates are regarded more as juveniles than mature adults. Although draped with the legitimacy of management theory, direct supervision and control are legacies of another era. Today's fast-moving business environment requires innovation and quick response to crises. Traditional control is delayed, retroactive, and retrospective—qualities that are altogether ineffective in directing the modern enterprise. The role of senior management is not control per se, but real-time coordination of action aimed at achieving the best outcome for the organization's stakeholders and, by extension, the organization itself.

Serving contemporary changing customer needs in real time differs fundamentally from the stable mass production of products and services. Today's dynamic marketplace has changed senior management's role from hands-on, line-level organizational design, to having a birds-eye view of organization design or architecture. This view enables knowledge workers to create the appropriate specific design for the marketplace of the moment, exploiting the dynamic flexibility of the network form.

Why couldn't the architect principle work in the industrial economy? Today's real-time information systems provide immediate feedback on the consequences of decisions. When real-time control was impossible, traditional control techniques made the best of significant delays, relying on geographical proximity to enable face-to-face communication and maintaining control retroactively, in a negative-feedback manner designed to stop an existing impulse. Such responses to the technical limitations of yesterday's information technology are ridiculously inappropriate in the context of today's information systems.[12]

Cross-functional IT includes managerial modeling and decision-support systems that can facilitate the sharing of information vertically as well as horizontally. DP era mechanisms by which hierarchical firms leveraged information included managerial reporting structures and MIS that attempted to recreate production processes in virtual fashion. The technology to support such models was somewhat lacking, and the early models were not exact; unexpected disturbances, for example, did not show up in the managerial model.

Nevertheless, the more consistent the production environment, the better the correlation between the virtual and the actual factory. Clinging to manual production techniques introduces unnecessary noise into management decisions, reducing correspondence between model and reality and leaving the factory in a low leverage position despite sophisticated managerial modeling techniques.

To expend enormous amounts of effort to improve management's information position without first justifying the production process is inefficient. Concentrating on management information puts the cart before the horse, confusing cause and effect. Sophisticated management tools do not make the shop floor manufacturing task easier, but simpler shop floor processes do ease the task of management reporting. Hence, the most efficient course is to first make the process consistent and thereby simplify the management tools needed for control. Savings from a more focused MIS-improvement effort will more than cover the cost of business process redesign on the factory floor.

Extending the Resource Allocation Infrastructure

The New Set of Management Principles

12. Strategic orientation principle: The strategic orientation of the firm is serving customers' needs, versus manufacturing the product or service.

The rise of managerial capitalism centered on the alternating goals of maximizing production and generating demand.[13] The customer in the industrial economy was the masses, not well-defined individuals; consumers as individuals played an insignificant role. Large groups of customers known as market segments were the smallest aggregates that industrial economy companies recognized in their manufacturing and marketing activities.

Corresponding production strategy shifted to meeting the market segment demands of specific groups, provided demand justified building a plant of minimum efficient scale—a production technology-based criterion describing the point at which long-run average production costs are minimized for the first time in the growth of a firm. But it is the more strategic market-based concept of minimum efficient size that establishes how small a firm may be and still compete successfully with industry rivals. These measures share little more than an acronym, differing fundamentally in their prescriptive scope. Minimum efficient size is concerned with competitive circumstances, minimum efficient scale only with the engineering relationship between fixed and variable costs. Put another way, minimum efficient size relates to profitability, on both the cost and revenue side; minimum efficient scale refers only to cost efficiency. Firms that build to minimum efficient scale set production capacity to drive average production cost down, but do not consider the impact of that capacity on market price. There was no need to do so in the industrial economy, when capacity was so scarce that even massive additions could only partially slake consumers' thirst for industrial goods.

Asked why maintaining high production levels was important to profitability, industrial economy managers would likely have responded "economies of scale." What these managers would have meant by this ambiguous statement was that increasing volume sufficed to dilute large fixed costs of production thereby lowering average accounting costs. This simple picture misleads when variable costs change with output level or experience. If variable costs increase as production rises, this interpretation of scale economies can significantly reduce profitability: the rise in variable costs will increase average costs more than the dilution of the initial fixed investment will lower them. A firm's overall average costs may increase with volume, cramping profitability as price is held constant or declines.

A second component of economies of scale is the learning curve. The presence of a learning curve implies that the last unit of production costs less than the first by virtue of being last, that the organization has somehow reduced production costs through experience. A genuine learning curve is a true example of economies of scale; incremental costs really do decrease, the average cost goes down without resorting to the dangerously naive fixed-cost dilution argument cited above. Indeed, a learning curve pushes producers toward larger and larger scale, as fixed costs are diluted and variable costs decline simultaneously.

But the circumstances of the first half of the century, when demand for industrial economy goods greatly exceeded supply, could not last forever. Commoditization of traditional products and services forced firms to take into account the effects of their production decisions on market prices. As more and more undifferentiated competitors piled into the markets, prices were driven downward to the point that only variable costs were reimbursed. This downward price spiral not only effectively stifled entry, it also canceled rewards to incumbent firms. In a traditional corporate finance setting, this translates roughly into being able to break even on operations, but unable to pay interest on the bonds that fund capital expenditures. Firms can persist in such an environment only as long as their capital remains productive. The rest must exit, and thereby improve the profitability outlook for those that remain.

Information technology enables firms to add value through customized product differentiation. The notion of using productive capacity to create value for consumers as individuals is at the very heart of the strategic orientation shift from a production-driven orientation to a customer-driven orientation. Customer satisfaction, rather than efficient use of productive capacity, becomes the interim goal of the product manager. The firm achieves profitability by focusing not on cost reduction, but on revenue enhancement.

Low cost is no longer the crucial issue when competing through differentiation. Customized products cannot, presumably, be produced in batch sizes sufficiently large to lower unit costs to the absolute minimum through the dilution of set-up charges. Moreover, the learning curve for highly customized product offerings reflects experience with customers rather than experience with a production process. Accordingly, it is less important that a product be created in the most efficient manner than that it be sold to the right customer. Attention shifts from the cost side of the profit equation to the revenue side and marketing relieves manufacturing at the helm.

A 10% change. Have senior managers spend three days per month directly serving customers. United Airlines had managers work at airport ticket counters.

A 10✕ change. Evaluate each activity of every worker with respect to direct value added in the firm's customer relationship. Tie rewards directly to adding customer value. Nordstrom's "sales per hour" commission and control system, for example, encourages employees to focus on creating value by serving customers.[14] When shaping strategy, concentrate on serving customer segments rather than figuring out how to use organizational capabilities.

Extending the Performance Management Infrastructure

> **The New Set of Management Principles**
>
> 13. Team principle: Teams are formed by leaders offering compensation packages intended to attract knowledge workers with the expertise needed to achieve project objectives.

The old industrial economy principles of functional independence, compensation determination, and the role of supervision give rise to new information economy principles that call for intrapreneur-led teams. Intrapreneurs organize individuals into teams to exploit members' diverse sets of skills through mutual commitment; the bulk of these members' compensation comes as formal recognition of their contributions to those teams.

The team performance-management infrastructure must evolve to enable the efficient functioning of the team-based structure. The only nonnegotiable aspect of teams is the dispute-resolution mechanism, which must be handled by networked executives, as Principle #18 will address; all else can be amicably negotiated according to the needs of the teams in place at any particular time. Both the purpose and practice of team management depends on the activities of other teams in an organization. Cross-functionality follows naturally from intrapreneurial team-based activity: to speak of "functional independence" when both functions and independence are absent is clearly not meaningful.

IT that enables cross-functional process integration contributes to an organization's information leverage. Common forms of cross-functional information technology include materials requirements planning (MRP) and computer-aided design and manufacturing (CAD/CAM) systems. The cross-functional relationships encouraged by such systems are anathema to hierarchy, but vital to the network organization.

Instead of offering rigidly structured jobs with fixed salaries, managements will offer menus of responsibilities and corresponding compensations. Instead of having to choose a job and stick with it, employees will be able to select from these menus over and over. Intrapreneurs will themselves be offered a smorgasbord of menus in the form of the constant inflow of opportunities afforded by various internal and external marketplaces.

The sole remaining responsibility of the "supervisor," strictly construed as "overseer," is to interact with the performance management infrastructure in evaluating team results as an evolving pattern of performance rather than focusing on any one success or failure. Intrapreneurs are concerned with efficiency, relieving senior management of that responsibility. Team members join teams voluntarily and thus control their own destiny.

Why couldn't these teams work in the industrial economy? The industrial economy lacked performance measurement systems needed to make team-based compensation work. With a credible performance management infrastructure and a demonstrated commitment to rewarding superior performance, significant productivity gains can be realized indirectly from IT expenditures, which unlock the gains from monitoring and evaluating other processes. The transaction costs of pencil-and-paper monitoring would swamp any gains from continuous contracting, team formation and dissolution, and surplus division; not so in the information economy.

In the self-designed network organization characterized by evolving teams, voluntary and deliberate withholding of vital skills constitutes the only veto-like power. The network organization counters this form of "hold-up" by rewarding rare abilities and structuring compensation on a project-by-project basis in a way that makes participation highly attractive.

Implementation Lesson from Market Access: Look in Your Own Back Yard

The preliminary downsizing essential to transformation improves consistency through automation and frees up resources to fund quality and cycle time initiatives. Moreover, it forces the organization to adopt a "lean mentality." Being on the efficient frontier and under siege is a challenging environment that can, if framed properly, foster feelings of comradeship and cooperative desperation. Quality initiatives channel employee effort in a positive direction and reward performance over both the short and long term.

Information technology has engendered an organizational environment entirely different from that of five or ten years ago. Organizations under siege have no alternative but to acknowledge and incorporate it. Management information systems that expand knowledge about business processes enable management to introduce consistency and thereby greatly simplify control. In practice, it makes economic sense to first make underlying processes simple and consistent, as this greatly simplifies the management tools needed for control. Savings from focused improvement efforts at the information systems level more than make up for the costs incurred by business process redesign on the factory floor.

Firms that leverage existing product-market strengths frequently discover valuable (and previously overlooked) redesign skills in their workforces. But by and large, organizations seeking market access simply forget to look in their own back yards first. The number of personal computer manufacturers that do not know how to effectively use the machines in their own business is astonishing; the number of banks that devote billions of dollars to portfolio risk management, but no time to analysis of competitive risks, is incredible; the number of information-service providers that exhibit poor information leverage about their customers is shameful.

Frito-Lay, a division of PepsiCo, knows how to look in its own back yard for guidance. To prevent snacks from getting stale while sitting on the shelf, drivers make sure that information does not get stale while sitting in the delivery truck. These knowledge workers, who happen to drive trucks as part of their logistics management duties, punch in the information on daily sales in their handheld computers, which is then transmitted via satellite to a central database in Plano, Texas. The daily sales information is acted upon immediately to schedule production in the plants. Keeping its information fresh enables Frito-Lay to keep its product fresh. The leaders in extracting business value from information technology need not be high-tech startups, but any senior management team that takes the time to understand what is happening in the transitional business environment and seriously probes the implications for the way they need to compete in the new environment.

Getting CAM caught up to CAD, quickly, before market share was lost forever, required further coordination among engineering and manufacturing as the automated production machinery was itself subjected to intense CAD scrutiny with an eye toward improving its design. We see this motif over and over: product-driven organizations can improve their competitiveness by looking in their own back yards, bringing the very strengths that make them formidable in the product-market arena to bear on their internal organization.

Chapter Six

Stage Four: Become Customer Driven

OW DOES a firm deliver customer-driven quality at the level of companies such as Toyota? Perfectly consistent production achieved through statistical process control (SPC) does not win Baldridge awards. SPC and automation assure consistent quality at prescribed levels. What ensures that levels are set high enough, and what distinguishes quality from consistency, is customer-driven orientation. Without it, the most brilliantly planned customer initiatives, though they produce technically excellent products, are doomed to long-term unprofitability. The difference is focus. Consistent technical quality is achieved by looking inward, customer-driven quality by looking outward. It is achieving a customer-driven orientation that is the fourth stage of the transformation process.

Toward a Customer-Driven Orientation

Integration of technical excellence—that is, consistent quality—and customer orientation can be illustrated by the difference between functional quality and technical quality as measurement tools of IT performance. In organizations with overly tight budgetary controls, functional and technical quality tend to suffer together. Organizations characterized by uncontrolled IT spending, on the other hand, tend to exhibit high technical quality, but low functional quality. To achieve both simultaneously requires a top-down approach to IT spending. Similarly, simultaneous realization of both technically excellent quality that meets rigorous engineering standards and functionally excellent quality that uncompromisingly meets customer demands relies on a senior management focus on organizational design.[1]

A Customer-Driven Orientation in Manufacturing

Consider two major quality initiatives in the automotive industry: one aimed at technical quality, and one aimed at functional quality. Both initiatives involved product and process improvements, but their end results were very different.

Automakers that excelled in technical quality were not necessarily the same firms that excelled in functional quality. Ford, after long struggles with quality and cost control, has achieved consistent quality. Its cars rank as high as Japanese cars, around 130 on the industry's 135-point quality scale, a considerable improvement over the 100-point scores it achieved before competition from Japanese imports forced adoption of rigorous technical quality standards. But significant capital and training expenditures notwithstanding, Ford's achievement is on a purely production-oriented scale, designed to measure not customer satisfaction or preferences, but technical performance.

Technical quality and consumer choice are related—certainly consumers prefer higher quality to lower quality cars when all else is equal—but the traditional quality scale omits many attributes of customer satisfaction while incorporating many technical details not particularly useful to consumers. Ford's customers are hardly dissatisfied with their consistently low-defect automobiles. That few U.S. consumers are even aware of, never mind consider, the 135-point quality scale, renders it at best a limited indicator of functional quality, however.

An alternative standard scale used to measure quality is a benchmark: a comprehensive and objective set of measures of customer satisfaction with particular vehicle attributes. This type of quality measure in the automotive industry was established by the independent J.D. Power & Associates. Attributes were selected not for ease of observation, but on the basis of the importance customers attached to them.[2] The measure of functional quality on this alternative scale being customer satisfaction, the Power scale measures functional, not technical, quality. Moreover, the Power rating criteria are fluid to accommodate changes in customer preferences and requirements. As demand for anti-lock brakes has increased, for example, the Power survey has more heavily weighted consumer perception of braking power.

Meeting customer-driven quality standards is more difficult than meeting production-driven quality standards because (1) customer expectation and preferences are moving targets, and (2) expectations and preferences are measured relative to the competition, not to an absolute yardstick such as the "perfect 135."

A Customer-Driven Orientation in Services

The financial services industry offers a good example of how a customer orientation developed from the perspective of cycle time improvement, which is a characteristic market access tool for service industry firms. History has made clear the trend toward disintermediation, the replacement of banks as deliverers of financial services with direct links between consumers and financial markets.[3] The first major blow to banks was dealt by money-market accounts, which offered consumers an opportunity to earn high yields in relatively safe, liquid, short-term securities. Deposit principal was not government insured, but the higher yields apparently more than compensated consumers for any sleep deprivation from worrying about losing their money.

Merrill Lynch added customer convenience to the money-market account with the introduction of its Cash Management Account (CMA), a broad package of financial services, integrated with the company's traditional securities brokerage and research businesses, that included checkwriting privileges and a debit or credit card. The CMA stressed easy access. The services were promoted as an integrated package; customers could easily transfer funds among accounts and received one statement summarizing account activity. Merrill Lynch in effect created and served a previously nonexistent market. This was an early instance of institutional innovation. Moreover, its innovation satisfied three essential criteria for a customer orientation: value creation, surplus sharing, and self-selection.

The structure of the short-term debt market satisfied the first two criteria for the CMA. The money-market funds' practice of pooling individual customers' deposits to purchase commercial paper and high-value premium-return CDs created value, earning returns sufficiently high that some of the surplus could be shared. Sharing this surplus enabled consumers to earn higher returns than they could from their banks. Few customers could assemble the $100,000 necessary to achieve equivalent rates of return on their own, and benefited from the coordination service of the fund. Value creation occurred through consolidation of deposits; paying an interest rate to consumers between the consolidated rate and the banks' rate represented a sharing of surplus.

Finally, to discourage low-balance accounts that would be frequently tapped for everyday expenses, Merrill Lynch charged a fixed fee for CMA maintenance. Banks' earnings had traditionally come from the spread generated from lending money borrowed from depositors to loan customers. Banks also charged customer maintenance fees on low-balance accounts. The CMAs charged a larger fee but almost no spread, attracting large-balance customers with higher effective yields, with the fee diluted across a larger principal base. Even larger banks, constrained by regulation and bureaucracy, could not compete with the CMA for these high-value accounts. CMAs managed to grab a large quantity of short-term deposits in medium- to large-sized chunks. Merrill Lynch had successfully skimmed the cream by targeting bank depositors with reasonably large accounts, leaving the banks to struggle with unprofitable small accounts.

Merrill Lynch's previous prowess in providing consistent technical quality served as an important precursor to customer orientation. People wouldn't put their money into the CMA unless they had confidence in Merrill Lynch's transaction processing system. Despite other financial services firms' introduction of imitation CMAs, Merrill Lynch managed to gain 70 percent and maintain almost 50 percent market share simply by having been the innovator. A reputation for accuracy might get customers, but Merrill Lynch needed to deliver on that reputation in order to keep a substantial market share. That some firms are now offering CMA-type products with no annual fee suggests that the self-selection property—the ability to attract the "right" customers—is paramount; firms are willing to exchange a substantial amount of their share of surplus in order to attract such customers.

One approach to customer orientation in the air travel industry was to distinguish between the business traveler and the pleasure traveler (a customer orientation that did not necessarily benefit all customers). American Airlines led the way by aggressively tailoring its services to the business travel segment, devising convenient routes, striving for on-time arrival, and enticing new, and creating switching costs for old, customers through frequent-flier incentives. American Airlines, like Merrill Lynch, singled out and offered a superior class of service to a particularly desirable customer segment, leaving the less lucrative segments to their competitors.

Similar observations can be made about the distribution channels for personal computers. Differences between IBM's relationship with Computerland, which distributed IBM products, and Dell's mail-order strategy, are notable in terms of surplus division and customer-driven orientation. Computerland distributed relatively expensive IBM systems with a premium service package. Dell offered high-quality personal computers (without the IBM brand name) at competitive prices. Mail-order companies such as Dell took considerable market share from Computerland-type distributors when consumers gained confidence in third-party computer hardware. Once it was obvious that the "IBM premium" was not entirely for increased hardware quality, consumers figured out the superior surplus bundle very quickly; to pay a premium price for superior product durability is one thing, for Computerland's set-up-and-plug-in help quite another. Dell continued to earn handsome profits, while both Computerland and IBM experienced serious competitive problems. Why? IBM and Computerland's industrial economy customer orientations were upstaged by Dell's market-access strategy of consistent quality coupled with the simple surplus-sharing arrangement of lower prices.

If the customer-driven innovation process is as simple as 1-2-3 (value creation, surplus sharing, and self-selection), why is customer-driven orientation a major transformational initiative? Precise target marketing and service expertise appear on the surface to be unrelated to organizational structure and networking, but they share a common characteristic: both are information intensive. Information technology is needed to ensure that the technical quality of services is not strained. Organizational networking and a network-enabling IT infrastructure are essential to monitoring, connecting to, and communicating with target customer segments. In addition, constant updates on value creation, surplus sharing, and self-selection maximize the momentum of the targeting process, as well as provide customer service in real time. It is these transformation steps which must be undertaken before pursuing a customer-driven orientation, and which constitute the necessary barrier to entry.

Which Strategy to Pursue?

The practical implementation of customer-driven quality measures follows after consistent quality has been achieved for pragmatic reasons. An organization that cannot build products or deliver services on a consistent basis at competitive costs will find it difficult to reorient toward customers. The organization that can successfully deliver consistency can then make use of those technical skills to manufacture the products or services desired by consumers. Managers must especially keep in mind that Total Quality Management is only a method, not a goal; quality that does not address customer needs will not lead to product-market success.

The rare organizations that achieved consistent quality before starting down the transformation path, approximately 20 percent of industrial economy firms, can employ this ability as a market-access tool to attain customer-driven status directly, but need to improve response time to preserve customer loyalty. Because the customer-driven orientation is inherently unstable, long-term customer relationships, and rational loyalty, cannot be maintained against imitators' incursions in the absence of a market foreclosure strategy. Customer orientation is thus an interim goal, not an end in itself.

The reason the remaining 80 percent of manufacturing organizations need to implement consistent quality in advance of pursuing customer orientation thus becomes clearer. In the quest for customer orientation, firms must embed value in their products and services. This value is maximized through balanced attention to quality and cycle-time considerations. "Quality first" is generally mandated for manufactured goods. Customers are singularly unimpressed by quick response to product failures when the failures reoccur in replacement products. Fidelity Electronics, a manufacturer of chess computers, found this out the hard way when it introduced the Fidelity Travelmaster, a breakthrough product in terms of price/performance and portability. Unfortunately, severe design problems plagued the Travelmaster, eventually forcing its recall even as hundreds of orders continued to pour in daily. Fidelity's customer service was more than adequate and its marketing effort and response tremendous, but it was tripped up by poor technical quality and suffered accordingly.

In the service sector, the situation is reversed; 80 percent target cycle time rather than consistent quality. The typical customer-driven service business, if one exists, has already achieved super-responsive cycle time, albeit not at the expense of quality. Unlike manufactured goods, customers' perceptions of quality in services are defined by the value of the delivered service, not the consistency of the process by which it is delivered. The meticulous design of a service delivery process is, and should be, transparent to the customer, who perceives the value of a service in terms of speed and consistency.

Toward the Network Organization

A survey of the technology and applications of customer-driven IT reveals the familiar lag between the availability of information technology and its implementation in customer-driven organizational structures. How can a firm that desires a head start on customer orientation accelerate the adoption process?

Being customer-driven implies consistently direct, timely, and generally non-routine, responses to updates in customer information frequently gathered through customer queries or complaints. To execute their responsibility for "routinely non-routine" customer interaction effectively, customer contact employees must have significant latitude and decision-making autonomy. Within the narrow discretionary authority pattern characteristic of the functional hierarchy, employees operate under management policies or "standard operating procedures" that dictate the intercession of a supervisor in customer service encounters that involve discretion. This intercession lengthens the time of the interaction. Leading customer services companies have combined responsibilities for customer contact and decision making, creating new positions or job descriptions within their hierarchies that put decision makers at the point of customer contact and empower employees in traditional roles with more incremental authority. This transformation, from authority into accountable autonomy, represents a step toward establishing a virtual network of equals, which is what is wanted given that superior responsiveness tends to be achieved by customer service employees who work as a team. Supervisory and managerial positions are converted from monitoring and directive functions to training and conflict-resolving functions, respectively.

Being forced to shuffle knowledge around hurts a firm on the revenue side rather than the cost side of the profit equation. Involving supervisors in service encounters necessitates a transfer of information, that even if otherwise costless, lengthens response time. Slower response annoys consumers, and is thus a competitive product/service disadvantage that must be offset by more competitive pricing, which reduces revenue and, hence, profitability.

The Role of IT in Enabling a Customer-Driven Orientation: Extending the Information Technology Infrastructure

Development of a customer database is generally the first step toward creating a direct interface with a target customer segment. The requisite database collects, stores, processes, and reports in a manner that does not swamp management with extraneous information about customer characteristics, needs, and competition-supplied alternatives. This simultaneous compression and filtering describes the crucial position of information technology in the relationship between provider and customer. The difficulty of developing such a database can be traced through the history of database design and the internal treatment of customer information.

Early Databases in the Functional Organization

Consistent with the familiar approach to automation as a substitute for existing processes, transaction processing systems were automated with the intention of perpetuating their existing functionality. Little consideration was given to what new applications of available information might be possible. The walled-off functions characteristic of hierarchy inhibited the development of information standards such as uniform customer identification numbers. The nature of the technology that supported business' first cut at functional systems gave rise to an archive mentality that emphasized storage over access. Development of random-access storage media provided a liberating mechanism on which database software was slow to capitalize; the prevailing database product preserved sequential organization, thereby keeping the function of database technology essentially static even as its form changed.

Lack of innovation in software development was entirely consistent with firms' internal treatment of information. Like the sequential access mentality that governed database organization, the hierarchical mentality that prevailed in the organization of firms greatly restricted the distribution of information, however organized. Customer files were "owned" by the functions responsible for them. This equivalence of collection and ownership resulted among other things in: duplication of customer information; inconsistencies in customer information; slowness to update customer information; and lopsided distribution of customer information among production, marketing, and management.

Allocating the lion's share of the budget to the function most efficient at collecting customer information led to competition for funding and ongoing reluctance to share information with other functions competing for the same budget. Moreover, information-collecting functions not only were not reimbursed for their efforts through some sort of royalty arrangement, but were tacitly penalized with shrinking budgets when they shared information voluntarily.[4] Such ownership without a price system for trading it led information gatherers to clam up when they found something of importance.[5] In addition to the budgetary disincentives for sharing was a general reluctance to open one's database to meddling by other functions. Flat refusal to transfer responsibility, coupled with trepidation over transferring data without responsibility, led to a near total lack of data transfer.

Even when database organization moved beyond the sequential ordering of information, it continued to be constrained by the need to serve the functional hierarchical structure of most organizations. The resulting functional organization of customer information confounded early efforts to integrate and share databases; essentially customer files had either to be tailored to one of the participating functions' needs to the distinct disadvantage of the others, or organized in a manner so generalized as to be of minimal utility to all functions. Hierarchical database technology generated reports in only one way, characteristic of the hierarchical structure of the records within the database. Further evolution of the integrated customer database had to await substitution of relational for hierarchical database technology.

Relational Databases, Object-oriented, and Parallel Processing

Relational databases, object-oriented development, and parallel processor computers are flexible and powerful enough to generate customized reports and support multiple data-entry formats for millions of multimedia records—text, pictures, voice, and video. One might think of a relational database as a collection of structured databases that can be "rotated" to present any of a number of combinations, much as a network structure can, through self-design, emulate any given hierarchical structure. Object-oriented development is a technology used by an operation that allows data such as "place an order" to be embedded in a unit called an "object." Once developed the object can be reused in other object-oriented programs. Further, object-oriented development technically tracks what data exist in what objects so that when a data administrator updates a data element, all the occurrences of the data element in all objects are updated automatically. This requires a great amount of computer power, which is available from parallel processing computers. Parallel processing is a computer architecture in which up to many thousands of computers operate together, each processor computing a small piece of the solution, to solve a highly complex problem, such as updating a large customer database.

What remains is to shift the emphasis of control systems that document the sources and uses of information from security and restriction to distribution. This shift is needed to promote compensation of information gatherers commensurate with their contributions to the knowledge pool, and to introduce priorities and prices into the collection effort by assessing the usefulness of information as measured by frequency of access. When rewards for information-gathering can be aimed at individuals rather than diluted over a large group, greater individual effort is encouraged. It is through the resulting alignment of incentives between information gatherers and firms that the integrated customer database has secured its place in the provider-customer relationship.

Customer-Accessible Databases

Ultimately, the customer-oriented manufacturer or service provider opens its customer databases to customers. Customer interface technology has assumed many forms, from grocery store checkout scanners to airlines' computerized reservations systems. On-line teller systems that enabled bank employees to provide customers with up-to-the-minute account information, relegating the passbook to a quaint symbol of old-time banking, have been expanded through network technology to nationwide, indeed worldwide, scope, and made directly accessible to customers through ATMs and interactive telephone link-ups. With most banks now participating in global networks of financial institutions offering cash at thousands of sites worldwide, U.S. travelers in Europe can receive a favorable exchange rate by accessing their domestic bank account through European ATMs and receiving cash in the local currency. Such services are a tremendous convenience to travelers and a source of fees for the financial services networks that provide them. Banks may finally have caught up to brokerage firms in their use of customer-oriented technology.

Successful Users of Customer Database Technology

American Express Corporation has exploited its strengths in one area of financial services to develop new strengths in another. The company is using its mature, sophisticated customer database to develop specialized financial products targeted at its credit card customers, thus adding value to its diversified portfolio even as the card business that generated the database declines in profitability—a strategic use of diversification, as discussed in the previous chapter. One component of that portfolio, the

American Express Centurion Bank, although only a few years old and existing only as an electronic entity, is one of the fastest-growing banks in the world. This virtual bank, sans branches, potted plants, marble counters, and muzak, exists exclusively through the medium of information technology. American Express has also developed a successful insurance company that employs information technology to generate gains that it splits with consumers in an effort to draw them from competitors. The company's entire customer service organization is technology-based and its scrupulously selected customer service representatives, highly trained in the use of its integrated customer database, can solve problems in real time while the customer is on the phone.

With significant gains still to be had from coordination in the financial services industry, successful insurance companies such as USAA and Capital Holding have consciously redesigned their fundamental business processes around new advances in information technology to enable them to operate largely as network organizations, with autonomous business units supported by centrally administered information collection, management, and dissemination services. This centralized use of IT can be supplemented with agent-level computing power, as in the case of Mutual Benefit Life, whose agents use personal computers to provide tailored, personalized services to customers.

In a very real sense, such technology adds information value to the manufactured product itself, outside the manufacturing process—an automated service rep in every vehicle. Today it is possible for "informated" automobiles to communicate in real time with company service centers to secure assistance in the event of a breakdown.[6]

Ford and other automobile manufacturers are currently exploring opportunities for adding customer involvement to the information-updating process. One idea is to have each automobile's distinctive information signature recorded on a removable card that could be inserted into an ATM network. This smart card would incorporate an embedded microprocessor capable of updating information stored in it. Potential applications include alerting drivers to warranty information, distributing tie-in marketing efforts from after-market suppliers of gasoline, tires, or motor oil, and supporting economic analyses of continuing ownership versus trade-in. A logical extension of this technology would be to replace the removable smart card with a direct satellite connection to the car, and periodically provide messages on a monitor or voice communication device, and even download information to give the car a real-time tune-up.

Smart telephone debit cards, only recently available in the United States, have been in use by the French for years. Prepaid account balances are read by public telephones and the cards are automatically canceled when balances are used up. This debit feature has made use of France's relatively advanced national information network to avoid in a practical manner many of the collection problems and outright fraud borne by U.S. calling-card providers.

Management Principles Central to Customer Orientation

Becoming customer driven entails the creative destruction of three industrial economy management principles and the creative construction of two new information economy management principles. Communication, worker focus, and supervision principles must be fundamentally redefined to support the customer-driven organization. Moreover, two new management principles, dynamic authority and information accountability, are essential to achieving and sustaining a reorientation toward customers.

Completing the Shared Knowledge and Database Infrastructure

> **The New Set of Management Principles**
>
> 14. Communication principle: Communication is swift, spontaneous, and point-to-point, unlike paper memos and formal face-to-face meetings.

In hierarchical organizations, having access to information is like finding gold bullion; subordinates who uncover the precious stuff are expected to relinquish it immediately to their superiors for evaluation and dissemination. To exchange information at their own level in any but the most informal ways, to dare to "go over a supervisor's head," or refuse to surrender information, subjects subordinates to reprimand or even demotion and dismissal.

Hierarchies enforce this perception of information through channels of communication and chains of command. Information in an M-form organization flows upward through functions until it reaches the first divisional level, which may, in the largest organizations, be as many as ten levels removed from the point of origination. Only at the divisional level does information begin to move horizontally, among the division heads who will ultimately send some of it on the long journey down to the functional areas that need it. Henry Ford observed of Alfred Sloan's new hierarchical organization: "It takes about six weeks for a message from . . . the lower left-hand corner of the chart to reach the president or chairman of the board."[7]

Chain of command is rendered unsteady by the elimination of organizational layers in the downsizing process, and further challenged by organizational restructuring aimed at achieving the total quality orientation; it is finally toppled by the need to distribute decision-making rights and discretion to customer-contact employees. Distributing on-the-spot decision-making rights to eliminate the competitive disadvantage that attends lengthy response times further erodes communication patterns and authority structures associated with hierarchies.

Structural factors make "going through channels" both necessary and efficient in a hierarchy. Chain of command defines these downward channels of authority and upward channels of communication. Each subordinate is linked to one supervisor, each supervisor to multiple subordinates, but not to other supervisors or their subordinates. In theory, there is exactly one link (direct or indirect) between any two individuals in the hierarchy. As most organization members do not have direct links to most other members, this single link is often not only indirect, but painfully so.

Paper-based technology requires physical transfer of the medium; the memo cannot be read until someone takes it upstairs. Information that must travel through traditional channels, like materials that travel by conventional production lines, accrues idle time; work-in-process (WIP) accumulates in production, and information-in-process (IIP) is communication that has accumulated. Manufacturers that become leaner in an effort to transform WIP into cash realize a one-time gain much as they would from downsizing; improving the efficiency of the system eliminates a large chunk of resources.[8] Improving communications initiates a similar one-time rush of information and reduces cycle time for future information flows. Information, like inventory, has time value and carrying cost; its value decays as it sits unused.

The ideal network organization provides direct links among all network members. Assuming a small, ten-person network, this means that there are more than 250 different ways to communicate information. Moreover, physical networking technologies such as teleconferencing and electronic mail support originator-designated distribution. The traditional hierarchical communications structure typified by the so-called "memo culture" will hopefully be among the first casualties of business transformation because, as Nobel laureate Kenneth Arrow has pointed out, information propagation is a key limitation on organizational growth.[9] In a rigidly hierarchical organization, everyone in the chain of command between the originator and recipient is privy to the contents of a memo. Targeted distribution preserves individuals' free expression, ensures dissemination of information without fear of censure, and reduces the information load on others not directly involved. Uninhibited communication is vital to the functioning of the feedback process; employees frightened of the consequences of saying what they think will remain silent, depriving the organization of useful commentary.

Centralized authority, perfectly natural in a hierarchical structure, does not fully employ the cross-functional communication capability of a network structure. Information integrity is also at risk with traditional channels. Repeated handling and interpretation by workers many levels removed from its genesis can do to information what the children's game of "Telephone" (also known as "Gossip") does. The consequences range from honest misunderstanding to deliberate withholding or distortion.

Fast, unfiltered, point-to-point, peer-to-peer communication across functions eliminates garbling and delay. Allowing the originators of information to communicate in this way also reduces supervisory workloads. Monitoring of communication, if dictated by security considerations, should be conducted in a manner transparent to communicators. Nothing should impede the sharing of knowledge.

A 10% change. Install electronic mail, make it universally accessible, and encourage its use for all routine communication, particularly that which involves distribution lists. Mandate that routine reports be submitted electronically. Insist on getting copies of critical meeting announcements and team project reports by electronic mail. Actively promote communication in whatever form, whether by fax, voice mail, or electronic mail.

A 10✕ change. Make communication dynamic. Install electronic mail comprehensively, including links to customers and suppliers. Substitute electronic mail for a significant quantity—80 percent—of fax and memo-based communication. Personally use electronic mail as a priority means of communicating with workers and customers. Emphasize and reinforce its quick-response characteristic by checking your electronic mail frequently and responding factually and quickly to questions. Penalize those who do not use electronic mail rather than those who do. Stress peer-to-peer communication and dismantle the traditional chain of command entirely.

Opportunities for sharing knowledge will increase not by 10 percent, but by 1,000 percent in the network organization. Hierarchy resembles a plumbing job, a host of vertical pipelines constricting the flow of information and insulating information flowing through one function from that flowing through another. A network organization resembles more a reservoir, to which everyone in the organization contributes and from which anyone in the organization can draw.

Emerging human resource concepts relevant to customer orientation include empowerment, a vaguely defined catch-all term that refers to an overall increase in autonomy at many levels of an organization. True empowerment involves shifting comprehensive decision-making rights downward, not merely dumping additional decision responsibility on lower echelon workers while preserving supervisors' decision privileges. Empowerment does not precipitate dissolution of the traditional hierarchical command-and-control relationships; rather, it results from a firm's commitment to expedite and improve the quality of customer-service encounters. It is thus not, as some organizational theorists view it, a good thing in itself, but a means to productive balance among the goals of shareholders, customers, and employees.

> **The New Set of Management Principles: Phase II**
>
> 7. Information Principle (revisited): All organization members have open access to all information versus restricted flow based on "need-to-know."

The industrial economy principles that govern information access, worker focus, and compensation combine to reinforce the new information economy management principle that mandates accountability-based information access. An information technology infrastructure enabling universal information access, initiated through the downsizing process, is a prerequisite to information accountability. Provisions for crediting sources must be implemented to discourage freeloading. Citation, the process of crediting one's sources, is enforced in the network organization by documenting who knows what; the old need-to-know philosophy for information access is replaced by need-to-give-credit-where-due. Benefits from the successful use of information must be shared between the provider and the user of that information; this system of pricing information balances the incentives to disseminate it for public use against the privately borne costs of collecting it. Broad-based access to a sparse database of information yields little benefit.

Because the functional hierarchy treats information as a scarce resource that needs to be conserved and protected to create value, employees who seek information encounter many obstacles. The notion that "information about other functions is at best unnecessary and at worst distracting" is incorporated into hierarchical management through parallel chains of command and communication.

The hierarchy's need-to-know principle can be effective in an environment geared toward achieving perfect consistency, but breaks down dramatically when called upon to support innovation or quickly respond to crises. The reality is that it is simply not obvious to just anyone in the organization which manufacturing information is relevant to design and which design information is relevant to manufacturing. Yet the need-to-know principle assumes that someone—whether a design or manufacturing engineer or, more frequently, a supervisor—can and will decide which information is to be gathered or shared.

The only way to ensure that information is available to those who need it is to create a cross-project environment in which it can flow freely. No information administrator can possibly know what the complete information requirements of a process will be, and most will err on the side of accumulating and releasing too little information. Yet the costs of making too much information available are extremely low, and the costs of making too little available extremely high.

The need-to-know principle made sense when pencil-and-paper was the dominant information-transfer technology. Because the transmission process was slow and costly, restrictions that minimized its use were in the economic interests of the firm. But with tremendous IT-driven reductions in the cost of data storage and transmission, the incremental cost of transmitting the same packet of information to one more user becomes insignificant. In the network organization, restrictions on access are warranted only in the most vital strategic areas. Broad-based voluntary communication and information sharing among employees is most attractive when knowledge is distributed throughout an organization. These conditions are, not surprisingly, two tenets of networking with a customer orientation.

Such a JIT approach to information is easier than a JIT approach to materials for two reasons. First, the organization's electronic infrastructure makes information in the knowledge pool easier to transport than corresponding physical materials in inventory. The technology delay for providing information, the last essential bottleneck in the system, corresponds to only fractions of a second in transmitting information from the central pool to the decentralized workstation.

Audit rights for information access—a means for controlling information access—traditionally assigned to white-collar workers through the authority relationship will devolve to the citation-enforcement process. All others must observe the information-market rules. Thus, for example, knowledge workers who want to know about the information access to specific customer information of other workers will have to pay for the knowledge explicitly, as they would for any other information. It will be in everyone's best interest to ensure that information about "who knows what" does not require constant monitoring. The savings from eliminating monitoring can then be shared.

In the context of information access, long-term efficiency is different from short-term efficiency. Short-term efficiency advocates free access to all information on the grounds that collection costs have already been incurred and are thus not relevant to the current usage decision. To achieve long-term efficiency, some method to transfer benefits from the user of information to its collector (i.e., a negotiated price system) must be attached to information usage to provide incentives for information collection, even if the charge is only a citation requirement. Equity does not bear on this problem directly. Just because one person possesses some information—paid for either by effort in collection or citation—does not mean that, to ensure a level playing field, another should receive the same information gratis, only that each should have the same initial opportunity to purchase it. Information is made freely accessible not to improve workers' happiness, but to improve a firm's competitive position.

Why couldn't information accountability work in the industrial economy? Universal information access could not have been implemented in the previous economy because the security technology of the day provided no way to verify access to information without limiting the information available. Security today is ensured by computers that track data access in real time, 24 hours per day, 365 days per year. Access need no longer be restricted by clumsy verification methods.

Extending the Human Assets Infrastructure

> **The New Set of Management Principles**
>
> 5. Worker-class principle (revisited): All employees are treated as a uniclass of knowledge workers, versus the two-class system of white-/blue-collar workers.

Customer orientation further erodes the blue-collar/white-collar distinction first attacked by downsizing. With the growing empowerment of the workforce and accelerating popularity of initiatives that put managers in direct contact with customers, this traditional two-class paradigm is giving way to the notion of a single class of employees, knowledge workers. The term refers not only to employees in the traditional sense, but also to contractors, consultants, and volunteers who embed their own relevant learning and expertise in a firm's production processes and products. A knowledge worker's status is related not to position, but to capability.

Centralization and decentralization, so long the hallmarks of the M-form hierarchy, are no longer the key organizational drivers when knowledge workers dominate the value chain. Distribution of autonomy does not imply decentralization of control. Just as a centralized database can act as a server to individual workstations, the central control group can supplement individualized controls at the production and customer-interface levels. Any focus on centralization or decentralization that does not address the motivations behind the reconfiguration is a red herring. The proper role of centralized control in today's organizations is to experiment with standards, implement measurement and feedback systems, and distribute information, not create micro-level policies or intervene in routine decision making. It doesn't matter how long the arm of the corporate office is, as long as "hands off" prevails.

A true network organization selectively builds significant autonomy into every position. Workers make routine decisions automatically and contribute to decisions and projects they do not control. This selective autonomy amounts to a pragmatic distribution of authority along with the knowledge to make decisions; when a network member's knowledge is sufficient, external authority is not required.

When local knowledge is insufficient, a query to the network usually yields a suggestion that, if taken, has an outcome indistinguishable from a process-specific command. The crucial difference is that authoritative opinions are solicited by knowledge workers rather than imposed on direction takers. The complexity of planning and apportioning work in the context of selective autonomy can be accommodated by dividing the task among many intrapreneurs, effectively implementing parallel processing within the organization.

A 10% change. Introduce workplace diversity by hiring people with non-traditional profiles. Hire more women into white-collar positions and more managerial trainees from the ranks of technically-skilled workers rather than fresh from Ivy League universities. Hire part-time and flexible-time employees, at appropriately proportional pay and benefits.

A 10× change. Create a knowledge uniclass by matching skills to needs at all levels. Define needs creatively to match skills available in the labor market. Name a musicologist as the president of a research university. Hire a soft-drink executive to focus an innovative, customer-driven computer company. Let everyone know that your organization offers rewards to those who can motivate teams, and let these people come to you. Pay for results and contributions to team productivity, not for the amount of time spent in the office. Follow through on promises. Building a diverse set of skills in an organization is for naught if the organization cannot retain the satisfied employees who possess those skills.

Extending the Performance Management Infrastructure

The New Set of Management Principles

3. Supervision principle (revisited): Supervision is indirect through results assessment, versus direct worker observation.

A customer-driven orientation reinforces the new role of supervision by making supervisors responsible for maintaining the day-to-day runnings of the performance measurement infrastructure and ensuring that results are assessed quickly and accurately to provide motivation. The functional hierarchy, in contrast, assumes a somewhat inconsistent view of motivation. At the line level, workers are deemed to need supervision to exert maximal effort in pursuit of the firms' goals. Such supervision represents a philosophy of direct control, with rewards and punishments tied to job effort and meted out swiftly. Indirect control predominates at the staff level. Competition among managers for a limited number of slots at the next higher level was believed to maximize effort at this level.[10] This competition, which focused on maximizing such indirect performance measures as budget control (or size), represented an earnest attempt to achieve defined goals rather than to redefine goals to meet new opportunities.

IT provides the means to rapidly learn the consequences of decisions made by workers through a myriad of dimensions. For example, the decision of a lower level customer contact person who responds to a customer complaint can be evaluated later by analyzing whether the customer's buying patterns change, whether new customers might have resulted, or whether possible product defects were uncovered. Quick feedback on all of these possible outcomes can have important effects on the performance of the firm.

A 10% change. Adopt peer-review techniques. Develop an understanding of employee performance by asking coworkers about effort and attitude. Compensate employees based on their importance to the firm; update assessments annually to ensure that compensation keeps pace with professional development.

A 10× change. Respond, do not enforce. Make the concept of promotion irrelevant by implementing a performance measurement system that is based on actual performance rather than measures of performance. Broadcast the results of this system. Because peers already know who is performing well and who is not, costly supervisory interference is unnecessary. Demand for top performers and the tremendous rewards commanded by truly outstanding achievement will mean that individuals' formal recognition is defined by what other team members, not parallel-function employees, perceive to be important. Stick to pay for performance even when overall results are poor. This incentive system makes efficiency self-enforcing. Reorient supervisors to the task of ensuring that knowledge workers have the tools they need to meet self-set goals.

Extending the Resource Allocation Infrastructure

The New Set of Management Principles

15. Authority principle: Authority for resource allocation is continuously changing and is awarded to workers who are the most effective decision makers.

The industrial economy management principles related to compensation, role of supervision, and worker focus can be combined to form a new management principle that prescribes that authority be distributed with value-creation ability. Authority in a hierarchy is structural, deriving from relative position. A supervisor higher up in the hierarchy automatically possesses authority over a subordinate, relative seniority and knowledge notwithstanding. Moreover, authority relationships in a hierarchy are usually static and fairly enduring; seldom does a supervisor end up working with, let alone for, a former subordinate.

The genesis of authority in a network structure derives not from position, but from expertise with respect to the task at hand. Authority falls upon intrapreneurial "rainmakers"[11] who creatively combine employee talents for mutual gain. Consequently, authority relationships shift quickly when tasks change. Authority may rotate in erratic fashion or remain firmly with one expert coordinator made highly accountable by vastly intensified performance monitoring. Talented members with critical or rare skills, whether intrapreneurial or not, will eventually be in great demand. The most successful network organizations, to maximize the productivity of rare skills, create and destroy project teams as the need arises. Linkages among human resources in a network are made explicit, authority relationships left fluid. Expertise, because it is available to all but captive to none, can be effectively tapped when and where needed.

Whereas a Hay kind of structure rewards hierarchical position and number of subordinates, a network structure rewards individual and team contributions. The shift from the blue-collar/white-collar dichotomy to the knowledge worker "uniclass" paradigm is implicit in the network organization, as neither locus of authority nor compensation levels can be established until a task is specified. Because rewards for performance reflect success in applying expertise to the work of the organization, individuals' compensation is likely to be highly variable, as skills alternate in importance from project to project. Individuals stand to reap substantial rewards from projects that rely on their particular expertise. Variations in the compensation of individuals on the same team to a large extent replace variations in the fixed salaries of individuals across hierarchical levels.

Permitting market forces to determine resource allocation does not guarantee workplace equality. Remunerating skills on the basis of their worth to the organization guarantees that they will be efficiently utilized, but not with any particular regard to equity. Because some skills will inevitably be needed more often than others, inequality in average compensation will persist with, and perhaps even be exacerbated by, pay for performance. Matching compensation to skills rather than position and permitting the call for particular expertise as dictated by market demand, rather than by social custom, represents the ultimate opportunity for democracy and for elitocracy.

Once an electronically enabled network is in place, an organization needs a coherent superordinate design to specify the rules of the game. When this superordinate design has made clear that those who contribute will be rewarded, the shift from static hierarchical thinking to expertise-based authority is like wildfire. This is one transitional principle the implementation of which management need not worry about: the conditions are set and the rest happens automatically.

Senior managers should concern themselves with the sustainability of this principle, not its immediate inception. Those with historical, position-based power are likely to offer fierce resistance. If senior management compromises the transition to expertise-based authority to appease the historical power base, the transition will be smoother in the short term, but its sustainability will be seriously undermined.

If rewards are equitable in the long run, the market dynamics of creating value by rewarding expertise will be respected. The role of supervision shifts from a negative monitoring to a necessary coordinative function concerned with the bountiful rewards from leveraging expertise and cooperative team work.

Why couldn't this sort of supervision work in the industrial economy? One must remember that the distribution of workers in the traditional functional hierarchy of the industrial economy was 60 percent blue-collar and 40 percent white-collar. The computer having not yet been invented, routine tasks still required physical labor or heavy machinery. University-level education was still reserved for the privileged few. The most effective organizational-design paradigm for this environment was that the white-collar worker design work and the blue-collar worker execute work. This design, which incorporates a best response to yesterday's knowledge conditions, must be completely repudiated to gain the full benefits of enhanced education, job skills, and collective managerial wisdom.

Implementation Lesson from Companies Striving to Be Customer Driven: Customer Orientation and Culture Change

The completion of the shift from a traditional production-driven to a customer-driven orientation is potentially both dramatic and traumatic. It frequently requires major investments in retraining workers, the installation and debugging of information technology, and concerted efforts to establish new cultural norms and sanctions more appropriate for a customer-driven focus. There is also a transition period during which the organization is in some hybrid state, vulnerable to trauma.

Companies approach this transition in different ways. United Airlines' bottom-up, process-oriented program that required senior managers to spend several days per month working directly with customers at reservation counters was mentioned earlier. Executives' direct experience with change is presumed to provide valuable feedback to policy makers and supply management guidelines for establishing appropriate levels of authority for dealing with customer-service encounters. Managers' models of reality are expected to be improved by experiencing customers' overall satisfaction or dissatisfaction first-hand; facing an irate customer is a good reality check. IBM took a top-down, vision-oriented approach, bringing in a guru on paradigm shifts and holding executive training sessions worldwide. It remains to be seen how effective these approaches will be. Of one thing, we are sure: a customer-driven orientation can not be arrived at incrementally. Only the adoption of a new set of management principles—and not just a few days wearing a different hat or listening to seminars—will suffice.

Becoming customer driven marks a fundamental transition in the culture of an organization. It is at this point at which an organization becomes more network than hierarchy, more "sense and respond" than "make and sell." Management might contrive to lose the customer orientation, but to recapture distributed decision-making rights requires enormous effort. A customer-driven firm will either prosper or fail as a transformed organization; it cannot restore its former hierarchical structure.

To negotiate this shift in balance without undue organizational trauma, management must undertake and encourage aggressive culture-change programs. IBM's top-down, paradigm-based executive education program is an example of both an effective message about transformation and a particularly hierarchical approach to it (by a company with a venerable history as a hierarchy). Although IBM's message seems to have been received, we confess to being skeptical that top-down, executive-based motivation can work without significant commitment from knowledge workers who, after all, are responsible for the bulk of a firm's productivity. Centralized control of the transformation process can be surprisingly effective, especially when it is in keeping with a legacy of strong central control—the case at IBM—so long as care is taken to strike a balance between controlling the direction of the transformation process and conserving its momentum.

A less traditionally centralized organization might devote a project team to network evangelism. In providing such a team with the requisite resources and then turning it loose, management would be practicing the distribution of decision-making rights and responsibilities that it ostensibly advocates. Individuals' choices to attend lectures and participate in seminars would be accompanied by the caveat that responsibilities and compensation in the transformed organization will be allocated on the basis of promised productivity, not past accomplishments. Such a tabula rasa approach to future compensation would ensure employee participation without heavy-handed mandates.

Decentralized control does not guarantee success. Nor is it without cost. Centralization concentrates on careful steering at the expense of loss of momentum. Decentralization economizes on control at the risk of a runaway transformation. It promises a wilder ride and, if successful, a more complete transformation. The ultimate target of decentralization, in the spirit of exchanging control for opportunity, is to look beyond current markets to the challenge of global scope. A judicious amount of prophylactic market foreclosure, however, is in order before giving the organization free rein.

Chapter Seven

Stage Five: Develop a Market-Foreclosure Strategy

A MARKET-foreclosure strategy, like a market-access strategy, is concerned with ensuring a fit between an organization and its environment. Whereas a market-access strategy attempts to fit an organization's capabilities to the requirements of its competitive environment, a market-foreclosure strategy completes the circle by attempting to tailor the competitive environment to the organization's capabilities.

Before the firm can make an intelligent decision about *how* to alter its environment, it first needs to collect an enormous amount of information about its surroundings. We might think of the firm as an extremely complex information-processing entity much like the human body.[1] To maintain itself in good working order, an organization performs certain tasks at regular intervals much as the human body's autonomic nervous system routinely attends to such homeostatic functions as respiration and temperature maintenance. The rhythmic flow of information and materials necessary to sustain "business as usual" can be likened to the flow of blood; accordingly, we refer to the impulse that starts and sustains this flow as an organization's heartbeat.

A successful implementation of a market-foreclosure strategy will define the competitive environment in terms of the level of performance required to participate in the firm's markets, and that which is needed to discourage all but the most determined challengers. To stabilize at an insufficiently challenging level will amount to a delaying tactic, no more. If market access opens doors for the firm, market foreclosure slams them shut on competitors, after the firm has safely entered. To extend the prior metaphor, market access accelerates an organization's heartbeat; market foreclosure stabilizes it at the new rate. Without market foreclosure, market access initiatives beget tremendous spurts of energy followed inevitably by fatigue and collapse.

Successful investments in market foreclosure crack down on inefficient processes that waste valuable resources such as time, money, or information. Only by eliminating inefficient processes can an organization ensure that its competitive position is safe against imitation.

Market Foreclosure: Failure and Recovery

We refer to the use of market-access tools to help a firm hurdle competitive barriers as "leaping," and tailoring the environment to a firm's existing skill base as "lowering." Similarly, we call using market-foreclosure tools that increase organizational sophistication to deal with future competitive threats "learning," and the tools that prevent access by others, "locking" (see Figure 7-1).[2]

Too Much Lowering, Not Enough Locking

The ability of foreign competitors to use consistent quality as a market-access tool was evidence of U.S. firms' neglect of quality as a market-foreclosure tool. U.S. firms had spent too much energy trying to preserve the existing not-very-competitive environment (lowering) and too little energy developing the sophistication they would need to contend with new challengers (learning) or establishing a stable level of performance sufficiently high to dissuade would-be challengers (locking). The sophistication of corporate strategy research advanced at precisely the wrong time for Detroit; once Toyota and Honda took advantage of the unlocked door,

Focus of Strategy

		Access	Foreclosure
Scope of Strategy	Firm	**Leaping**	**Learning**
	Environment	**Lowering**	**Locking**

Figure 7-1. Leaping, Lowering, Learning, and Locking

around 1980, and noted that U.S. automakers were not prepared to leap, their increased emphasis on speedy model changes (locking) made it unlikely that the U.S. automakers' quality initiative (leaping) would make a large competitive difference, no matter how effective or image-redeeming. Quality had become a necessity; the platform of competition in the automobile industry had shifted to cycle time. Fighting this war with the strategy and tactics that won the last war means almost sure defeat.

We suspect a learning strategy, on the order of GM's experiment with Saturn, will turn out to be a safer response. Learning ensures an organization's ability to leap in the future, and just the ability to leap is often sufficient to dissuade competitors from trying to woo a firm's customers. How does a firm profit by stealing customers it cannot hope to hold even long enough to recover the expense of luring them away? The threat is more powerful than its execution.[3]

We have been picking on the automobile industry, but it is hardly alone in is plight. Very few U.S. firms accustomed to relatively stable, low-competition markets in the mid-1970s were prepared for fiercely intense competition. Moreover, they could not have implemented rigorous quality standards even if they had been technologically capable of doing so, as their cost structure was not competitive with that of their new opponents. They had not invested in reduced cycle time or extra capacity, established war chests to sustain them through price wars, or implemented other strategic market-foreclosure initiatives. In the absence of competitive pressures sufficient to force extraction of organizational slack, they held on to inefficient manufacturing practices.[4] No radical innovation was necessary to beat these firms, just incremental improvement over their existing, well-documented practices. Had U.S. firms attempted to boost quality in response, they would almost certainly have lost money.

Other companies were inadvertently constrained by human resource practices. IBM's full-employment policy, for example, although it generated favorable public opinion and contributed to retention of valuable employees, greatly restricted short-term efforts to downsize in any but a slow and controlled fashion. Companies saddled with such self-imposed restrictions had not completed the process of automation-motivated downsizing when the first wave of quality challenges washed over the West from the Pacific. Such policies might have been sustainable had these companies plowed some fraction of their extraordinary earnings back into strategic market foreclosure, but they did not. Efforts to continue getting something for nothing eventually admitted entry and incurred losses.

It is hardly surprising that both foreign and domestic competitors, when choosing entry points, targeted markets with such observable weaknesses in conduct (as opposed to structure) as competitive complacency and full-employment policies. Suffering from the growing number of competitors, incumbent firms were unable to respond. The battleground on which new entrants mounted their attack against insufficiently foreclosed U.S. markets was providing more value to customers, who were rapidly coopted. New entrants provided more value to customers (in other words, increased consumer surplus) with quality improvements and lower prices. With incumbents' manufacturing techniques and capital investment optimized for tolerance-based production, they could not achieve a 10 percent quality improvement without incurring a 20 percent cost increase or a 10 percent cost reduction without suffering a 20 percent degradation in quality. In short, they were stuck. To move either up or down the quality spectrum would consume surplus; staying at the same quality level would inevitably result in the erosion of their market share.

Being stuck is no fun, especially in a business that is commoditizing; that is, all products that meet well-known standards of performance and compatibility are becoming perceived by the consumer as equivalent, and products that do not meet these standards are not considered at all. Mature products such as automobiles, copiers, film, and certain types of computers are especially subject to commoditization. Paper clips are paper clips; their purchase is based on cost without regard to manufacturer. Aggressive pricing by entrants to commoditized markets immediately reduces the twin streams of earnings and cash flow needed for a stuck firm to finance a competitive response. Consistently higher quality performance by entrants redefines quality standards, leaving incumbents saddled with both inappropriate manufacturing technologies and high costs due to previous indiscretions. Worse, the stuck firm develops a reputation for bad quality, and customers stop buying its products. There seems to be no way out.

For stuck firms, aggressive management action at this point in a market share war is imperative for survival. Under the gun for a quick solution, faced with restricted resources, and rising cost of funds due to decreased revenues from price competition, management must ponder its options: fight or flee. Japanese firms that invaded U.S. markets in the 1980s correctly perceived domestic firms as unready to do either.

Japanese automobiles, for example, not only equaled, but exceeded, U.S. quality standards in 1980, the point at which we think of them as having "caught up."[5] Domestic consumers not only accepted Japanese autos as adequate, but began to prefer them over U.S.-manufactured vehicles. Fuji's value-based entry strategy against longtime dominant player Kodak was built around film that was at least equal in quality to Kodak's, but priced considerably lower. By sharing surplus with value-conscious film consumers, Fuji managed to enlarge its market share to 40 percent in 1992.

Canon's introduction of a photocopier superior in quality to Xerox's equivalent offering was accompanied by a price that added insult to injury, which was approximately equivalent to the U.S. firm's cost of manufacture.[6] Targeted as vulnerable in the product-quality arena and hardly able to counter with a pricing strategy (the traditional method of preserving market share) Xerox, the model of American ingenuity in manufacturing, research, and human resource management, had to scramble to discover an entirely new method of redirecting competition.

By extensive strategic benchmarking against competitive products and services before attempting a dramatic restructuring, Xerox avoided a common functional pitfall associated with information-based process redesign, by allowing consultants to address problems at their factory-floor roots. Reverse-engineering its competitor's product revealed that there was no way Xerox, using its initial manufacturing configuration, could manufacture a competitively priced copier of equivalent quality. This humbling realization pronounced in eight-foot high letters the need for dramatic change in its production process. Xerox subsequently undertook the needed transformation in an appropriately holistic way, embracing new technology, new organizational structures, and new management principles. Key to getting the company back on its feet were the abilities of its scientists and engineers. The voluntary and enthusiastic contributions of such knowledge workers are critical to transformational success.[7]

Firms that do not solve their problems at the roots find themselves in the uncomfortable position of clinging to their old technology at a very high cost. Over the past twenty years, shop floor data processing equipment used to expedite turnover of inventory stocks, and MRP systems, founded on such practices as buffer stocks and economic order quantity (EOQ), have flourished as the heartbeat of manufacturing accelerated. Suddenly, it became critical that sufficient raw materials be on hand to feed assembly lines; a calendar day with systems down had come to represent a much greater loss than in less technology-dependent times. Potential gains from substituting person-hours for clock hours were accompanied by opportunity costs of downtime. Management attention accordingly focused on methods for avoiding process interruptions. Scheduling applications suggested specific capital investments or process-redesign efforts to circumvent production bottlenecks. Shift structures can be reoptimized to reduce reliance on unscheduled overtime and avoid overtime wage premiums.

Even though management time spent fine-tuning MRP systems will still be more than repaid by material-to-labor savings, its opportunity cost is enormous at this stage. This is the appropriate time to interface production scheduling applications with MRP systems to improve capacity utilization, as many companies have done. Data germane to cost/benefit analysis must be communicated to spreadsheet users who control investment decisions, closing the loop between investment and productivity. Omitting this important step of closing the loop leaves the data from the factory floor (or back office) in limbo, divorced from real-time decision making.

Cycle Time and Management Control

The "homeostatic" functions of organizations are maintained through the traditional responsibilities of the management control system, independent of the information technology in place. Companies' traditional information-collection heartbeat is the annual budgeting process. Planning information from divisions comes in once a year and major resource allocation decisions are made based on that information once a year. Once the major resource allocation decisions are made, the rest of the year is devoted to carrying out the activities required to execute the plan.

The involvement of computers notwithstanding, the annual budgeting cycle—a product, in part, of external auditors' reliance on end-of-fiscal-year financial statements—remains institutionalized in the functional hierarchy and poses a formidable obstacle to increasing the speed of organizational response.

Accelerating an organization's heartbeat to make major resource allocation decisions more frequently than once a year is analogous to increasing a personal computer's clock speed; it enables the set of tasks to be changed more frequently and done more often in a given period of elapsed clock time. Companies that cut out ticks of the clock by taking advantage of knowledge workers' expertise can dramatically change the way they do business, not only saving time as a resource but gaining tempo as an opportunity for strategic movement—the competitive equivalent of sneaking in a few extra moves at chess while your opponent is thinking. Once the structural substitution of person-hours (time) for clock-hours (tempo) has been made, different efficiency-inducing technologies go to work to reduce the number of person-hours required to complete a given task. The difference between such structural substitution and the incremental improvements that naturally follow it cannot be overemphasized. The former is a one-time fundamental change in the way work is accomplished, the latter a continuous search for improved efficiency. Acceleration, therefore, makes the most sense in an environment in which clock time (tempo) is of the essence in creating and marketing a product.

IT systems aimed at improving workflow on the shop and trading floors indirectly and serendipitously altered relationships between functions. MRP applications that incorporated manufacturing simulation capabilities designed to provide feedback to design engineers encouraged cross-functional applications and coordination between engineering and manufacturing. But although they facilitated efficient use of machinery, such systems did not solve the more general problem of efficient capital utilization. Equipment utilization was optimized at the expense of highly padded raw material inventories. JIT systems, a new managerial technology appropriated from Japanese manufacturing firms, offered a means to control inventory if information leverage could be designed into the procurement process. Such appropriation is an example of learning as market foreclosure.

Patterns of Defensive Competitive Responses

By Stage Five of business transformation, the firm has reached the point of no return in terms of creatively destroying industrial economy management principles and creatively constructing new information economy ones. At this point, the firm's default defensive response to competition is fundamentally different from before. Figure 7-2 illustrates five types of competition, and the pattern of defensive responses typical of firms that operate with industrial economy management principles.[8] Figure 7-3 illustrates the parallel contrasting defensive responses of firms that operate with a critical mass of information economy management principles. Comparison of the two figures illustrates that the defensive responses of the information economy firm are more robust, and more complicated, as well. Having

Source of Trauma	Management Response	Effect on Shareholders	Effect on Employees	Effect on Suppliers	Effect on Customers
Increased Competition	Cut Costs	Increased rivalry lowers ROE **—** Best response is price competition	Wage cuts **—** Management plays "hardball"	Tougher price negotiations **—** Management plays "hardball"	Lower prices **+** Consumers benefit from competition
Increased Supplier Power	Vertically Integrate	Fewer contracting costs **+** Efficient prices and investment	Less pressure for parts efficiency **+** More opportunities for coalitions	Lose business **—** Renegotiate or dip below MES	Lower rivalry means high prices **—** Increased upstream concentration
Increased Buyer Power	Long-term Contracts	Lose flexibility **—** Cannot exploit future events	Higher job security **+** Solid bargaining position	Tougher price negotiations **—** Management plays "hardball"	Lower rivalry means high prices **—** Contracts lock out entrants
Increased Threat of Substitution	Price Promotion	Lower margins **—** Declining market nixes cooperation	Emphasis on efficiency **—** Tighter monitoring; coalitions squeezed	Strategic jeopardy: might be displaced **—** Declining market nixes cooperation	Lower prices **+** Consumers benefit from competition
Increased Threat of Entry	Limit Pricing	Lower margins **—** ROE may not exceed capital cost	Emphasis on efficiency **—** Tighter monitoring; coalitions squeezed	Volume increased **+** Good bargaining position	Low rivalry, but low prices too **+** Partially competitive

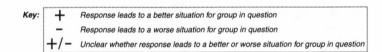

Key:
+   *Response leads to a better situation for group in question*
—   *Response leads to a worse situation for group in question*
+/—   *Unclear whether response leads to a better or worse situation for group in question*

Figure 7-2. Industrial Economy Responses to Organizational Trauma

the information technology infrastructure in place to analyze, respond, and tune defensive strategies is essential.

Pitfalls in Accelerating Work in the Hierarchy

Speeding up work in the hierarchy, the traditional automation role of computers, made work more efficient in terms of production per hour. Automating general ledger, for example, enabled companies to close their

Source of Trauma	Management Response	Effect on Shareholders	Effect on Employees	Effect on Suppliers	Effect on Customers
Increased Competition	Differentiate	Monopolistic competition **+** Good structure deters rivalry	Low emphasis on efficiency **+** More opportunities for coalitions	Good bargaining position **+** Creative pricing	Broader product choice **+** Better fit with products/needs
Increased Supplier Power	Multisource	Lower contracting costs **+** Efficient prices and investment	Avoid share dilution **+** Keep surplus "in the family"	Bad bargaining position **−** Price competition	Keep costs down **+** Low cost, high innovation
Increased Buyer Power	Micromarket	Increase precision of dynamic balance **+** Stay on the smooth path	Smaller share of larger profit **+/−** Net results are indeterminate	Less waste; more products **−** Bad side effect of higher cost	Smaller share of larger pie **+/−** Net results are indeterminate
Increased Threat of Substitution	Continuously Redefine Product	High R&D costs, but low rivalry **+/−** Dynamic differentiation	Easy to get funding but high stress **+/−** Consulting firm syndrome	No assurance of sourcing **−** Poor investment	Broader choice, but higher prices **+/−** No results are indeterminate
Increased Threat of Entry	Continuously Redefine Entry Requirements	High R&D costs, but low rivalry **+/−** Dynamic entry deterrence	Little emphasis on costs **+** More opportunities for coalitions	High stress and low volumes **−** Renegotiate or dip below MES	Low rivalry means high prices **−** Pizzazz instead of value

Key:
+ Response leads to a better situation for group in question
− Response leads to a worse situation for group in question
+/− Unclear whether response leads to a better or worse situation for group in question

Figure 7-3. Information Economy Responses to Organizational Trauma

books monthly instead of annually, effectively accelerating their heart rate by a factor of twelve. Sophisticated software packages enabled financial institutions to quantify their risk profiles on a continuous basis and close their books daily. Spreadsheet software automated variance analysis, once the bane of cost-control jobs, and facilitated the virtually immediate generation of "what-if" budgets. More timely information speeds up the circulation of resources, permitting managerial attention to turn from internal manufacturing problems to the more challenging global task of coordinating suppliers and customers.

In Japan's famous *kanban* (literally, "signpost") system of assembly, the movement of goods conveys information independently of explicit vertical or horizontal communication channels. The presence or absence in the very small buffers between assembly stages of work-in-process (WIP) is sufficient information to balance the cycle times of the line processes. Tasks moving too fast for the rest of the line would be starved of inputs and forced to slow down. WIP piling up in front of slow tasks signals a need for more workers, before tasks at normal speed are starved for inputs. JIT, the U.S. interpretation of *kanban*, encourages both explicit and implicit connections with and among suppliers, relieving management of a great scheduling burden by outsourcing responsibility for raw material availability. Firms that use JIT to substitute the market force of incentive alignment for vertical integration and explicit contracting are effectively employing pay for performance with their suppliers while getting a head start on organic boundaries, as we will see in Principle 20. Organic boundaries are fluid and shift in response to the competitive environment in contrast to the relatively fixed boundaries of the traditional hierarchy. Freed by JIT from internal concerns, management can focus its abilities outward, in search of new methods for coordinating material, capital, and labor resources to produce surplus and new ways to distribute surplus in the short term so as to maximize long-term shareholder value.

Expediting speed of decision making eliminated idle time on the factory floor, which translated directly into productivity gains, but the benefits of such improvements were limited by other bottlenecks in the organization. These shifting bottlenecks constrained overall improvement. The speeding-up lost its punch because the rest of the organization lacked the excess capacity to absorb the increased output of the newly technology-assisted process. Worse, organizations were often at a loss for what to do with new resources. Accountants, for example, found that they were able to generate hundreds of budget revisions—busy work that eventually used up excess capacity in previously slack areas, but created new bottlenecks as management digested their increased output.

Within a traditional hierarchy, the natural ability of computers to speed up work hits a functional wall. Improvements realized in one area have little effect on overall organizational performance because other constraints quickly become binding. This frequently derails IT investments that might improve organizational design because previous, function-specific IT investments, frustrated by lack of organizational attunement, yielded no benefits. Had organization-wide IT investments been made, the unrealized benefits of previous investments would quickly be obvious. Unfortunately, until senior management grasps the link between targeted current investment and the benefits of previous investment, necessary organization-wide investments are not likely to occur.

The hierarchical organizational structure was not designed to coexist with modern information technology. IT introduces stress in the hierarchy that brings about a system reaction consistent with Le Chatelier's principle; the hierarchy acts to relieve the stress by damping the effects that motivated the investment. Only through thorough, system-based organizational reengineering can this negative feedback loop be resolved into a self-sustaining transformation process obsolescing the functional hierarchy and creating the IT-enabled network. This rationale is exactly the opposite of the traditional view of reengineering; here, system redesign complements incremental improvement, it doesn't substitute for it. This point becomes obvious when the issue of organization inertia is separated from the issue of managing creative destruction of the hierarchy.

Some managements, in mandating cross-functional connection with teams in quality initiatives, unwittingly induced the mutation of the functional hierarchy into a network structure, a sort of half-hearted organizational redesign that, because it focused exclusively on quality improvement without regard to such other critical factors as cycle time, removed only some of the functional barriers that held technology gains in check. When, for example, it was observed that early cross-functional systems such as MRP were generally under utilized because of their incongruence with hierarchical structure, MRP was separated into MRP I, a partial functional integration that could accommodate itself to a hierarchy, and MRP II for organizations that had already moved beyond the hierarchy. Unable to distinguish MRP II's direct effects from the onslaught of previously unrealized benefits of other technology investments left many managers with an exaggerated view of MRP II's contribution.

Business Process Redesign Revisited

Business process redesign (BPR) focuses on alternatives to traditional assumptions about the way work ought to be carried out with respect to functions, tasks, and budgetary control. BPR initiatives frequently involve alternatives such as network-style notions of teams, projects, and project management control.[9] But BPR alone is insufficient to motivate an organization to transform. Part of the problem is with the terms: "reengineering" and "redesign" connote fine-tuning and tinkering in the context of scientifically mechanical processes. The senior executive's responsibility in the transformation process is as visionary, not oil-can carrier. The visioning process is an art in search of a new paradigm, not a science. Reengineering and redesign efforts take guidance from, but are necessarily secondary to, the executive's overall vision of the transformed organization.

Toward the Network Organization

To achieve superior quality, management had to break down the walls that separated function from function within the hierarchy. These walls represented divisions of responsibility that impeded cooperative intrapreneurial ventures, that encouraged, for example, "throwing the bear over the wall," the practice of striving to complete assigned portions of a project as quickly as possible without regard to impact on the subsequent function's task.

The notion of cross-functional teams of design and production employees, cooperatively designing products for manufacturability, came to symbolize the breakdown of the functional organization. Hard-hitting management-led quality initiatives forced continuous contact across functions to achieve ambitious improvement goals. Many organizations found that IT networks established to support this contact were self-sustaining, that cross-functional liaisons tended to last well beyond the quality-improvement campaigns. They evolved from formal and strong ties to informal and weak ties. Unfortunately, management's awareness of the gains to be derived from this new network organization lagged behind its awareness of the strategic product-market threat; with their crises behind them, many firms neglected to take steps to preserve their hard-won total quality orientation. This addiction to episodic management persists.

Informal, weak ties across functions constitute a shadow network floating on top of the formal hierarchical organizational structure. Recognizing that the information leverage such networks afford was an essential ingredient of competitive organizational performance, management experimented with informal networks across other functional areas, prompting a proliferation of electronic networking technology and more influential shadow networks.

To ensure the intensive cross-functional networking needed to sustain superior quality levels, new management principles that clearly communicate to employees the extent of the firm's reliance on networks are essential. These principles open the firm's information resource in its entirety, and encourage employees to exploit their access to this resource to advance the firm's competitive position.

Whether aided or hindered by management, shadow networks will continue to grow within organizations. Perceptive managements will eventually legitimize them as supplementary components of the existing communication and control function. Formal organizational charts may persist, but, ultimately, the network will win out, supplanting the functional hierarchy as the locus of decision-making authority. Whether management explicitly recognizes this shift or not is irrelevant; it cannot stem the tide by refusing to acknowledge it.

What happens to cycle time when the network is formalized? Remaining benefits from existing technology are made available for capture as organizational bottlenecks are exposed and treated. An organization's cycle time shifts from the lowest common denominator of the annual budgeting cycle to a system of variable and concurrent cycle times specific to key business processes. Fast processes, free to solicit external resources, need not wait for slow internal processes to catch up. This freedom leads to evaluation of slow cycle-time processes; those strategically necessary are maintained, the remainder contracted out. A continuous learning and feedback loop is institutionalized with the goal of improving cycle time for individual strategically important business processes or redesigning the overall process to eliminate the strategic necessity of retaining them within the organization.

Management Principles Central to Market Foreclosure

Market foreclosure entails the creative destruction of one unsalvageable and one salvageable industrial economy management principle and the creative construction of two new information economy management principles. The principle underlying the corporate/divisions structure must be discarded and the operating cycle dramatically changed. New management principles governing real-time performance monitoring and dispute resolution are also needed.

Unsalvageable Principle

Centralization/decentralization principle: Organizations are divided internally into a corporate group and divisions—the M-form. Centralized shared activities are carried out by the corporate group, and decentralized operations activities are carried out by the divisions.

As industrial economy firms add products and distribution channels, they typically integrate multiple functional hierarchies for individual products, geographical locations, or market segments into an M-form hierarchy coordinated by a central corporate staff. Except for their common dependence on the centralized corporate body, divisions operate independently. The body of management literature on centralization and decentralization provides the logic and guidelines for separating the activities into corporate and division activities.

A 10% change. Grant individual divisions autonomy to make their own operating and tactical decisions, keeping strategic and financial decision making centralized and incorporating financial results into a consolidated balance sheet. Practice hands-off management by not pulling the strings.

A 10× change. Reject centralization/decentralization relationships driven by economic considerations such as internal markets permitting project managers to bid for attractive knowledge workers. Blur the boundaries between the inside and outside of the organization, treating strategic alliances across divisions as if they were arrangements with independent firms. Use strategic outsourcing and internalization interchangeably, as dictated by the circumstances. Within divisions, emphasize "work-outs," a term originating from General Electric, meaning the process of work simplification, over mandating specific solutions to conflict. If the strategic alliance framework does not fit in this internal environment, consider three explanations:

1. The division itself belongs outside

2. This particular alliance does not deserve to work

3. The idea is good but "inside" is the wrong place to look for its execution

This test constitutes a stand-alone set of criteria for internalizing activities or, alternatively, an acid test of the ability to outsource. IT increases both internal and external opportunities available to a firm; there is no reason to limit the search to one or the other, but many firms consider outsourcing without reconsidering the fit between the proposed alliance and the rest of the organization.[10] Each of these three failings must be correctly diagnosed if a firm is to eventually achieve global scope.

Extending the Resource Allocation Infrastructure

> **The New Set of Management Principles**
>
> 16. Cycle time principle: Resource allocation decisions are made in real time instead of on the fiscal year cycle.

The heart of the functional hierarchy beats only once per year, with this periodicity institutionalized in the frequency of both the planning process and annual budget cycle. The fiscal year governs the planning and budgeting process. The network plans as it goes and uses budgets ex post to self-benchmark performance. Annual planning in this environment is less competitive analysis than a combination of goal-setting for motivation and target-generation for mobilizing organizational support for these goals.

A 10% change. Prune half of the corporate headquarters' staff responsible for planning and control. Leave 10 percent of the corporate staff in place to coordinate financial management, and decentralize the other 40 percent to the operating business units.[11] Instruct the business units to carry out planning and control as they deem most effective. Evaluate the continuance of each business unit on its economic performance: divest underperformers; invest in those that satisfy targets.

A 10X change. The operating cycle of the information economy firm must be effectively zero, that is, real time. The firm can determine its current economic position and performance between any two points, generating instantaneous balance sheets and income statements. Planning is driven by real-time simulation models that immediately correct future plans based on actual and anticipated events.[12]

Make electronic communication within and outside the firm the dominant form for important matters. Paper and telephone will survive at the extremes, as informal and emergency communication.

Be explicit with your external auditor; demand an outside opinion of your organization's success in realizing these new principles. Make the report available to the financial community and organizational stakeholders, and perhaps to competitors as well, to engender a high level of healthy competition in your overall industry.

Embrace structural control. Structural control relies on incentives rather than formal budget-based authority to ensure both surplus creation and capture. A wide range of structures from pure marketplaces, which rely on prices and voluntary participation to assign tasks, will appear inside the network organization. Hierarchies and markets, previously thought to be mutually incompatible, will often appear together as suborganizations within the larger networked whole.[13]

If self-design techniques are applied, a network of hierarchies will perform much better than a hierarchy of networks. Even when hierarchy is guaranteed to be appropriate for a specific task, the uncertainty of which task will be performed—and, by extension, which hierarchy will be required—mandate investments in structural flexibility. The extra tool of structural choice at the team level guarantees that the self-designed organization will work at least as well as the centrally designed firm.[14]

Extending the Performance Management Infrastructure

The New Set of Management Principles

17. Control principle: Control is made efficient through extensive performance feedback information, and self-interest-based reward systems which act to motivate workers to maintain high levels of performance.

From the industrial economy principles of operating cycle, compensation determination, and the role of senior management, is formed a new information economy principle that calls for the continued monitoring of organizational performance along with real-time evaluations.

The power of the accounting-driven hierarchy, motivated by periodic performance evaluations, promotions, and budgetary control, to manage complex organizations should not be underestimated. This organizational form became almost mystical as it created the best, largest, and most productive organizations ever—AT&T, Shell, General Electric, General Motors, Ford, Sears, and IBM, to name a few. The accounting profession rose to provide an objective opinion of how well organizations were performing. Balance-sheet benchmarking afforded small organizations contextual clues about how to exploit economies of scale, mass distribution, and functional organization. As managers, we thought that we had the answer: we could just manage all companies like the "best-of-the-best."

Senior managers need to let go of the old and begin looking for new diagnostic tools. They need to develop real-time performance monitoring to improve their understanding of marketplace dynamics and provide feedback on their organization's performance.[15] Performing the old diagnoses twice as fast is not enough.

Management control must be accomplished by continuously monitoring a firm's activities and performance. Superior performance comes about through use of a credible performance-measurement system; organizational learning is generated by continuous improvement in employees' skills. As all parties begin to feel comfortable that "nothing is forever," bargains will be struck that distribute surplus in various ways to achieve dynamic balance as employees' needs, firms' competitive positions, and their relationships change in tandem.

Why couldn't continuous performance monitoring work in the industrial economy? Existing technology—column paper, green eyeshades, and EBIT (i.e., Earnings Before Interest and Taxes)—dictated that complex organizations be controlled through elaborate and formal planning and budgeting systems. Managers limited their expectations to the control system's capabilities. Given hierarchy's sheer structural sluggishness, retrospective and retroactive control systems were sufficient in the industrial economy.

It wasn't until increasing numbers of firms embraced communication technologies and transformed into network organizations that these lumbering hierarchies were transformed into juicy prey. Real-time evaluation of operations is a necessary defense; knowing to stop when you're knee-deep is just as important as not stepping in the mud in the first place.

Extending the Project Tasking Infrastructure

> **The New Set of Management Principles**
>
> 18. Conflict resolution principle: Conflict between the firm and customers, employees, shareholders, or suppliers is expediently mediated by senior managers; use of third party mediation is the exception.

The industrial economy principles of compensation, roles of senior management, and supervision are the basis for the information economy principle of conflict resolution, which mandates that senior managers quickly mediate disputes and equitably distribute rewards with an eye toward long-term value creation.

When intrapreneurial teams routinely divide millions of dollars of surplus, some disputes are inevitable. A tempting pitfall in handling the first few disputes is to treat conflict resolution as a salvaged principle from the industrial economy. Only a partial refinement of the industrial economy approach would result in too heavy a management focus on ensuring equitable division, making stakeholder analysis part of major decisions. Managements that go halfway institute a policy of good "corporate citizenship" and stick to it even when it means lower earnings. They may claim to put employees first. They reject a short-term surge in profits in favor of a long-term relationship with the customer, and so forth. But true adoption of the conflict resolution principle, combined with the earlier principle of dynamic balance, focuses senior management's attention on the balanced distribution of surplus for future gain, not on efficient operations geared toward current surplus generation. The efficiency burden is shifted to leaders of intrapreneurial teams, and managers must restrain from intervening in ways that undermine the process being carried out by the teams.

Consider efficiency and equity together rather than separately. Managers administer equity toward a greater goal: the long-term value of the firm to all its stakeholders. A quick score in profits, like a quick score in customer satisfaction, quality, or market share, is wonderful in the short term, but, unless it can be sustained, adds little to a firm's long-term value for any of its constituencies. Similarly, intervening in team matters may create wonderful benefits in the short term, but it's far more important to be viewed as impartial in the long run. Nobody should enter a dispute knowing that they'll win because you're sympathetic to their side; everyone with short-run goals must fear and respect the conflict resolution process, which focuses on fostering the long-term cohesiveness of teams.

Implementation Lesson from Market Foreclosure: Integrating Market-Access and Market-Foreclosure Initiatives

The Easy Way: When Cycle Time Improvements Follow Quality Initiatives

Changing the cycle time of a traditional manufacturing organization is difficult, if not impossible, without first initiating the mutation of the functional hierarchy through a quality or customer-driven orientation initiative. Attempts to improve organizational cycle time often are accompanied by high expectations for cross-functional applications such as MRP. Such expectations often come by emphasizing the functional part that is being modified rather than any overall difference in the performance of the system after the change in cycle time.

Yet it is just this system-wide performance improvement that should be compared to the incremental cost of making the improvement. Projections that assume no feedback response to a change in one component of the system are likely to be significantly divorced from reality. Systemic analysis of suboptimal results will generally lead an organization to conclude that the roots of the suboptimization lie not in the technology, but in the interaction of the technology with the basic structural tenets of the hierarchy.

Because cycle time improvement relies on eliminating bottlenecks, the first transitional changes in the quest for improved cycle time tend to be significantly more successful than later changes, and even more successful when their primary objective is something other than cycle time improvement per se. Quality and customer-driven initiatives provide initial experience and evaluative benchmarks that can serve as initial data points for a later cycle time push. Two effects are at work here. First, the early initiatives pluck the low-hanging fruit, making obvious improvements, leaving later, dedicated cycle time improvement projects with more difficult challenges. Second, if cycle time is targeted first, the systemic reaction will inevitably dampen any benefits, perhaps to the point of absorbing virtually all benefits and setting back the transformation process for lack of resources. This system feedback frustrates the initial use of cycle time as a market-access technology in most manufacturing organizations.

But to attempt to fix all the problems through a complete system redesign, all at once, is too ambitious. To try to compress the stages of transformation into a single enormous organizational redesign effort is folly. Management, even if it were to try to carry out two stages at once, would inevitably run out of resources and fail to achieve the momentum needed to make transformation self-sustaining. Figure 7-4 chronicles the failures and successes of four historical examples: MRP, on-line order processing, integrated payroll systems, and integrated financial reporting.

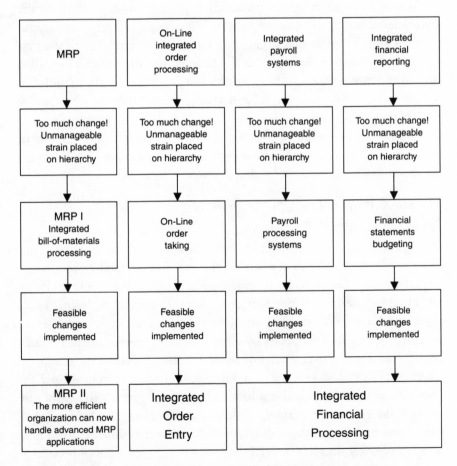

Figure 7-4. Effects of Too Much Change on Cycle Time Improvements

Management that chooses to pursue market access through a quality initiative deliberately postpones cycle time improvement initiatives. This salutary neglect allows potential benefits from cycle time concentration to accumulate without competing for limited managerial attention and financial resources. Typically, the initiative imposes too much change, and is scaled back into more manageable change over time. However, if the cycle time principle is not explicated and adopted, the initial change never progresses to the more beneficial change originally intended. For example, the majority of companies that implemented MRP initiatives remain stagnated with MRP I. These companies generally failed to understand the need to broadly adopt the cycle time principle as the overall umbrella for the MRP initiative.

When management does eventually explicitly target cycle time, the accumulated benefits can be released in a "cashing-out" process. Because the cycle time improvements that accumulated as a byproduct of the first three major initiatives have not been accounted for, the benefits they yield constitute a minor windfall when realized, much as the downsizing initiative provides a wellspring of financial and management resources. These newly available resources fund the large initial restructuring investment in cycle time improvement; pent-up benefits stored during previous initiatives should prove sufficient to fund the cycle time initiative and thereby bring the organization to a viable IT-enabled network.

The Hard Way: When Quality Improvements Follow Cycle Time Initiatives

Management that chooses the cycle time initiative for market access pursues cycle time improvement as an interim goal in the broader objective of improving responsiveness to customer needs. Salutary neglect of consistent quality allows the organization to pursue customer orientation by providing quick and dirty solutions, through the market access technology of cycle time improvement, unimpeded by distractions. Improvements in product consistency respond to customer demands for less customization and lower prices; they occur as processes are refined, and are not targeted per se. These improvements establish a base of expertise upon which a firm can draw in the future, an example of learning (see Figure 7-1). Firms that stress customer service through quick response over product consistency, for example, will find it beneficial to standardize their response process— not for cost-control purposes, but to ensure that basic, often-repeated services are handled with 100 percent accuracy. This investment in process control will eventually lay the foundations for a quality push by encouraging development of the necessary process-analysis skills "on the fly."

A firm that has successfully employed cycle time as a market-access tool will reach a point at which costs are increasing past the point of competitiveness. Everything is a prototype, and little or no learning carries over from project to project. When customer satisfaction is high, but production costs are out of control due to lack of process consistency, the time is ripe to target consistent quality. The quality initiative begins with a cashing out process that realizes, in accelerated fashion, the accumulated benefits of previous initiatives. By seemingly relegating quality considerations to secondary status, management builds a foundation for the "real" quality initiative that will serve as a strategic defense against the entry of low-cost imitators—the operational realization of the market-foreclosure strategy.

Chapter Eight

Stage Six: Pursue Global Scope

G LOBALIZATION must be one of the most overused, indeed, misused, terms in management parlance today. Tradition- ally, global scope has connoted multinational presence. We have found a more compelling concept of global scope in the mindset of executive leader- ship. The concept is more than geographic diversification in market and resource base, more than establishing branch offices in exotic locales; global scope is the ability to seize opportunities wherever and whenever they are found.

The global presence of an organization may be virtual, its influence felt in geographical locations where it has neither physical presence nor assets. The productivity of an organization with global scope is uncon- strained, in effect, frictionless—independent of geographical space, of the speed of its component processes, of the scale of production of its physical outputs. The principal constraint on the productivity of an organization with global scope is its management's aim; the ability of management to point the organization in the right direction.

Management tools for aiming the enterprise in a global direction are commitments—contract-like ties of varying strength and formality. These may range from legally binding (e.g., employment contracts or outsourcing agreements) to informal (e.g., maintaining a quality reputation or entering a strategic alliance), but they share a common basis in that

1. All emanate from the firm.

2. All are relationships between management, acting as the shareholders' agent, and the firm's customers, employees, suppliers, and competitors.

3. All are incentive-based in that they establish explicit connections

between performance and rewards in order to elicit continuing cooperation among these diverse stakeholder groups.

A global organization's first response to a problem is informational, using its powerful information and network position as a primary problem-solving tool rather than as an afterthought. Consider a clothing manufacturer unable to furnish stores with sufficient quantities of a very popular item. The traditional, nonglobal-thinking response would be to accelerate shipments of the product to warehouses, and from warehouses to stores, using a next-day delivery service. Ten years ago, such a response was deserving of a promotion, but no longer. A global-thinking firm would instead consider using the same next-day delivery service to ship directly to customers from its factory. It may be much less costly to ship five thousand items from a factory directly to customers than to distribute twenty items to each of five hundred stores and have half returned because of wrong size or color. Identifying this kind of alternative, and expediently calculating its cost/benefit must be done in the normal course of business.

By transmitting the information about the customer—size, color preference, and shipping address—from the store to the factory, the clothing manufacturer can bypass the illusory "necessity" of shipping the goods to the store. The store provides consumers with informative advertising, but the physical distribution occurs directly from the factory to the customer. The information shipment obviates the goods shipment, instead allowing the store to ship the customer—or at least the relevant attributes—to the goods.

Global scope frees the firm from the confines of its organizational resources. As the proportion of value added by heavy industrial production declines (the very word implies transportation difficulty and thus location dependence), the firm is becoming increasingly a system of formal contracts and informal treaties that organize resources toward a value-maximizing end. The intellectual resources a firm needs to make decisions about where to add value can be tapped as required from the network organization, thereby separating the firm's vision-driven objectives from the requirements for achieving them. This division of objective and means is difficult to quantify; it involves unobservable organizational capabilities (like manipulation of databases and accessing electronic communications) rather than observable organizational actions, leading us to distinguish between expansion and "blurring" of traditional firm boundaries.

The Transformation of Organizational Boundaries

Globalization as a transformational initiative deals not with the mechanics of making links with diverse locations or learning how to speak four languages, but with dedicating organizational resources to continuously monitoring and taking advantage of opportunities that emerge throughout the world. In changing what organizations do, globalization expands existing boundaries to encompass more potential resources. In changing how they do what they already do, it renders boundaries permeable, "blurring" them into a conceptual continuum.

The continuously updated and expanded portfolio of assets with which management takes advantage of momentary opportunities is controlled by the network of weak ties that an organization substitutes for asset ownership.[1] Control is exerted through ownership not of these assets, but of information about the attributes of the assets, where and in what quantities they are available, how they might best be exploited, under what terms they might be acquired or leased, and so forth. Many avenues exist for transcending traditional firm boundaries in this scheme. Opportunities abound for improving productive scale and coordinative scope, expanding geographically to embrace more customers or resources, extending coordinative domain and enhancing innovative capability.

Opportunities for Expanding Productive Scale

Manufacturing capacity can be viewed by the global firm as a commodity that can be contracted for in much the same way that home-delivered heating oil or court time at a racquet club are.[2] Recall the top fashion retailer described earlier. Once having accumulated an elaborate store of information about the quality of the manufacturing processes available to it, the firm no longer needs to worry about hands-on manufacturing challenges. It can concentrate on leveraging its fashion knowledge to generate new styles and negotiate production contracts that match product-market requirements with production-market capabilities.

Capacity-as-commodity represents the logical endpoint of the productive scale aspect of global scope. As more and more manufacturing industries organize this way, economy of scale in manufacturing will cease to be a competitive advantage for all but the most basic goods, as most production will naturally be farmed out to the most efficient producers. Unfortunately for aspiring global strategists, this aspect of globalization does not seem to accrue any sort of nonimitable advantage to early adopters unless these commodity producers with unique abilities (already a contradiction in terms) can be so full of your product that they lack the capacity to contract with your competitors—an unlikely result for all but the largest current organizations.

Opportunities for Expanding Coordinative Scope

Economy of scope refers to the cost advantage realized by performing more than one activity at a time. Like the notion of capacity-as-commodity, economy of scope has implications for the natural end state of industrial organization in an economy where physical location matters little.

Coordinating for economy of scope argues for organizing activities that jointly generate positive spillovers. The extraction of gold and copper, because they are often found in the same ores, exhibits significant economies of scope; a firm that mines one realizes some cost subsidy in producing the other.[3] Conversely, activities whose joint execution would bring about negative spillovers should be organized independently. This decision depends little on the apparent "sameness" of the two activities. Pizza making has little to do with dry cleaning, but both can be delivered.

How to organize the sharing of lumpy, multiuse core assets is an aspect of economy of scope that has been hotly debated in the mergers and acquisitions and diversification literatures.[4] Core assets can be shared through contracts (in the absence of reputation-based trust) or strategic alliances (that presume such trust) without requiring common ownership.

Opportunities for Expanding the Geographic Domain of Customers: Market Scope

Early efforts to tap foreign markets through aggressive international integration in manufacturing and service industries resulted in a spartan global presence for many M-form hierarchical organizations. With few exceptions, these international offices existed as subsidiary arms of their parent companies rather than autonomous business units. Most international subsidiaries were strictly forbidden to compete for clients with one another or with the parent organization; such strategic behavior was left to top management "back home."

In their 1989 book *Managing Across Borders,* Bartlett and Ghoshal refer to firms that are organized and controlled at home, but that own assets in foreign countries, as "multinational" organizations.[5] Multinationalism is only peripherally related to global scope. Viewing international subsidiaries as subordinate to the home office results in the suppression of networking benefits. Expansion is exclusively vertical, adding another layer to the hierarchy without redistributing any decision-making rights.

Multinational presence may show up on a company's consolidated balance sheets, but does it affect the way the organization's domestic subsidiaries do business? We think not. Moreover, we view such interaction to be the acid test for strategic expansion of geographic market scope. With no changes to its competitive condition, all a multinational firm achieves is economy of scale by diluting the fixed costs of management and production—hardly a strategic coup unless used aggressively to cut prices in domestic markets.

Globalization becomes strategic only when an organization's presence in global markets improves its performance in its home market or in other global markets, as when learning in a European facility enables a U.S. firm to lower prices and steal market share at home.

When a network organization's market domain becomes global, additional benefits accrue in all geographic areas in which the organization has a presence. Because the network structure internalizes competition for resources through intrapreneurship, there is no need to restrict nondomestic network members. Internal competition across the organization's units should already have ensured that organizational assets are located where they are most productive.[6] A global organization internalizes the so-called "economic nationalism" evident in Japan's industrial policy; the incentives of the organization's intrapreneurs are explicitly aligned with those of the firm as a whole by the performance-measurement and compensation system. Since network members are compensated as individuals or members of temporary project groups rather than as geographic entities, network cooperation is much easier to achieve than corresponding cross-office cooperation in a multidivisional hierarchy.

Opportunities for Expanding Geographic Availability of Resources

The global organization has the potential not only to become bigger in the classic sense of revenue gains, but also to become broader in the sense of investigating many and varied opportunities. The need for global organizations to augment the resources available to them becomes clear when one considers the extraordinary demands global consumers can place on an organization's resources.

The major barrier to foreign sourcing of goods today is not high transportation costs—information is easily transferred and high-value items are inexpensive to transfer relative to their base cost—but complications arising from laws, payment policies, and customs associated with contracting. The global network retains agents to handle contracting problems. When an agent agrees to mediate a deal, a company has effectively signed a contract that it understands with the agent, rather than a contract that it does not understand with the foreign source.[7]

We see again the pattern of focus observed in connection with "capacity-as-commodity": all activities, unless they revolve around an organization's idiosyncratic strengths, are contracted out to other organizations. Critical resources can be mobilized from around the globe to satisfy a need for special expertise as well as for the more mundane consolidation of production capacity.

Expanding the resource domain may look like the traditional coordinative function, but it is also strategic and reflexive. It is strategic in the sense that it affects the productivity of the firm's existing resources; it is reflexive in that it is affected by its own expansion. Mobilizing new resources increases the availability of potential intrapreneurs. Applying intrapreneurs' coordinative energies to the incremental resources a global firm mobilizes, as well as to the more effective use of a firm's existing resources, brings about a clear strategic gain for the firm.

When the only condition for assembling a project team is direct or indirect association with a given network, the number of intrapreneurs who might consider a given coordinative task is greater than the number available in a localized network. Whether in London, New York, Tokyo, or Timbuktu, every intrapreneur in the network has equivalent access to resources. Given a dramatic increase in the number of participants in the global market, the operation of market mechanisms should be improved. If the prices of valuable assets are driven up by competition, more valuable assets should become disposed to participate in the bargaining process. The process of mobilizing resources to accommodate increased activity is thus self-reinforcing, another positive feedback loop that constitutes a reflexive gain from the mobilization process.

The strategic implication of resource expansion is that globalization will improve the efficiency of allocating network resources. The reflexive implication is that networks made to operate more efficiently through global awareness will gradually come to command more resources by extending packages that ensure the participation of network members with crucial skills. Taken together, these effects can be expected to accelerate the evolutionary process of global networking.

Opportunities for Expanding the Coordinative Domain through Flexibility

The strategic and reflexive expansion of the resource domain expands opportunities for action. This increased flexibility does not end with the coordinative function. The global entity in an evolutionary environment exhibits a distinctly organic characteristic of adaptation—it seeks out opportunities that will nourish it and strives to avoid circumstances that cause discomfort. In addition to being able to change in small ways to mitigate stress—the homeostatic resilience implied by Le Chatelier's principle as discussed in the previous chapter—the dynamic network organization can increase its flexibility in dealing with unexpected circumstances. By relying on markets and reputation rather than authority to close the gap between the very short-term contracts—required to achieve perfectly harmonious partnership among shareholders, employees, and customers—and the longer-term contracts dictated by contracting costs, the network organization can have the best of both worlds. Any network can substitute home-grown markets for authority, but the global organization has a much wider array of markets to choose among.

The notion that relying on markets to command resources gives an organization greater control over its potential, and obligations, than relying on insourcing, runs counter to traditional wisdom—that outsourcing constitutes a strategic risk. "Better make it at home," managers argue, "because you can never be sure about what's going to happen." This strategic rule-of-thumb may have been appropriate in 1965, but it is seriously dated in today's globalizing economy.

Insourcing is no longer the only alternative to strategic dependence on suppliers. Tacit or explicit vertical integration is, as illustrated in Figure 7-2, a knee-jerk industrial economy reaction to supplier power. Strategic multisourcing (Figure 7-3) is an information economy alternative to insourcing. A firm that must decide whether to make or buy an essential input must still consider which mode of procurement is more secure—insourcing or outsourcing—but the default choice has changed. Japan, for example, lacks oil reserves, but has a global network of oil sources. If Japan were to sweeten its offer for crude oil by $1/barrel, dozens of producers would flock to supply its needs. Venezuela, on the other hand, a country with plenty of oil, would have played the insourcing game against Nature and lost were something to happen to affect oil productivity, such as a general strike, natural disaster, or national civil disorder. Venezuela's currency, without the major export backing of the petroleum industry, could probably not command much import of oil, whereas Japan's strong yen, a product of its comparative advantage in electronics manufacturing and a persistent trade surplus independent of its lack of oil, ensures it not only a secure supply of oil, but whatever goods it requires from the global market.

The Role of IT in Enabling Global Scope: Completing the Information Technology Infrastructure

No incremental capital investment or expansion of network membership is required to access the global network. Telecommunications providers can maintain high service quality at reasonable cost through economies of scale in infrastructure maintenance, most of which come through the efficient utilization of lumpy, multiuse assets such as satellite-repair teams.

The fixed-cost structure and economies of capacity utilization inherent in infrastructure maintenance give consumers significant market clout even when only a few firms compete in the industry. To retain the critical mass of customers necessary to sustain reasonable utilization levels, producers must offer the most attractive consumer-surplus package possible. As substitute technologies emerge, existing networks must improve their service quality just to retain customers.[8] This technology-consumer-scale triangle ensures that value-seeking customers will self-select the best technology, and thus completes the three-part incentive-compatibility cycle, consisting of value creation, surplus sharing, and self-selection, discussed earlier.

Outsourcing through relationships of varying strength gives a firm opportunities to expand its virtual presence while contracting its physical presence. This outsourcing can either substitute for self-manufacture or enable purchase of a previously unsuppliable commodity. In the telecommunications example, few firms elect to lay dedicated lines over accepting a proffered commercial package, but many firms collect their own market data. In addition to third-party data links between two network members, for example, third-party information sources provide an attractive alternative to localized data collection. The increasing scope of interorganizational systems such as electronic markets, Internet, and third-party databases provides a resilient infrastructure for the market for information itself. In the same way that the global telecommunications system provides an infrastructure for the market in data transmission, high initial quality and initial consumer value in this burgeoning information-as-product market should ensure both accelerating adoption and continued consumer value if incentive compatibility can be maintained.

The IT that enables physical and virtual expansion to global scope grows throughout the transformation process. This technology is only infrastructure; it does not become an architecture until executives permit it to influence decision making. To implement the infrastructure as a coherent whole, that is, to create an architecture, requires a master plan. Senior management must formally incorporate the ability to "act globally" into its tactical arsenal and the notion of "being global" into its business strategy.

Of the technologies that contribute to establishing an organization's virtual presence, several stand out in terms of integrating global capabilities with previously successful initiatives to leverage existing organizational strengths. On-line systems, for example, support expansion of an organization's activities beyond traditional boundaries. The speed of Federal Express pales by comparison with that of point-to-point data transfer. Terminals and personal computers are merely the visible endpoints of infrastructures that interface directly with knowledge workers who are already networked within the local organization. Adding nodes, or tapping into an established global presence such as Internet, explicitly expands the network horizon and thus organizational boundaries.

Database technology provides a universal format for classifying and storing data, essentially a collection of events looking for a structure. Organizing data to provide structure yields information; interpreting information yields knowledge. Figure 8-1 is an expansion of what we saw in Figure 1-3. The information technology infrastructure began by capturing records of events (observation) during downsizing, extended itself to incorporate analysis during customer-driven orientation, and now completes its duties by linking with the shared knowledge and databases infrastructure to leverage the accumulated organizational learning.

The local area network (LAN) technology that supports knowledge transfer within organizations is also the basis for global reach when employed in conjunction with universal public and proprietary global networks. The economics of access to universal networks makes LANs preferred for all but

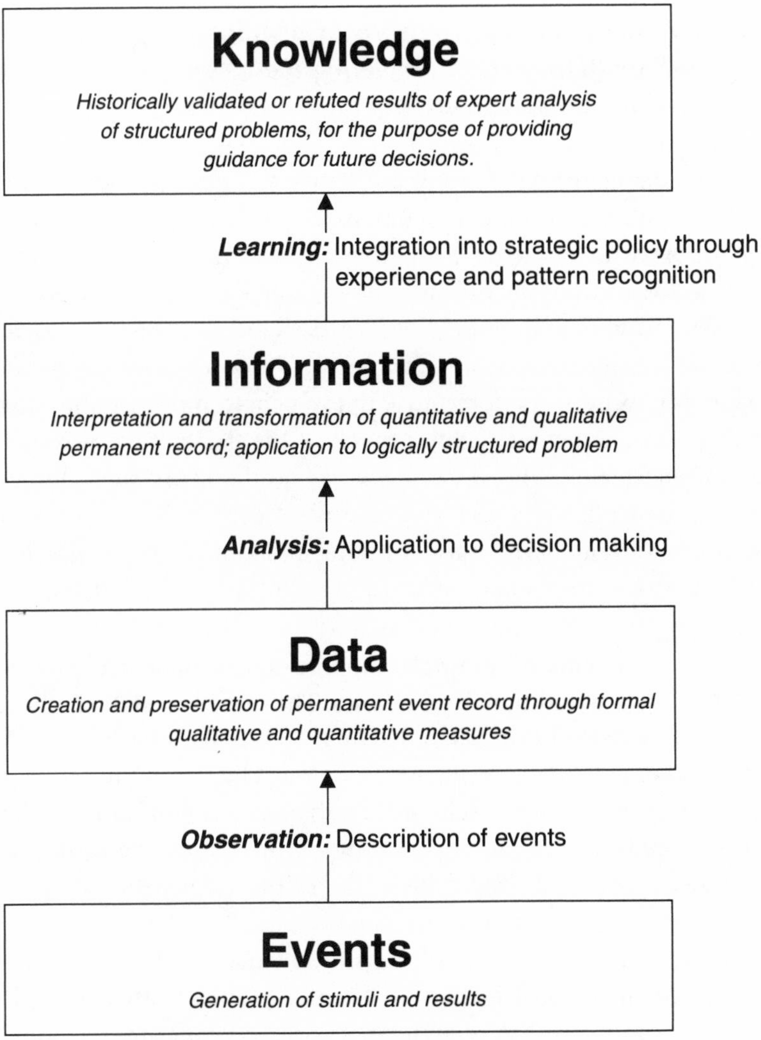

Knowledge

Historically validated or refuted results of expert analysis of structured problems, for the purpose of providing guidance for future decisions.

↑

Learning: Integration into strategic policy through experience and pattern recognition

Information

Interpretation and transformation of quantitative and qualitative permanent record; application to logically structured problem

↑

Analysis: Application to decision making

Data

Creation and preservation of permanent event record through formal qualitative and quantitative measures

↑

Observation: Description of events

Events

Generation of stimuli and results

Figure 8-1. Data, Information, and Knowledge Revisited

the most security-intensive applications; firms that buy global telecommunications services have fewer technical problems than firms that attempt to design their own systems. To rely on a multibillion-dollar company to get one's calls to London is likely to be strategically safer than to lay one's own cable or launch one's own satellite. Now the creed on outsourcing should be, "You ought to consider making that outside—you never know what might happen to your manufacturing facilities!"

Opportunities for Expanding Innovative Capability through Skill-Based Diversity: Completing the Core Competencies Infrastructure

In order to build a global portfolio of distinctive abilities, an organization must generate diversity among its human resources to permit a better match of people with tasks via the intrapreneurial market mechanism. Economics, in the form of the full-time-or-nothing employment relationships typically found in traditional hierarchies, forecloses this strategy to hierarchies. Even as hierarchical organizations are now learning to tap into the growing part-time work force to employ people more flexibly, the inherent drag of its structure nullifies much of the flexibility that comes from such arrangements. The global network, on the other hand, forges temporary bonds with employees as a matter of course; it can perform the calculations to fairly price these options and can afford to pay for flexibility because it corrected the structural lag of hierarchy through market foreclosure.

The network challenges the hierarchical notion of the fungibility of workers. Knowledge workers possess specific skills profiles that uniquely qualify them for membership in different combinations of teams. Moreover, these workers' skills and interests change over time. The role of the network as a coordinating mechanism is to match the needs of intrapreneurial teams with the skills of its knowledge workers. Only if it can perform this matching process effectively will a network realize the benefits of scale, scope, coordination, and resource domain.

Assembling a diverse portfolio of skills means making difficult short-term choices. Organizations inclined to keep employees with rare skills for which the organization has no immediate need can offer motivational incentives to encourage these employees to aggressively seek opportunities within the firm or at other firms to use their skills. This frees the executive group responsible for the design of the network to concentrate on assembling and maintaining the organization's skills portfolio without regard to how specific skills might be employed today. This skills portfolio must be continually updated to reflect changes not only in the workforce, but also in individual knowledge workers' changing skills and motivations, an ideal application for IT.

An organization that coordinates a diverse portfolio of human assets is positioned to respond to unique customer requirements; it has learned to leap. It is positioned to support zero-wait delivery and flexible customization and integration of cross-functional information into products. This is a powerful customer-relations tool that offers opportunities for highly creative pricing.

Expanding organizational boundaries permits more productive matching of resources with their most effective uses, a capability particularly important in the case of innovation. Coming up with a good idea was not enough in the industrial economy. The capital "partners" who funded innovations frequently appropriated large portions of the innovators' productive surplus. In the information economy, innovators and intrapreneurs have access to capital as a matter of course. A good idea will command attention. The matching of reward and innovation encourages future innovations, ideally those that the old performance system could not induce.

Management Principles Central to Global Scope

By the time the organization has achieved global scope, the search-and-salvage process begun by downsizing is complete. All industrial economy principles have been critically examined for sustained relevance and either repudiated or rehabilitated. The adoption of new principles, however, continues.

Completing the Project Tasking, Performance Management, and Human Assets Infrastructures

---

The New Set of Management Principles

19. Opportunity principle: Activity is oriented toward fast-changing global market opportunities rather than overcoming organizational inertia.

From the industrial economy management principles pertaining to the role of supervision, compensation determination, and senior management responsibility, we derive the information economy principle that decisions are motivated not by inertia, but by opportunity. Because supervision in the industrial economy punished bad outcomes, supervised employees avoided risk. Supervision in this sense was a contributor to the inertia that kept employees from capitalizing on fleeting opportunities.

In the absence of emphatic and unmistakable signals that rewards will be commensurate with assumed risk, employees are unlikely to take risks. Performance-based reward systems that base compensation on average performance over time are mandatory for the network organization. Statistical fluctuations will even out, but effort and ability will shine through. Equity sharing is also important, inasmuch as overall compensation must be aligned with the long-term benefits of risk taking. Motivating organization members to pursue innovative opportunities brings little to a company unless the right opportunities are targeted.

Opportunity-seeking environments are created by senior managers functioning as internal consultants. Senior managers are often those who have succeeded at, and experienced the benefits of, opportunity seeking, but past performance is no guarantee of future results. The expert opportunity seekers' role today is that of experienced guide: to exhort the value of and provide counsel on the pursuit of opportunity seeking.

Why couldn't the opportunity principle work in the industrial economy? Market opportunity was ever-present in the industrial economy; the challenge was to supply products and services at acceptable costs. Today, with the mass market largely satisfied, opportunity lies in niche markets that require customized and tailored products and services. Economical mass customization relies on a high level of opportunity seeking, or targeted innovative activity. Shotgun techniques are not sustainable. As a first step, aggressively seek out complementary processes and conduct "minimergers" inside the organization to exploit lumpy multiuse capabilities.

Completing the Resource Allocation Infrastructure

The New Set of Management Principles

20. Boundary principle: Organization boundaries are organic—continuously expanding and contracting—as various network relationships are added and subtracted from the firm.

Integrating salvageable principles with new principles expands the organization's productivity to the point that all limits become self-imposed. This enforced scope discipline, in turn, requires that the limits of organization be set by choice, not by necessity. The most intriguing aspect of global IT-enabled networks is defining what lies inside the organization, what lies outside. In the industrial economy hierarchy, the boundaries of organizations were clear and firm: a resource was either internal or external; all mergers were acquisitions; relationships with other economic entities invariably had a partially adversarial component and were formalized in lengthy contracts. Routine employment contracts were typically ominous, requiring the employee to agree to sign all intellectual property over to the firm regardless if the property was developed on company time or employee personal time. Employees generally had few alternatives to acquiescing to such contracts because of the imbalance of their market power compared to the firm. Nevertheless, resentment by employees to this exercise of power would fester.

Organizational boundaries can lose their rigidity and yet remain the same shape and size. This phenomenon, blurring, changes not what is within these boundaries at any given moment, but rather the rules that govern migration across them. The absolutes "in" and "out" are replaced by the notion of "in-ness," in effect, a continuum. The answer to the question "is resource X within the organization?" is neither "yes" nor "no"; all resources are partially "in" and partially "out" of an organization with fuzzy boundaries.

In practice, organizations blur their boundaries by gradually substituting weak ties or partnerships for strong contract-based ties. The notion of "fuzziness" is bounded; an organization that relies entirely on either authority or markets is not fuzzy. As can be seen in Figure 8-2, both contract-based organizations and organizations that mix and match, seeking the optimal proportion of strong to weak ties, are fuzzy on the practice-based "Fuzzy Laffer Curve," which originally sketched a supply-side theory relating average tax rates to total tax revenue.

In practice, fuzziness is a relative state, defined by the ability to steer through the substitution of internal and external resources. Degrees of fuzziness reflect strength of contracting ability, not the internal or external location of resources. Information technology, through databases, electronic communications, and real-time monitoring, markedly expand knowledge of, and improve the ability to enforce, both internal and external contracts over relatively brief time horizons.[9]

The firm has the option to transform weak ties into strong ties, at the right price and time, of course.[10] Collecting these options into a strategic portfolio, a manager resembles a puppeteer working a marionette. A firm with option ties in hand can bide its time, waiting for an opportunity

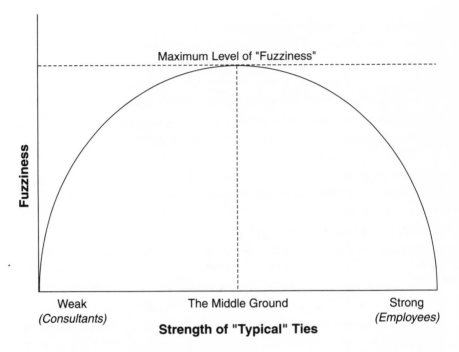

Figure 8-2. The Fuzzy Laffer Curve

that matches one of its option-bound assets. When one arrives, the firm manipulates its option as it will. Competition among potential puppeteers drives the prices of exercising these resources up to their maximum value, sometimes a very high price indeed. An example of acquiring options and opportunistically converting weak ties into strong ties can be seen in various LBO situations, in which a firm retains experts solely to prevent them from advising the other side.

Since strong ownership ties are more expensive to maintain than weak ties, managers must use weak and strong ties simultaneously to achieve the desired capability at reasonable cost.[11]

Negotiation and partnership. The marionette analogy clarifies the difference between negotiating a contract and establishing a partnership. Contract negotiation defines a strong relationship between the desired marionette-asset and the puppeteer-firm—the asset agrees, for a price, to yield all rights to the fruits of joint efforts. The puppeteer-firm assumes responsibility for evaluating opportunities for this collaboration and establishes a strong (and presumably enforceable) tie through the contractual relationship.

The weak ties between the asset and its network are not shared by this contracting; they cannot usually be contracted upon at all because they are not well-defined. Thus, the contract principal and agent still have individual weak-tie networks but these networks are not merged by the strong tie. These strong ties are thus intrinsically limited in their coordinative scope; they cannot pretend to join what can be neither observed nor contracted upon.

A partnership has a different flavor altogether. In a partnership, two potential puppeteer-firms join forces and form a new weak tie, agreeing to share weak as well as strong ties. Commitment of the weak-tie network is the distinguishing characteristic of partnership; the fuzziness of definition need not matter in a partnership, since each partner has a genuine interest in making the collaboration work. The observability problem has been circumvented by an incentive-based solution.[12] Partnerships thus have greater potential scope than formal contracting, as they can do everything contracts can do plus solve the information-performance problem of unobservable weak ties.

Establishing and maintaining a partnership is usually much more difficult than bidding for or soliciting bids for a contract. Partnerships require trust; an organization demonstrates that it deserves its partner's trust by repeatedly forgoing opportunities to gain short-term advantage at its partners' expense. This requires time, making it entirely reasonable for partnerships to evolve from traditional contracting relationships. Partnerships need to be renegotiated or adjusted to retain incentive compatibility and short-term reward equity, as partners' conditions and contributions change.

The employee and the consultant: strong and weak ties in human resources. Employees sell to employers the residual rights of control over activities they are willing to perform to employers in return for wages.[13] A traditional employee is thus defined by the set of tasks that he or she will not do, the relationship taking the form of complete contractual commitment with reservations explicitly stated.[14]

For years, external consultants have cultured a distinctively different type of relationship with corporations. Figure 8-2 distinguishes consultants from employees. Whereas an employee's contract is usually of the form

"I will do anything for you except . . . ," a consultant typically negotiates a contract that stipulates "I will do nothing for you, except . . ." or "I will not work for you, unless. . . ." Consultants' contracts presume that management will specify a set of tasks or goals attended by an offer of compensation. In some management consulting firms, contracts are anathema, and have been replaced by reputation and mutual trust. These consulting firms have established a reputation for being the best at what they do, for example, "strategic information technology consulting." The professionals of the consulting firm work together with the professionals of the client firm until they mutually agree that either further work should be terminated or redefined in terms of scale or nature in order to maintain requisite value-added. Not to do so hurts the client firm economically, damages the reputation of the consulting firm, or both.

Consultants on fixed-fee schedules can resist expansion of the scope of their projects unless they are given appropriate additional compensation; employees on fixed wages cannot, unless the proposed added tasks are specifically identified on the short list of explicitly excluded duties and responsibilities. Longer-term employees who demonstrate to an employer that they will exercise caution and discretion in the interests of continuing employment may gain some say in what they are and are not expected to do. At this point the employee's relationship with the firm has shifted from an employee-type to a consultant-type relationship. Such employees reclaim some residual rights over their activities and gain some ability to design their own jobs. These most treasured employees often chafe the most in traditional organizations.

We expect an increasing number of work agreements, from shop floor to executive suite, to be of the consultant type in the future. Informal arrangements that mitigate opportunism through long-term relationships can, as they become the norm, combine the benefits of flexible short-term agreements with the stability and security of long-term relationships. Managers of transforming organizations can facilitate this shift for mutual benefit by implementing performance measurement and compensation systems that encourage all employees to take the plunge into self-designed work.

Global Scope in Practice

It is difficult to identify "best-practice" and "worst-practice" examples of global scope. Since global scope is a mindset that alters an organization's perspective and abilities without necessarily changing its actions, it is possible that an obscure Tallahassee faucet maker might be the world's best global company. What we can do is cite some examples of firms that are known to us that illustrate key facets of global scope.

The press has served up an ample portion of shortsightedness by U.S. companies abroad, often portrayed comically, although shareholders seldom perceive the episodes so. Disney, for example, which apparently failed to take into account the average height of customers when building Disneyland East near Tokyo, has seen poor concession sales. Chrysler's AMC Motors division neglected to offer its popular Jeep with a steering wheel on the right-hand side and then wondered why the vehicle did not sell well in Japan. But simply to choose one or two anecdotes would be to miss an opportunity to point out a more fundamental shortcoming of U.S. business.

Too many U.S. firms, content to make incremental improvements in local markets and reluctant to expose themselves to the risk of embarrassment in foreign markets or loss in domestic ventures, elect, through inaction or ignorance, not to pursue global scope. Is it worse to have tried, failed, and learned, like Disney and Chrysler, or never to have tried at all? Disney and Chrysler will make better choices in the future. Chrysler did install right-hand drive steering wheels on their Jeep vehicles exported to Japan, and the Jeep became a hot seller in Japan. Firms that do not pursue global thinking will remain stuck in the industrial economy.

Global thinking begins at home. Xerox, for example, never explicitly targeted the personal copier market as attractive. Though the market was not very well developed at first and thus not particularly profitable to enter, it nevertheless harbored a hidden benefit. Competitors that had been manufacturing for the personal copier market for years had discovered cost-reduction techniques that they were able to apply to office-based machines. Having ignored the market that gave rise to these innovations, Xerox had no recourse against competitors that could price it out of the office market. Xerox, like U.S. automobile manufacturers during the early 1980s, had chosen to squeeze current profits out of its office market and suffered similar competitive difficulties as a result.

Implementation Lesson from Global Scope: The Self-Examination Process

We find that many organizations espouse globalization in their business strategies, but few have the enabling IT and network infrastructures to turn their rhetoric into reality. An organization that truly has global scope not only "talks the talk," but also "walks the walk." Consider the radical transformation of IBM since 1993. In the long-forgotten past, IBM's "global" strategy had consisted of printing its computer manuals in six languages and sending U.S. executives abroad for several years before bringing them back to Armonk to resume their climb up the hierarchical ladder. As IBM vice president Pierre Hessler admitted at a Harvard Business School colloquium: "We thought we were global (in 1982), but we were obviously not."[15] It has taken ten years for companies to realize that globalization is more than multinational presence. They didn't know what they didn't know.

Ten years later, not a single firm that participated in a joint Nolan, Norton Institute/IBM study considered itself global.[16] Critical self-assessment—the ability to know what you don't know—is crucial to the successful completion of a transformation initiative. The next step in the self-assessment process is to take stock of organizational strengths by looking in one's own back yard; you may not realize what you know. Only after it documents both weaknesses and strengths does an organization know what it knows.

Globalization As an Executive Mindset

The management principles that underlie a shift in the executive mindset from a local to a global focus are not new; they have been around for more than twenty years. As early as 1969, Howard Perlmutter described the evolution of the multinational enterprise as a shift in executive mindset.[17] Perlmutter hypothesized that the executive mindset, which he divided into three categories, was the main determinant of an organization's focus. Exhibit 8-1 attempts to integrate his categories into our transformation paradigm.

Bartlett and Ghoshal discuss in depth the building and management of what they term "the transnational organization." We shall not repeat their findings except to emphasize once more that the executive mindset is the stabilizing factor in the transformation process. An executive vision must have a tangible impact at all levels of an organization. Management must persuade all of the parties involved that their personal stake in transformation is high, that short-term pain must be endured to realize gains, and that "going global" is not the end of the world, but the beginning.

Perlmutter's Typology	Executive Mindset	Transformation Equivalent
Ethnocentric	Domestic Dominance Centralized Control	U- or M-form hierarchy Downsizing; Dynamic Balance
Polycentric	Country-by-Country Multicentralized	Hierarchy and shadow network Customer-driven Orientation
Geocentric	Global Embrace Decentralized	Globalized Formal Network Global Scope

Exhibit 8-1. *Classic Description of Global Scope by Mindset*

Global Scope As an Interim Goal

Achieving global scope is only partially, so to speak, "the big payoff" in the transformation process. Global scope reinforces and leverages lessons learned in previous transformational phases. It is the end of the first transformational transition experienced by a firm, but still only an interim goal, a stepping stone to the larger goal of continuous self-evaluation and improvement. We have so far traced the emergence of the network organization past two major milestones, or interim goals—downsizing and customer-driven orientation. Global scope is the third.

The first major interim goal was reevaluation of resource requirements through downsizing, enabled by automation technology. The milestone development was the establishment of the shadow network, which served to redirect many of the more difficult tasks of hierarchy, such as expedient response to competitive threats requiring major resource allocations to a network structure without dismantling the formal organizational structure. The shadow network comes about through implementation of cross-functional teamwork, often as the result of a quality initiative. New technology, combined with old organization, provides the productive capability.

The second interim goal was the substitution of a customer-driven orientation for the product-driven orientation of the industrial economy. The key development was formalization of the shadow network and recognition of that network structure as the designated successor to the hierarchy. This legitimization of the shadow network structure typically occurs during the customer-driven initiative, because it is not only convenient but imperative that the allocation of decision-making rights follows the distribution of specific knowledge, as an organization's focus shifts from the factory floor to the point of customer contact. When decision-making rights are transferred from hierarchical supervisors to customer-contact employees, the separation of hierarchical rank from decision-making rights is complete. This time new technology combines with new organization to increase productive capability.

The third interim goal is the network organization's achievement of global scope. The first- and second-order transformational initiatives allow an organization, at considerable cost, both the external focus and the internal wherewithal to interact openly with its competitive environment. With the next stage, globalization, an organization "cashes in" on its new-found focus and capabilities. Globalization by no means completes the transformation process, although it may appear to do so when transformation is involuntary and incomplete, forced by competitive necessity rather than deliberately instigated by value-maximizing managers. Transformation motivated by necessity often stops at downsizing or falters after a quality initiative. The complete treatment—all six stages, from downsizing to global scope—is barely enough; only fully transformed organizations have a chance at continued success.

Successful transformation managers live in the future. The goal of the transformation process for these futurists is simple: to create shareholder value by improving long-term profitability. They do so by "walking the tightrope" of surplus distribution.

Chapter Nine

Management Principles Essential to the IT-Enabled Network Organization

INFORMATION technology has enabled business transformation both directly and indirectly. Its role was not obvious at the outset, but it has been discovered, refined, and studied over three decades.

Now it is obvious that IT is responsible for the emergence of a powerful and flexible new form of organization: the IT-enabled network, which marries network organization structures with network technologies. And now we can boldly hone in on the dramatic importance of network technologies. Mainframes and microcomputers in organizations were important technologies, of course, and resulted in important, organizational learning that was the prerequisite for the marriage of network technologies and network organization structures. As we observe the epic consolidations and strategic alliances among computer companies, telecommunications companies, cable TV companies, and media companies, the word is getting out.

Our discussion of the six-stage transformation process has covered a lot of ground and many years. In this concluding chapter we try to crystallize our vision of the IT-enabled network organization and the information economy management principles on which its emergence relies.

First, we advance a framework for network organization design, an ominous task at which we feel compelled to make some attempt because of the inadequacy of traditional organizational design approaches. We then summarize and suggest approaches for putting into practice the new information economy management principles.

A Framework for Network Organization Design[1]

Most prevailing organizational design approaches were conceived for industrial economy environments. Traditional approaches were based on the assumption that senior management is competent to design the total organization. Certain business functions were centralized and others decentralized to divisional or lower business units. We believe that there is a definite limit to how much of the organization senior management can effectively design, and that this limit occurs at a startlingly modest level in today's organization.

In our opinion only high-level infrastructures (we identify seven; see Figure 9-1) can be effectively designed by senior management. The fundamental need to respond quickly to diverse customer requirements renders day-to-day decisions and operations too dynamic to accommodate direct senior management involvement. These activities are best left to knowledge workers in self-designed networks. Moreover, traditional approaches to organizational design implicitly embody restrictions on the flow of and access to information. Information technology has abolished these information constraints.

Finally, we believe that the information economy organization needs to be guided by effective and continuously-updated visions of what it needs to be and values instead of the more traditional formal articulation of objectives and strategy, which tend to be reduced to very narrow objectives for subsidiary business units. Ultimately, what we propose is that organizational structures be created through the explicit design of infrastructures that provide the context and boundaries within which transient and organic self-designed networks can be built and dismantled as needed.

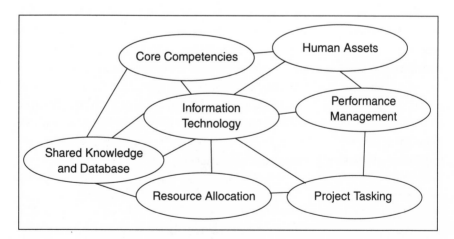

Figure 9-1. Seven High-Level Infrastructures

Superordinate Design

Superordinate organizational design establishes as points of stability the major shared infrastructures by which groups of knowledge workers, organized into self-designed networks driven by internal market forces rather than by managerial fiat, bring about coordinated outcomes. We will reexamine seven such infrastructures first shown in Figure 2-2, which are the foundation of the information economy firm.[2]

1. Information technology infrastructure. Built in Stage I (Downsizing), extended in Stages II through V (Dynamic Balance to Market Foreclosure) and completed in Stage VI (Global Scope.) The information technology infrastructure is the foundation for the other six infrastructures. The physical infrastructure of networking technology evolves throughout the transformation process, supporting the network organizational structure in two ways. First, it relaxes a binding physical constraint: the volume and speed of information transfer needed to fuel the network structure could not be supported prior to the development of networking technology. Second, networking technology changes the relative costs of information transfer and the consequences of ignorance. Communication among employees in a hierarchical structure is costly, because of both time and business expense associated with long-distance telephone, fax, and overnight mail of documents and diskettes. Electronic mail, a low cost and universal means of communication, effectively alleviates these expenses while increasing penalties for not knowing. This "ignorance tax" has grown with the pace of competition; the cost/benefit balance tips toward increased communication as a consequence not of cost savings, but of increased intelligence.

2. Performance management infrastructure. Built in Stage I (Downsizing), extended in Stages II through V (Dynamic Balance, Market Access, Customer-Driven Orientation, and Market Foreclosure), and completed in Stage VI (Global Scope). Senior management is responsible for establishing performance measures to assess how effectively resources are being utilized. These measures and information about them are also important to the self-designed teams that access the firm's resources. Measures of quality, customer satisfaction, innovation, human capital development, and competitive position are as fundamental to the network organization as financial measures were to industrial economy organizations.

The information technology architecture is the basis for performance measurement systems for senior management and pay-for-performance evaluation systems for employees. The performance management infrastructure also provides a mechanism for holding suppliers to higher standards. Interorganizational systems that connect companies with their suppliers and customers facilitate the joint flow of information and goods and services and provide a benchmark for continuous improvement.

3. Human assets infrastructure. Built in Stage I (Downsizing), extended in Stage II (Dynamic Balance) and IV (Customer-Driven Orientation), and completed in Stage VI (Global Scope). Establishing guidelines for recruiting, acculturating, and training employees is part of senior management's superordinate design responsibilities. Interpreting these guidelines into organizational norms is not. To achieve multinational flexibility requires, according to Bartlett and Ghoshal, "differentiated and specialized subsidiary roles." Information technology can be employed to develop screening mechanisms for recruiting, simulations, and programmed exercises for training.

4. Resource allocation infrastructure. Built in Stage II (Dynamic Balance), extended in Stages III through V (Market Access, Customer-Driven Orientation, and Market Foreclosure), completed in Phase VI (Global Scope). An organization's budgeting and capital budget processes and compensation system govern the allocation of its financial resources, based on expected returns as determined by previous performance and anticipated future opportunities. Responsibility for defining the processes by which allocation decisions are made is a responsibility of senior management; making the allocation decisions is the responsibility of intrapreneurs. Senior managers must ensure that the information technology identified in the organization's technological blueprint, essentially a map of its available information resources, is sufficient to gather and analyze information to support intrapreneurs' allocation decisions as well as account for resource decisions made by others.

5. Shared knowledge and databases infrastructure. Begun in Stage II (Dynamic Balance) and completed in Stage IV (Customer-Driven Orientation). Bartlett and Ghoshal identify "joint development and worldwide sharing of knowledge" as one of the key organizational characteristics of the transnational corporation. Senior management must ensure that mechanisms exist to make knowledge developed in geographically disparate parts of the global company what Bartlett and Ghoshal call "dispersed and interdependent assets and resources." Such mechanisms include large relational databases, database standards and communication protocols, data administration software to enable universal information access, and individual workstations for knowledge workers.

6. Project tasking infrastructure. Built in Stage III (Market Access), extended in Stage V (Market Foreclosure), and completed in Stage VI (Global Scope). Senior management is explicitly responsible for creating and making available project assignment and management tools, for example, a skills-based computerized organizational chart to serve as a directory for intrapreneurs trying to locate specific critical skills. Technologies such as E-mail, phone-mail, and publicly-accessible computerized resource-allocation calendars can help managers control tasks and identify available resources within the networks they assemble.

7. Core competencies infrastructure. Built in Stage VI (Global Scope). Senior management is responsible for identifying and articulating an organization's core competencies and for ensuring, through continuous learning and innovation programs, that skills inventories are continually developed and renewed.[3] Relational databases enable an organization to build cumulative knowledge bases; multimedia workstation-based JIT training facilitates the transfer of critical expertise;[4] global telecommunications support knowledge sharing, which enables firms to leverage existing information assets. The expertise infrastructure amplifies existing core firm capabilities. Superb facility in expertise-sharing can become an expertise in its own right.

Self-Design

An organization's knowledge workers utilize the infrastructures established by senior management as guidelines and resource maps to execute self-designed activities.

Structure. The structure of a network blurs boundaries between the firm and its suppliers, customers, and even competitors through strategic alliances, joint ventures, and other such "soft" forms of managing external relationships.

Resources, drawn from the resource allocation infrastructure and accessed on a task-by-task basis to form local networks, nourish the temporary relationships that form and dissolve as tasks and projects begin and are completed. As an aggregate of many local networks, the overall network structure is constantly shifting. A static hierarchical structure is not merely replaced by a static network structure. The constituents of a network may be located anywhere in the world; information technology and telecommunications architecture plays a central role in coordinating opportunities and allocating resources.

Systems. Like structure, management control systems have historically been designed by senior management, usually in the finance function. Such systems were typically manual and report-based, utilizing data generated by functional processes. The shared knowledge and telecommunications infrastructure allows workstation owners to design and redesign their own systems. Data secured from an organization's shared databases can be combined with local and external data accessed through telecommunications networks and analyzed at individual workstations. If workstations are powerful enough, and are outfitted with the right software, users can develop and refine an array of systems without the aid of information systems specialists.

Strategy. Strategy, too, has historically been the responsibility of senior management, often assisted by strategic planning staff and external consultants. Lower level managers and knowledge workers have been responsible for the implementation of strategy in which they have had little input. Today's information economy makes it clear that individuals closest to customers are in the best position to develop strategies for meeting their needs. Such grassroots location of strategy origination more fully utilizes the collective expertise of the infrastructure.[5] But there is a caveat; the sum of many individually made best decisions will not always yield the best overall outcome for the organization.[6] The purpose of superordinate design is to ensure that local decisions made by knowledge workers contribute to the firm's overall success and not lead it astray.

From decision making to decision framing. In the information economy, big decisions may be made at any level of the organization. Senior management may not even be aware of which decisions are truly big, as a decision's importance is often only revealed over time. Moreover, senior management never operates alone; other knowledge workers participate in decisions that impinge on the outcomes of projects in which they are involved.

This information economy treatment of decisions suggests a shift from decision making to decision framing as the primary responsibility of senior management. In the divisionalized functional hierarchies left over from the industrial economy, senior management makes the "big" decisions to establish a context for routine decisions at lower levels. Trying to build impetus for projects demands significant influence from senior managers.[7]

The overarching change in organizational philosophy required to accommodate an effective network lies in the procedural allocation of decision-making rights.[8] In the network organization, senior management's primary responsibility is to frame the context in which big decisions will be made. It does this by developing the superordinate infrastructures that ensure that the requisite information, resources, tools, and processes are in place. All decisions that affect elements of the infrastructure, no matter how routine, should be made by senior management. Hence, senior managers will make some decisions that are trivial in terms of direct financial impact. All non-infrastructure decisions, no matter how big, should be made by others in the firm, with senior managers included only under specific conditions. This reallocation of decision-making authority will result in some very low-level people making decisions that can have substantial financial impact. For example, the operation of a semiconductor manufacturing facility might be made the full responsibility of the employees operating the facility; some may have multiple doctorates, some no high-school diploma. As a result, an operating employee is given the decision-making power to shut the facility down if the employee suspects that a particular raw material might negatively impact quality. While the cost of a manufacturing facility shutdown might run into the millions of dollars, it is presumed that senior management has already assessed the cost/benefits of allocating this decision to operating employees, and is willing to accept the costs of a shutdown in exchange for maintaining quality standards, and avoiding other costs of shipping defective semiconductors to valued customers.

In order for senior managers to be able to distribute decision-making rights, elements of a firm's infrastructure must be clearly defined and decisions that affect the infrastructure distinguished from those that do not. The notion that senior management is responsible for decision framing, and local knowledge workers handle decision making, is easy to advance in principle, but difficult to implement in practice. The temptation to label all big decisions "infrastructure decisions" just to get executive hands on the tiller must be resisted if the distinction between superordinate and self-design is to be maintained.

This is not to say that senior managers must not participate in decisions at the self-design level. Because they are also knowledge workers, to exclude senior managers categorically would only reinforce a hierarchical distinction that would confound decision making: decisions related to superordinate design would come to be regarded as centralized, and those related to self-design teams would be labeled decentralized, a spurious demarcation that would hinder the organization's move from a divisionalized functional hierarchy to a network.

Senior managers, up to and including the CEO, are network members. Their participation in self-design team decisions must be in the role of knowledge workers participating in teams, not ex officio senior managers, and occur only by invitation. Senior managers must not invite themselves to participate, even if reasonably certain that a decision will be made that will have negative consequences for the firm. Those responsible for self-design teams must be given the opportunity to both make and learn from mistakes. Strategic patience—the art of observing and reflecting until it's time to move—is paramount.

Senior management intervention is warranted when poor decisions continue to be made, or when the pursuit of autonomy leads senior managers to be excluded inappropriately. For example, in the case of the semiconductor manufacturing facility, if plant shutdowns continued at a higher than expected rate, senior management might intervene to see if employee decision making is being hampered by the lack of critical expertise.

Senior management should not inject itself forcibly into decisions, but rather examine the infrastructure with an eye toward making changes that might foster improvement in self-design decisions. The organizational monitoring and feedback elements of the formal control system bring these improvement possibilities to management's attention; management's attention is focused on capabilities and guidelines, not on the specific decisions being made.

From Industrial Economy Management Principles to Information Economy Management Principles

Further perspective on business transformation can be developed by categorizing the 20 information economy management principles we have developed on the basis of the functions of the executive, nature of the firm, information resource management, and supervision and compensation. Grouping the information economy management principles into these four categories, as shown in Exhibit 9-1, highlights the distinctive characteristics of the network organization.

Group One: Functions of the Executive

Chester Barnard's classic treatise, *The Functions of the Executive*, reprinted 18 times since 1939, defines three executive functions: (1) providing the system of communication, (2) ensuring essential efforts, and (3) formulating and defining purpose.

Five information economy management principles pertain to the functions of the executive:

• Leadership principle
• Information principle
• Architect principle
• Conflict resolution principle
• Opportunity principle

The strategy formulator, organizational designer, and ceremonial top leader of the industrial economy organization must become a visionary and an organizational architect in the information economy organization, responsible for the design of superordinate infrastructure and the dynamic balancing of stakeholder interests. Day-to-day activities of the information economy senior manager include timely dispute resolution, internal consulting, and opportunity seeking.

The slower heartbeat of the industrial economy organization accommodated calculated actions achieved by consensus. In the context of such

	#	Principle	
Functions of the Executive	1	Leadership principle	Senior management formulates and coordinates firm's vision, and plays a central role in defining projects.
	7	Information principle	All organization members have open access to all information, instead of restricting the flow based on "need-to-know."
	11	Architect principle	Senior management shapes the firm's structure through the design and redesign of infrastructures necessary for the operation of self-designed teams.
	18	Conflict resolution principle	Conflict between the firm and customers, employees, shareholders, or suppliers is expediently mediated by senior managers; use of third party mediation is the exception.
	19	Opportunity principle	Activity is oriented toward fast-changing global market opportunities, rather than overcoming organizational inertia.
The Nature of the Firm	10	Task principle	Work is organized into projects, and carried out by team members assigned to these projects based upon their expertise necessary to accomplish the project goals.
	12	Strategic orientation principle	The strategic orientation of the firm is serving customers' needs, versus manufacturing the product or service.
	15	Authority principle	Authority for resource allocation is continuously changing and is awarded to workers who are the most effective decision makers.
	16	Cycle time principle	Resource allocation decisions are made in real time instead of on the fiscal year cycle.
	6	Value creation principle	All activities of the firm must be justified by their role in maximizing customer value.
	20	Boundary principle	Organization boundaries are organic—continuously expanding and contracting—as various network relationships are added and subtracted from the firm.

Exhibit 9-1. Principles for Survival in the Information Economy

Exhibit 9-1. (Continued)

<table>
<tr><td rowspan="5">Management of Information as a Resource</td><td>5</td><td>Worker-class principle</td><td>All employees are treated as a uniclass of knowledge workers, versus the two-class system of white-/blue-collar workers.</td></tr>
<tr><td>7</td><td>Information principle</td><td>All organization members have open access to all information, instead of restricting the flow based on "need-to-know."</td></tr>
<tr><td>14</td><td>Communication principle</td><td>Communication is swift, spontaneous, and point-to-point, unlike paper memos and formal face-to-face meetings.</td></tr>
<tr><td>9</td><td>Dynamic balancing principle</td><td>The firm's surplus is monitored in real time, and equitably distributed to shareholders based on current information.</td></tr>
<tr><td>17</td><td>Control principle</td><td>Control is made efficient through extensive performance feedback information, and self-interest-based reward systems which act to motivate workers to maintain high levels of performance.</td></tr>
</table>

<table>
<tr><td rowspan="5">Supervision and Compensation</td><td>2</td><td>Span of control principle</td><td>Span of control is variable, and limited by resource availability, not by supervisors' capacity to monitor workers.</td></tr>
<tr><td>3</td><td>Supervision principle</td><td>Supervision is indirect, through results assessment, versus direct worker observation.</td></tr>
<tr><td>4</td><td>Reward principle</td><td>Rewards are performance-based, not position-based.</td></tr>
<tr><td>8</td><td>Coordination principle</td><td>Firm activities are made purposeful and efficient through extensive flows of information, which enable workers to anticipate and expediently correct problems using informed discretion.</td></tr>
<tr><td>13</td><td>Team principle</td><td>Teams are formed by leaders offering compensation packages intended to attract knowledge workers with the expertise needed to achieve project objectives.</td></tr>
</table>

▨ Salvaged principle ☐ New principle

organizations, the annual budget sufficed as the core instrument for control. Ex-post organizational design entailing lengthy implementation periods is entirely incompatible with the "sense and respond" paradigm of the information economy. Today's senior manager must be a real-time player in organizational dynamics.

Group Two: The Nature of the Firm

Ronald Coase's classic 1937 article, "The Nature of the Firm," established the groundwork for analysis of firm functions and characteristics. The network organization exhibits dynamic and organic characteristics only now emerging in organizational science. Notions of boundaries and place are supplanted by a shared vision that serves to marshal resources in a way that contributes to the organization's value-added processes. Six information economy management principles bear directly on the nature of the firm:

- Task principle
- Strategic orientation principle
- Authority principle
- Cycle time principle
- Value creation principle
- Boundary principle

A definition of the firm that is both specific and robust becomes elusive in the information economy. The network organization's boundaries are complicated by strategic alliances, JIT supplier arrangements, and other network relationships that change with time. Moreover, the real-time operating cycle demanded by the information economy renders firms flexible rather than fixed entities.

Group Three: Managing Information As a Resource

Knowledge workers who effectively exploit information resources are a source of extraordinary value. Vast stores of readily accessible information provide leverage for utilizing other resources more productively. Industrial economy management principles related to resource management are universally misleading with respect to the new information resource. Information, unlike physical resources, is not consumed with use. In fact, the value of information as a resource may be directly correlated with its amount of use.

Resource-management principles are the least developed of the information economy management principles and will probably subsequently be refined more than those in the other groups. Five information economy principles bear on resource management:

- Worker class principle
- Information principle
- Communication principle
- Dynamic balancing principle
- Control principle

Group Four: Compensation and Supervision

The shift to an information economy alters the determiners of compensation from loyalty and organizational level to performance, and the role of supervision from monitoring human activities to mentoring and coaching of individuals bound together by common business objectives.

Compensation and coordination are governed by five information economy management principles:

- Span-of-control principle
- Supervision principle
- Reward principle
- Coordination principle
- Team principle

The shift from blue-collar/white-collar to a uniclass of knowledge workers necessitates a realignment of incentives and rewards that reflects a shift in responsibility for adding value from organization to individual. This shift has already occurred in leading organizations. Microsoft, for example, has created 2,200 millionaires with a current employment of approximately 12,000. The Limited clothing stores have an employee equity program and pay expenses to ensure that employees as well as financial analysts attend annual stockholders' meetings.

The Art of Network Management

We acknowledge, indeed, depend on, there being many ways to make things happen in practice. Consequently, we include a self-design component in the transformation framework with the expectation that management teams will craft their own ways of employing it.

We also offer three provisos to management teams that aspire to virtuoso performance in a transformation environment. First, the complexity of business transformation necessitates reliance on assumptions that keep uncertainty at manageable levels. Realistic assumptions can greatly simplify the analysis process; unrealistic assumptions almost certainly doom it to failure. Until we applied simulation modeling to several case studies of downsizing, we had not considered the importance of managing the distribution of organizational slack among workers, customers, and shareholders. In assuming that surplus creation and distribution were completely separate processes, we had initially oversimplified the model. If managers are to give coherent thought to the challenges of transformation, they must dust off such powerful but rarely-used tools as simulation, knowledge of agency problems, and a feel for internal markets.

Second, institutionalized experience with traditional management principles is a known impediment to making successful tenfold improvement. To overcome this impediment, managers must be exceptionally explicit about making new management principles the basis for their actions. When new principles are not clearly delineated in practice, 10 percent changes have a tendency to predominate.

Third, we cannot overemphasize the need for balance between flexibility and dogged persistence. If an initiative is not working, something else needs to be tried to conserve time and preserve momentum. Persistence in working toward achieving results—"keeping your eyes on the prize," so to speak—is crucial to maintaining the managerial attention and resource focus needed to keep a process moving. Transformation results show up on new multi-dimensional performance measures well before they appear on the traditional balance sheet; firms that persist in the face of stagnant or lagging performance stand to realize breakthrough achievements rather than incremental gains.[9]

The Two Scenarios of Transformation

Variations in the transformation process occur as early as the first downsizing stage—firms respond differently to undesirable initial states that motivate transformational change. An organization's starting point determines which of two scenarios it should follow. The first, and easier, takes an organization from a hierarchy with an established, but still informal, shadow network, to a fully IT-enabled network organization. The existence of a shadow network is a tremendous asset to the organization in its bid for transformation, facilitating the replacing of the management principles of hierarchy and the industrial economy with management principles more appropriate to a network structure and the information economy.

A second transformation scenario, rather more difficult than the first, takes a traditional functional hierarchy directly to a fully IT-enabled network organization, without passing through the shadow network to rest. In this scenario, organizational barriers associated with the traditional hierarchy must be overcome before a firm can change its competitive strategy to reflect information economy capabilities. When the functional hierarchy throws off its traditional management principles and formally establishes the shadow network as the accepted way to get work done, this scenario is reduced to the first—but any time spent relaxing in the shadow-network state is time during which the resources freed up by downsizing are being consumed, never to be seen again.

Key to the transformation agenda of successful companies that experienced growth during the 1980s such as Wal-Mart, Apple, The Limited, and Morgan Stanley, is the conversion of their highly successful shadow networks into IT-enabled networks. These high-growth firms have, by and large, migrated to shadow networks over time from entrepreneurial flat hierarchies. They incorporated traditional management principles to a degree, but also integrated IT into their efforts to grow in a controlled manner. The challenge for these firms in the 1990s is to further incorporate IT infrastructure into their thinking about the set of resources available to them. In doing so, they will combine existing knowledge and the ability to gather and act upon new information and make them an integral part of their product-market strategies.

Large, successful industrial economy companies such as General Motors, Ford, Chrysler, DuPont, General Electric, Exxon, and Sears must embark upon transformation by making fundamental changes at both the executive and customer-contact levels. To create a vision of transformation, the executive mindset must shift from a local to a global perspective, and the customer-contact body of the organization must transform from its traditional, multidivisional, functional hierarchy to an IT-enabled network structure.

This dual transformation is much more easily espoused than accomplished. Nothing fails like success; the historically high degree of success of institutionalized hierarchical structures has engendered a fundamental inertia that blocks successful transformation initiatives at every turn. Companies succeeded in the industrial economy by saturating every pocket of their organizations with the industrial economy management principles. Now these deeply seated principles need to be thoroughly flushed out. To accomplish this, management must impart to every member of the organization a sense of urgency. This urgency may derive from an external competitive threat or be instilled by a charismatic, forward-looking leader. Crisis-driven transformation is likely to provoke less resistance, but anticipated transformation is less destructive. Even organizations without visionary leaders will eventually be subjected to competitive trauma and forced to transform.

Experience suggests that the path these organizations take begins with disintegration, the breakup of highly integrated, traditional structures into smaller, autonomous structures. This initial disintegration is essential to galvanize the change in mindset from control to recovery. The breakup establishes a structure that is at once acceptable to existing managers who might still be in the thrall of old management principles and those hospitable to new principles. Chief among the drivers of this disintegration is relocation of decision-making rights and responsibilities from centralized top management to customer-contact employees. Unless distribution of decision-making rights precedes structural disintegration, the chaos resulting from trying to directly and centrally control the transition from complicated integrated structures to networks will almost inevitably culminate in a loss of control.

A Concluding Thought: Transformed Organizations Are More Fun

During our consulting and case research visits we have visited a lot of companies. We have been struck by the feeling we have come away with after visiting firms that are clearly successfully transforming to viable information economy competitors—firms such as Cypress Semiconductor, Microsoft, Intel, Motorola, Morgan Stanley, and The Limited. These and like firms repeatedly achieve impressive results in highly challenging competitive environments and exhibit extraordinary discipline in the consistency and efficiency with which they go about doing so. Members of these organizations show their dedication by performing at levels rarely observed in other organizations. Among a variety of motivators of exceptional performance is member perception of the tasks at hand. Employees in these firms are inclined to describe their work as fun; they seem to enjoy it. Moreover, such companies acknowledge their employees' commitment and hard work and encourage collective pride in their accomplishments by routinely and enthusiastically celebrating when they achieve new performance levels.

Celebrating and fun are the "art" counterparts of the challenge and discipline "science" elements of business transformation. What these firms seem to have done is create environments in which talented, high-potential knowledge workers can flourish: the embodiment of successful transformation.

Appendix

What Size Is Right Size? A Theory and Simulation of Firm Design

THE INSPIRATION for our simulation of the hierarchy's collapse came about while examining economic perspectives on the theory of internal firm organization. The economic literature on the fundamentals of hierarchy, beginning with Williamson in 1967, suggests that it is a "lesser of two evils" approach to organization.[1] Supervision is the essence of hierarchy. On the one hand, supervision discourages shirking and increases profitability; on the other, level upon level of supervision eventually dilutes the decision-making capabilities of executives. Williamson makes several interesting, albeit strict, assumptions about the nature of this process and derives a formula for the optimal size of a hierarchically-structured firm.

Williamson's original paper spawned a host of critical examinations of firm size and his model provided a convenient target for alternative theories. Three of his more controversial assumptions are of particular interest to us, given our hypotheses about the relationships between information technology and firm structure. We developed a model that simulated the automation process in a hierarchical organization and, by varying the conditions under which we permitted the removal of slack resource units, we were able to verify our organizational hypotheses with simulation data. Specifically, we were able to address each of the elements of the critical subset of Williamson's assumptions, namely: (1) static physical production technology; (2) static and constant span of control; and (3) constant information dilution.

Criticism of Static Technology: The Model Production Function

Our original simulation model of the production function included capital, labor, and technology in the Cobb-Douglas functional form. We were interested in keeping total production constant throughout the simulation, the better to observe effects on the cost function. The form assumed for production was $X = K^A L^B$, where the ratio A/B changes with improvements in technology. This model captures the spirit of a Cobb-Douglas production function at any given moment since the only aspect of production technology that changes through time is captured by the K/L ratio and the derived factor inputs.[2]

Since the purpose of this simulation is to examine the buildup and removal of organizational slack through automation, the logic of the automation paradigm suggested that we examine the gradual substitution of technology for labor. Accordingly, we held capital stock and production level constant at K_0 and X_0, respectively. When A and B were independent of time, the amount of labor required to produce a given output was inversely proportional to the level of technological innovation.

We purposely assumed a simple production function in which the level of accumulated technology determined the capital/labor ratio for a given production level. Note that the simplicity of this production function does not drive the outcome of the dynamics of organizational flattening; it serves only to minimize technical distractions in the production portion of the model, which is of only secondary interest. Although it is certainly true that the Cobb-Douglas technology can explain a good deal of productive behavior unassociated with its assumptions, the reasonable flexibility of this functional form proved to possess the necessary dynamic element without significantly complicating analysis.

Modeling Technological Innovation

The process of technological innovation is a sort of "black box" in this simulation (although we discuss sets of consistent motivations for and dynamics of practical innovation later). The effect of technology is to allow labor inputs for a given capital stock to be decreased without affecting output. This approach is in keeping with the treatment of the cost function as dual to the production function; since our focus is on cost, we are effectively simulating the cost function for a given production level rather than production capabilities with given factor inputs.

Accordingly, we added technology to the organization's production function first as a steady drip process, a simple additive method wherein each "tick" of the simulation clock added one new unit of technology; second, technology was added as a three-forward, one-back process, a random walk with trend, wherein each "tick" of the clock would, with equal probability, add three units or subtract one unit of technology. Note that three-forward, one-back is equivalent to steady-drip plus a random walk of two-forward, two-back with equal probability. Note also that although these two methods of simulating technological progress produce the same mean result of one unit of technology added per clock tick, the high variance of three-forward, one-back turns out to have a significant effect on the frequency of organizational change.

Modeling Organization

In our simulated organizational model, all production occurs at the bottom level. In line with Williamson's and others' assumptions of "no working foremen," upper levels of the hierarchy are assumed to perform purely supervisory and information-oriented functions rather than add value to a product. Since the assumption of constant productivity requires a certain amount of line-level labor at the beginning of the simulation, the hierarchy can be effectively assembled from the initial production functions andvector of spans of control. For example, if the span of control for each level in the organization is 2:1 and sixteen line-level workers are required, a natural (and wholly efficient) five-level hierarchy results (see Figure A-1).

Criticism of Span of Control: Modeling Supervision

We initially followed Williamson's assumptions of constant spans of control. Varying span of control across levels, however, produced interesting results, which we discuss below.

Criticism of Constant Information Dilution: Evolution and Revolution

If supervision of employees is a necessary evil, then layer upon layer of hierarchy must also be a necessary evil inasmuch as supervisors themselves require supervision. This principle of *qui custodiet ipsos custodes* underlies much of the recent literature on executive compensation and contract and incentive design.

The inexorable inflow of technology into line-level production processes, to the extent that it eventually eliminates discrete units of labor from the labor-capital combinations required to maintain critical production

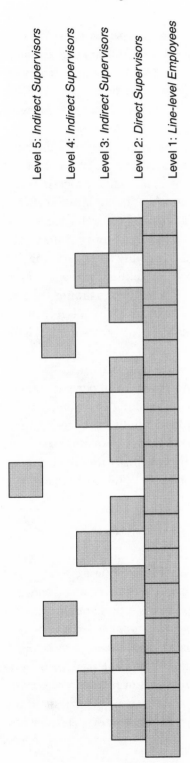

levels, will gradually reduce demands on the direct supervisors, which will, in turn, reduce demands on the indirect supervisors, and so forth. Gradual unit-by-unit redeployment of direct and indirect labor resources is termed *evolution*. The profit maximization goal of the firm demands that slack resources be eliminated whenever possible without loss of productive capacity, and that their costs be returned to the profit pool.[3]

A second, more dramatic, type of redeployment accounts for the bulk of the cost savings realized from the dynamic adoption of technology. Consider the following example. After much technological progress, eight line-level employees have been removed from the hierarchy without affecting productivity. In keeping with the 2:1 span of control, four direct supervisors have accordingly also been eliminated. According to the slack-elimination requirement specified above, responsibility for supervising the four eliminated direct supervisors will have been diffused across the four original level 3 supervisors such that each retains the maximum level of slack allowable before reassignment. Even though level 2 has been reduced by half, level 3 remains untouched by evolution. The hierarchy immediately after elimination of the four level 2 supervisors is as depicted in Figure A-2 (shading designates resources in use, white space slack).

Note that the Level 3 supervisors are underutilized; 50 percent of their capacity is slack. The four level 2 supervisors are handling a full complement of eight level 1 line employees, and the four level 3 indirect supervisors are managing only half their capacity of eight subordinates. Two organizational redeployments are possible, both attended by potentially traumatic consequences. One involves reassigning supervisory responsibilities horizontally, the other vertically.

Horizontal Reassignment

Theoretically, it ought to be possible to reach a more efficient state simply by horizontally reassigning level 3 supervisory responsibilities. By consolidating existing slack, two of the four level 3 indirect supervisors—and, by extension, one of the two level 4 indirect supervisors—could be eliminated, yielding the situation in Figure A-3.

Unfortunately, there is no way to eliminate half of level 5 since only one employee occupies this level. Hence, the 50 percent slack of level 5 will never be eliminated and an underutilized level of hierarchy will exist indefinitely. Moreover, the next horizontal reassignment (after four additional level 1 line employees are displaced) will result in 50 percent slack

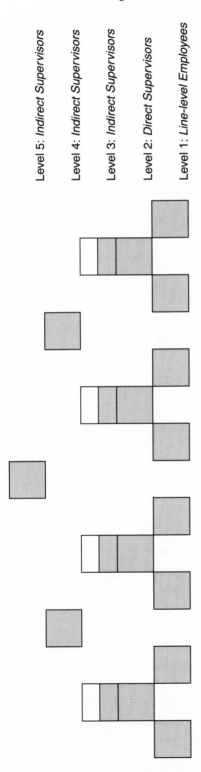

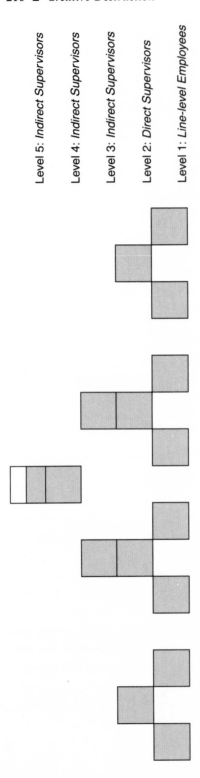

Level 5: *Indirect Supervisors*

Level 4: *Indirect Supervisors*

Level 3: *Indirect Supervisors*

Level 2: *Direct Supervisors*

Level 1: *Line-level Employees*

for the level 4 indirect supervisor as well. The amount of "hard-core" slack thus accumulates with this incremental downsizing technique, and the organization never reaches a new efficient level.[4]

Vertical Reassignment

We describe elimination of an entire level of hierarchy as revolution, as it immediately changes the nature of supervision in the remaining levels of the hierarchy. Vertical reassignment of responsibility breaks the chain of command, short-circuiting the authority relationship. The "long way around" can then be eliminated profitably.

Level 4 supervisors are fully capable of handling the four remaining level 2 supervisors, even without the assistance of the partially slack level 3 supervisors. Keeping the inefficient level 3 in place merely increases labor costs and the degree of information dilution.[5] Eliminating level 3 entirely from Figure A-2 results in labor savings plus a nonquantifiable gain associated with eliminating information distortion. The resulting hierarchy is shown in Figure A-4.

In this post-revolution hierarchy, which looks exactly like a pristine four-level hierarchy, all employee resources are fully utilized once more. Vertical responsibility reassignment has effectively exploited the opportunity to downsize generated by the accumulation of technology.

Graphical Description of Simulation Progress[6]

In Figure A-5, phase 0, or the basic hierarchy, exhibits a sharp distinction between middle managers (modulator-demodulators performing information transmission tasks) and line-level workers (creating value directly). This distribution, represented by the black bar in Figure A-5, reflects the blue-collar/white-collar industrial economy classification scheme. Some direct technical changes (shown as shading) can take place without having any effect on the area above the bar, as supervisors do not participate directly in value creation. The distinction between top upper management (decision makers) and middle management is left nebulous, as we show that this distinction is relevant only with respect to a specific technological change. Small changes generate little or no effect above the bar. The original area of the triangle is 16 units, representing (up to a proportionality constant) the total number of employees.

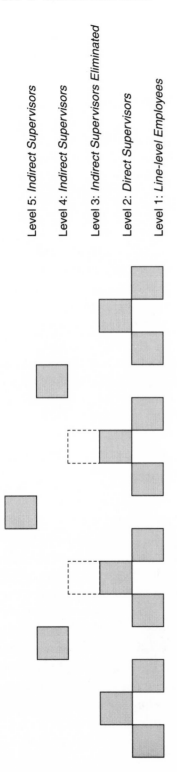

Level 5: *Indirect Supervisors*

Level 4: *Indirect Supervisors*

Level 3: *Indirect Supervisors Eliminated*

Level 2: *Direct Supervisors*

Level 1: *Line-level Employees*

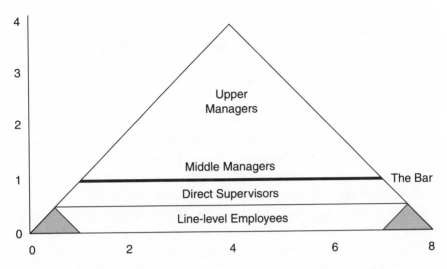

Figure A-5. Phase 0: Basic Hierarchy

Any technical change (no matter how small) will lead to direct savings through elimination of line-level workers. We assume that the direct benefit from automation accounts for 2 units of savings, making the remaining hierarchical size 14 units. The blue-collar/white-collar "bar" indicates the limit of direct technical progress (see Figure A-6). Note also that this fundamental technical progress need not begin at the absolute bottom of the hierarchy, the levels above any arbitrary point of change also have a

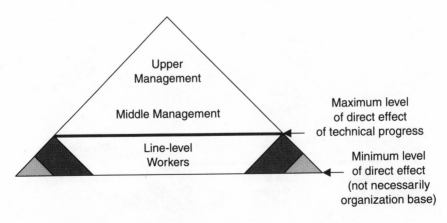

Figure A-6. Phase I: A House Divided

triangular shape; for example, the change can occur at mid-level in the hierarchy and only levels above the change will be affected.

Any technical change will result in a certain level of indirect savings through elimination of direct supervisors of the previously technically-displaced line-level workers. The 2:1 span of control assumption means that this indirect savings removes an additional 1 unit, leaving a 13-unit hierarchy.

This disruption of the automated diamond-shaped organization created by direct technical displacement (as in Figure 3-1) represents the leveraging of technical progress into organizational change, and thus the start of the process of creative destruction (see Figure A-7).

Indirect savings through elimination of indirect supervision (the middle managers responsible for expanding and compressing reports from the previously eliminated supervisors) amounts to 1/2 unit, again using the 2:1 span of control assumption. If organizational slack can be consolidated such that whole people can be redeployed, this benefit can be stretched to 1 unit, leaving a 12-unit hierarchy.

This phase of organizational transformation is the first in which the absolute size of unanticipated technical change is important, in that the indirect effects extend above the bar (see Figure A-8). The effects below the bar are over, while the elimination of inefficiency (or expansion of capabilities) continues. A feedback effect below the bar is that line-level workers, freed of redundant supervision, are treated as self-directed knowledge workers.

Indirect savings through elimination of redundant middle managers—"deleveling"—to decrease the information dilution between upper management and the newly-empowered knowledge workers accounts for 4 units

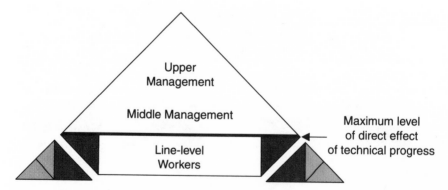

Figure A-7. Phase II: Diamonds Aren't Forever

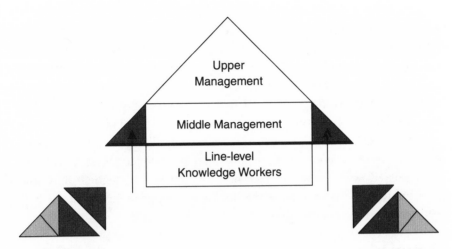

Figure A-8. Phase III: Crossing the Bar

of savings, leaving an 8-unit hierarchy. Note that if the consolidation in Phase III could not occur, this deleveling will not be possible under the existing span-of-control assumptions, and the 4 units will remain ungarnered (see Figure A-9).

This phase finally defines the previously nebulous distinction between middle and upper managers. The truly necessary decision makers experi-

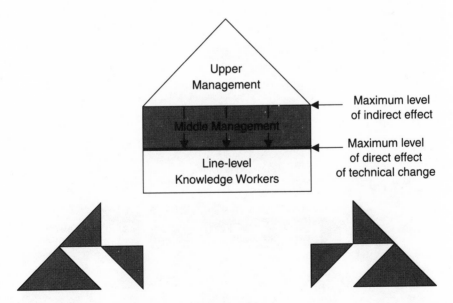

Figure A-9. Phase IV: Getting the House in Order

ence no direct effect of this change except for the increasingly direct interface (and blurring of task responsibilities) between themselves and the line-level knowledge workers. The bar has become a technological liaison.

The first stable organizational structure resulting from the effects of technical change has a new area of 8 units, a total savings of 50 percent over the initial configuration (see Figure A-10). The previous maximum level of direct effects and minimum level of indirect effects have been consolidated into a new interface between upper management and line-level knowledge workers. Note that the deleveling phase accounts for fully 50 percent of the total surplus.

Valuable Lessons from Simulation

Observing theoretical organizational behavior under a variety of assumptions over hundreds of situations yielded some interesting insights into how technology and organization gradually combine in the downsizing process. From these we derived a number of principles, which we present for the reflection of managers and academics concerned with the dynamics of organizational change in a controlled environment.

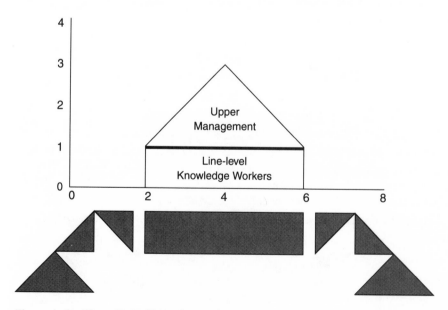

Figure A-10. Phase V: Half-Sized Is Right-Sized

1. The lion's share of gains comes from revolution, not evolution.
Chipping away at slack resources at various levels in the hierarchy—
essentially evolutionary behavior—can yield a satisfying flow of benefits
from technology. But removing these levels altogether frees a much larger
portion of resources for more productive uses. In the 2:1 span of control
example described above, fully 50 percent of the total savings is derived
from eliminating level 2. The lesson to management is obvious: evolutionary
change is not good enough; it leaves too much shareholder value on the
table.

2. Mixed span of control means more revolutions. When we varied
span of control across levels within the same organization, we noticed that
average span of control was not very good at explaining revolutions. Indeed,
an organization with an average span of control of 3:1, but wide variations
(i.e., some levels with 4:1, others with 2:1), experienced more revolutions
than a straight hierarchy of homogeneous 3:1 levels. This is, of course, an
example of comparative advantage: levels with high spans of control are
naturally better at administration, and so are kept on when levels are
eliminated.

3. Random technology means more revolutions. We also observed
more revolutions with the random three-forward, one-back process than
with the steady drip approach to adding technology. We attribute this
difference to the nature of quantum organizational change; once change
occurs (e.g., immediately following three-forward), there is no going back.
Real-world organizations that experience this sort of random give-and-
take technological progress should be more efficient, on average, than firms
that experience steady-drip technological innovation, as such revolutions
release cash surpluses that more than compensate for the possibility that
the next backward step will overtax the organization.

Clumsy Contracting: Management's Only Essential Problem

A perfect managerial agent has one clear goal: to maximize the long-
term wealth of the firm's shareholders. Pursuing this goal while deluged
with unanticipated challenges requires being prepared for constant re-
optimization, a very information- and effort-intensive agenda. In practice,
there exist two broad classes of barriers between real-world managers and

optimal decisions, barriers to comprehension and barriers to action, a distinction that divides omniscience from omnipotence.

Barriers to comprehension include information that is unavailable or cannot be collected or created before a decision must be made, and analytic procedures that are too costly or time consuming to employ. Managers employed by an automobile manufacturer, for example, would profit from knowledge of future competitive conditions, which can be estimated or approximated but never known. Moreover, a best estimate that incorporated all available information would be prohibitively expensive to formulate.

Barriers to action block the implementation of a decision already made. Managers, for example, might act on evidence that suggests that constructing automobiles of a metal having the weight of aluminum and strength of titanium would maximize profitability, only to discover that existing technology will not support their decision.

In combination, these barriers give rise to the problem of clumsy contracting. We rely on physical technology to surmount barriers to action, information technology to circumvent barriers to comprehension.[7]

Barriers to comprehension in an information-intensive environment relate to firm infrastructure. Better information today will lead to improvements in the infrastructure that governs future decision making. Moreover, knowledge today that better information will be available tomorrow will further improve management's position. For example, Frito-Lay's knowledge of overall market characteristics calls for workers in the field to have the freedom to exploit changing conditions. Managers who do not know on Tuesday what Thursday will bring—but know that they will know by Wednesday—can allocate contingent resources to be used on Wednesday, or not, as the case may be, after Fortune tips her hand. These "real option values" manifest themselves as strategic choices whenever flexibility is important.[8]

The Strategic Elements of Transformation

Here we treat the formal strategic aspects of the transformation sequence from the viewpoint of the economic discipline of industrial organization, as put into practice by such commentary as Michael Porter's work on competitive strategy.[9] Specifically, we examine how a firm that is building its resource base can tailor its competitive strategy to its product strategy through market access and market foreclosure. A step-by-step walkthrough of the strategic argument is followed by an explanation of the process and discussion of conclusions applicable to the transformation process in general.

Internal Argument: Desirability of Efficient Firm Design

Information technology and internal efficiency. We first argue that employing information technology within an efficient firm design is desirable from a profit-maximizing viewpoint and identify the economic forces that must be considered in firm design involving information issues.

The "new institutional" view of economic theory suggests that firms exist largely to mitigate transaction costs of exchange. But hierarchical institutions, being imperfect vehicles for eliminating these costs, incur costs of administration and information dilution. These imperfections derive from constraints imposed by managerial limitations on span of control; managers, having only a limited amount of time and mental energy, cannot perfectly coordinate all the tasks in the organization.[10] The quality of managers' coordination efforts declines as demands upon them increase, necessitating some institutional form of relief. Unable to control directly all these tasks, managers must delegate authority to others who may not be as committed to the welfare of shareholders.

In addition to limited decision-making time and managerial attention, hierarchical firms are hindered by incentive-compatibility constraints that arise from goal incongruence—competition for surplus among shareholders, employees, and customers. We discuss the struggle associated with dividing up short-term surplus to cement long-term relationships in Chapter Four.

All else being equal, if hierarchical complexity is largely a "lesser of two evils" alternative to even greater transaction costs associated with contract- or market-based exchange, then introducing technology that serves to lessen its cost will encourage external contracting over hierarchical complexity. Improvements in supervisory and information-transmission technology can substantially reduce the costs of performing all the functions of hierarchy and avoid the institutionalized slack inherent in the hierarchical form. Simplification of hierarchical structure is the 10 percent, not the 1000 percent argument. In this case, only industrial economy technology (e.g., DP-era systems employed to automate the data collection and transmission) has thus far been invoked.

Hierarchy's authority- rather than market-based structure precludes costless arbitrage of excess capabilities. That is to say, the authority structure prohibits the buying of inputs and selling of outputs on the open market, mandating instead reliance on a firm's internal markets. Moreover, transformation can incur substantial costs; shifting responsibility across hierarchical levels, for example, can occasion short-term disruptions in output as organization members' attention is diverted from the product-market to the restructuring effort.

Investments in organizational flexibility frequently appear justified only when they become essential to cope with adverse competitive circumstances.[11] Option values, which carry value determined by flexibility in their exercise, are particularly sensitive to distribution rules, as their value swings wildly if inefficient exercise decisions are made by people who don't receive their benefits.[12] They reside apart from the source of funds that purchased them or the recipient of the benefits that accrue to their exercise. Option investment is thus most efficient when decision rights and option ownership are located in the same place. Costs of moving these decision rights on short notice generates inertia in the organization, as some greater cost must justify their relocation.

Given a tendency toward short-term inertia, the technology that is gradually accumulated by an organization will not be fully utilized and the organization will actually become less efficient on paper. The constraint to keep the other stakeholders satisfied binds the manager, making the shareholders bear virtually all long-term costs of change.

In a purely market-regulated economy, such as one characterized by external, contract-based exchange, slack associated with underutilized technology could persist only to the extent that the transactions costs associated with eliminating it through reassignment of responsibilities exceed the benefits of doing so. But in a hierarchical, authority-based organization, inertia can sustain slack even when the benefits of reassignment exceed its costs. It is difficult for managers to control the distribution of slack because employees and suppliers can appropriate it before management becomes aware of its existence. Parkinson's Law will eliminate even the largest amounts of slack if managers do not monitor its generation closely.

Along with transaction cost can be added the potential inflexibility in an organization's surplus distribution policy as reasons to avoid reassigning organizational assets. To make this policy as flexible as possible is one of the goals of an organization's management control system.

Only the surplus that the managers' constituents—that is, the shareholders—get to keep will be considered in the reassignment decision. Once the other stakeholders have been persuaded to remain with the firm on a long-term basis, only the surplus that can be redirected to shareholders matters to managers. Subsequently, managers are likely to make investments that benefit suppliers, customers, or employees only to the extent that they also bring about some shareholder benefit. Some investment opportunities will be foregone.

The fundamental divergence between shareholder and social interest, without dynamic balancing, is reflected in the growing inefficiency of organizations constrained by long-term labor contracts, continued customer influence, and undemanding competitive environments (recall our five conjectures at the end of Chapter Four). Organizational inefficiency can persist indefinitely in the absence of dramatic shifts in technology or stakeholder expectations. Inertia resulting from the cost of organizational change does not disappear over time; although it builds up, it is never easy to extract no matter how long it has existed. In fact, other stakeholder groups try to sustain it. For example, a firm accustomed to having a large amount of finished-goods inventory, larger than needed, might want to shrink this level to free up cash. It is no easier to do this when the extra inventory has been there for ten years than it is when it has been there for ten hours; in practice, the factory may have become accustomed to the inventory level and resist the drive to rationalize it.

Technological improvement and potential solutions. Information technology employed in conjunction with organizational redesign can improve internal firm efficiency via two paths, 1) by improving the productivity of existing hierarchy members, and 2) by improving the scope of the firm's contracting capabilities, externally through environmental scanning and internally by improving coordination abilities. Information technology can improve the efficiency of supervisors' information processing and transmission functions. Even without direct, line-level technical change, a reduction in staff can be brought about by increasing the volume of information each knowledge worker can handle while keeping overall information input and output requirements constant.

Note that expansion of managerial expectations at this point can nip potential savings in the bud. Extra effort demanded of employees that does not translate into product or service quality improvements or cost reductions does not add value to a firm. Ad hoc increase in managerial expectations—demanding that overheads be printed in sixteen colors, requiring perfect spelling on internal memoranda, insisting that sixteen copies of every memo be filed—do not increase value by a single nickel, but instead constitute nothing but opportunistic appropriation by managers of surplus belonging jointly to shareholders, employees, and customers. Management expectations must be firmly controlled to realize true productivity improvements.

Information technology also, by making it easier to collect data and structure and transform it into information useful for management decision making, improves firms' environmental scanning ability, the ability, for example, to better monitor contractual obligations and thereby exert sufficient control over external activities to justify the outsourcing and subcontracting of tasks that it might otherwise have scrupulously maintained under the umbrella of "integrated manufacturing."[13]

In addition, improved monitoring can relieve subcontracting team members of the effort commitment problem discussed in Chapter Three. Individuals who dislike expending effort but are compensated on the basis of the team's product will not work as hard as they would if they were paid according to their individual performance; under the latter system they bear 100 percent of the costs of working, but only a fraction of the benefits.[14] This multiplayer Prisoner's Dilemma problem accompanying unverifiable individual effort leads to a particularly pernicious productivity problem.

As we observed in the "volunteering to be monitored" discussion in Chapter Four, management can circumvent this problem by setting up a performance-measurement system that can measure individual effort. With credible and constant monitoring of individual effort, this moral hazard problem vanishes. By improving the information situation, we can get something for nothing. By eliminating the market failure of unobservability, management can create surplus by operating the monitoring system. This created surplus can be shared between the purchasing firm and the subcontractor employees, in effect assigning profit and loss responsibility at the subcontracting team and individual levels.[15] This location of decision making and its consequences together achieves the correct incentives for productivity, resulting in more appropriate effort levels and at least some surplus for the firm.

Monitoring technology, if it can be implemented at reasonable cost, can create surplus. The decision whether to monitor, and at what level, executive or line, can then be evaluated like any other investment decision, weighing present costs against future returns. But the impact of monitoring technology is quite different from that of other technologies. Reducing the cost of monitoring encourages a firm to subcontract, with both outside vendors and employee-intrapreneurs. In an organization that relies heavily on contracts and monitoring, knowledge workers are 80 percent "consultant" and only 20 percent "employee." Increased willingness to invest in external monitoring and contract-enforcement technology can induce a pervasive shift from internal production to subcontracting and a quantum change in firm cost structure and strategic direction.

Improved monitoring of external contract performance is a powerful incentive to pare down the existing organization by outsourcing particularly supervision-intensive tasks. Coupled with judicious organizational redesign, IT can increase efficient span of control and ability to handle information flows and thereby reduce the need for managerial resources committed solely to the middle-management functions of summarizing and explaining data, ultimately rendering entire hierarchical levels redundant.

Seizing opportunities for market-based interaction created by improved information gathering and supervisory technology is likely to expose slack resources. Market forces encourage redeployment of underutilized, but nonetheless valuable, assets to more productive uses. Redeployment serves to sever formal vertical ties between the resources and the supervisors previously responsible for them. This redistribution of control rights effectively creates a "shadow network" in the midst of a formerly rigid hierarchy. Since decision-making responsibility remains with the control rights, the internal market for resources has served to redistribute supervisory responsibility. Such reassignment is costly within a hierarchy, less so in a market setting. Exposing slack resources to market sunlight first, before resorting to heavy-handed downsizing techniques such as explicit command-based redeployment, can spare a firm's management and human resources time, pain, and unnecessary effort.

Eliminating redundant supervisory levels reduces information dilution by making top decision makers privy to current organizational capabilities as observed directly at the line level. The feedback process created by constant monitoring of top-level plans with an eye toward feasibility and optimality provides planners with a constant reality check on capabilities and focuses managerial efforts on existing information channels.

The union of information technology and organizational redesign can improve a hierarchical firm's transaction-cost structure with the result that external market-based transactions will largely replace dependence on the authority relationship. This ultimately serves to decrease a firm's "right size."

External Argument: Necessity of Efficient Firm Design

This argument addresses issues of taking the offensive positions to argue that adapting firm design to exogenous market conditions can, to the extent that competitors do not respond, yield competitive advantage, then addresses defensive issues, to argue that, if competitors are employing technology to alter firm structure and competitive capabilities, firms that do not respond will be driven out of the market. Combining the forward and backward arguments suggests that technology-based firm design is a dominant strategy in the face of changing competitive conditions; that is, it is better to redesign the firm when the market changes whether or not your competitors are also redesigning theirs.[16]

Forward argument: efficient structure generates competitive advantage. The core organizational abilities necessary to compete successfully in the information economy are quite different from those crucial to survival in the industrial economy. Specific skills and slow learning processes dominated the industrial economy, yielding a fragmented knowledge base and impeding knowledge transfer. Learning curves for some basic processes have been much compressed by the ready availability of vast stores of information. The availability of information eases barriers to entry, abbreviating the time a new product can reap extraordinary gains in attractive markets before entry inevitably occurs.

With the period between innovation and challenge compressed, markets have become less hospitable to incumbents, demanding constant evaluation of competitive strategy. Firms are constantly called upon to decide whether to "fight" or "flee" in the face of new entrants. Taking neither position dooms a market to rapid devolution into overcapacity and accompanying price-based competition, in which the only winners will be the consumers. A long-term strategy centers on anticipation of employing either a fight or flight tactical response to each new entrant. Preparing for a fight strategy involves accelerating the innovation process so as to compete directly on innovation and new product attributes rather than in the primary product market. Flight involves, in addition to the possibilities of harvest or meek exit, concentration of design effort on differentiation so as to forestall direct price competition.

As we have seen, improvements in consistent quality and cycle time can be useful as both offensive and defensive tools, market access and market foreclosure, respectively. A firm can invest in consistent manufacturing technology, for example, without tipping its hand about whether it intends to compete on the basis of cost or features. Among other strategic tools that grow in importance despite the fact that they commit a firm to a particular strategy is heavy investment in R&D, an offensive tool with limited defensive capabilities. R&D expenditure is a sunk cost, but can yield cost reductions or feature enhancements that improve a firm's future competitive position. A firm that continues to pour money into R&D is almost certainly going to stay in, rather than exit, the market, the costs having already been incurred and the benefits tied to continued market presence. Commitment to continued market presence may deter entrants, but it tips one's hand.

A defensive tool with limited offensive capability is a broad customer service network with a comprehensive warranty and service agreement that would be too costly to provide for low-quality items. Such a network signals to a firm's customers and competitors that it will be around for some time if it wants to be—that is, that it is competitive on a quality basis and will not be forced out of the market—without making any irrevocable promises of continued sales.

In an idealized economic world, firms can costlessly reorganize resources in any way they please to adjust to changes in competitive conditions. In the real world, of course, this is not the case. In particular, rigidities in firm structure impose constraints on flexibility in dealing with accelerating changes in the competitive environment. Competitive advantage in a time of compressed entry requirements will go to organizations that can quickly act on their strategic choices. A firm plagued by information dilution will, at the margin, seek flexibility over suppression of transactions costs. A shift in priorities toward flexibility can take on empirical presence in the form of increased choice of "buy vs. make," lower-level decision-making authority, and generally contractual, network incentive-based rather than fixed-wage, authority-directed structures.

The cost of this strategy-enabling organizational shift is the increased cost of monitoring and contracting to perform the previously-internalized hierarchical functions in the absence of the hierarchical form. It costs more to have "strong eyes" to expand the firm's contracting horizons. Technology that reduces information dilution and goal incongruence thus represents a potential strategic application. Implementation of such technology becomes more desirable as flexibility and responsiveness become strategically crucial.

Though a shift in competitive intensity may render the alternative of not implementing a technology less attractive, it does not alter the gross benefits of the technology. Thus, we ought to see some previously foregone opportunities reviewed as evolutionary speed increases; organizations should occasionally "advance to the rear" and reevaluate previously rejected technologies in light of new competitive circumstances. If the prevailing competitive situation, for example, demands 24-hour toll-free customer service, supporting technologies that might not have been cost-effective five years ago need to be reevaluated even if their costs have not changed.

New competitive circumstances should make technologies that mitigate the costs of contracting (i.e., that are "hierarchical substitutes") much more popular. Technologies that substitute for the hierarchical form while maintaining its coordinative functions are precisely the technologies that enable transformation.

Organizational reluctance to invest in information technology stems, in part, from uncertainty about future competitive conditions. The first barrier to investment in IT and structural change is that they constitute an irreversible sinking of large amounts of capital. If the benefits of previous investments have been appropriated by other stakeholder groups, potential funders are likely to be loath to make a commitment. A second barrier to investment is potential appropriation of option values by stakeholders that do not make the sacrifice at the time of implementation. A competitive crisis gives a firm an excuse to renegotiate previous commitments—whether labor contracts, product prices, or promotion expectations—without losing its reputation as a good-faith bargainer.

Information cannot pass through an organization in unaltered form. Just as engineering cost projections must be translated into a particular measurement system to make sense to accountants, the vast flow of potential information from a generic physical process must be compressed and summarized by intervening mechanisms (human or computer) before being presented to decision makers at higher levels of the hierarchy. The summation and transfer of information comes at a cost. Information tends to be diluted by each level of a hierarchy that it passes through. Dilution thus tends to be greater in more complex hierarchies and, all else equal, greatest in hierarchies with greater goal incongruence between levels.

Although technology that improves goal congruence or reduces hierarchical complexity will reduce information dilution, the full effects of any such reduction will not be observed until decision rights are reallocated through the process of organizational redesign. Two opposing forces are at work: increasing span of control eliminates levels of hierarchy and thereby reduces information dilution, while less intensive monitoring permits goal incongruence, which increases information dilution.[17]

Information technology that complements existing management structure serves to reduce resource requirements. If one clerk plus one computer can do the work of two people, the clerk's productive capacity has doubled. With the technology-aided knowledge worker able to do the work of two computerless clerks, only half as many clerks are needed. This reduction masquerades as automation, but in fact substitutes for the old-style "human information channel," changing not only the form of information transfer, but also the substantive content of the information being transferred—an informating change.

Such informating renders the hierarchy more conducive to information flow. An increasingly information-intensive control structure should then be chosen for firm governance. Competitive market risks are the same, even though the information position of the firm is improved. Firms that seek to avoid risk will use more information-intensive methods to compete in product markets. This structure often takes the form of increased reliance on contract- and market-based methods rather than traditional vertical integration. Reduced reliance on integration leads to further reductions in the size and complexity of the hierarchy, which leads to further substitution and simplification as previously required monitoring functions are replaced with incentive systems. This creates a classic positive reinforcement feedback loop, in which the incentive to further transform the organization arises from the tangible benefits that result from the previous stage of transformation. While this feedback loop is in effect, IT investment in information technology yields increasing returns to scale; the more invested, the more the next unit of investment will generate.

Information technology, in conjunction with organizational redesign, can thus reduce overall information dilution without adversely affecting an organization's information-processing capacity. In the absence of organizational redesign, however, the positive reinforcement feedback loop will not develop. To realize the dynamic synergies from combining information technology and organizational redesign, the efforts must be undertaken concurrently.

Backward argument: firm efficiency is necessary to survive. Given that efficient restructuring is individually desirable for each firm, all firms should eventually overcome their inertia and change according to the forward argument. If there are many firms in an industry, however, it is unlikely that all will have the same agenda or collection of capabilities. With a heterogeneous distribution of potential gains from adoption of information technology and organizational restructuring, for example, some firms would prefer to delay adoption of the new technology and structure because their own particular cost/benefit tradeoffs make inertia the preferred state to be in.

Because firms start off with different sets of resources, they must evaluate the cost/benefit tradeoffs of restructuring individually. Restructuring takes on added importance in the face of an accelerating pace of competition. Incumbent firms have little time to rest before being challenged by new entrants. Availability of information dissolves traditionally high knowledge-based entry barriers in many industries. Increased threat of entry provokes continuous assessment of the fight-or-flight response.

Flight strategies that involve immediate or delayed exit (sometimes called "harvest") do not require organizational change in the same manner in which fight responses do. Flight can mean either "get out" or "move on." For a firm that will exit an industry anyway, the transformation process should be dictated by the harvest strategy and not by any six-stage model designed to promote ongoing concerns. A prospective flight strategy designed to shield against the ravages of a prolonged price war would involve product differentiation and thus will mean changing the nature of the product.[18] This "move on" change will require at least as much awareness of and short-term reaction to the competitive environment as would a comparable fight strategy.[19]

An important strategic difference exists between a differentiation strategy and straight "fight" product-market strategy. A differentiation strategy will permit more downsizing than a fight strategy, as the excess capacity that exists solely as a threat to sustain cooperative outcomes will not be needed. The surpluses generated by the adoption of differentiating technology and subsequent restructuring will not be seized by consumers and thus accrue to shareholders and employees, the very stakeholders responsible for the decision. This seems to imply that restructuring would be more likely in differentiation than in pure one-dimensional (often cost-based) "fight" strategies. Empirical research would seem to be warranted here.

In a fight strategy, competition among producers with excess capacity in an undifferentiated marketplace is expected to lead to wholesale price cutting and transfer of surplus from shareholders and employees to consumers. Indeed, although traditional economic theory smiles upon competitive equilibrium as welfare-maximizing, the welfare surplus accrues entirely to the consumer in the long run, forced from the producers' grasp by the constant threat of entry. The structural characteristic of commoditization—increasingly homogeneous product competition—leads either to destructive price competition or to some sort of uneasy truce among low-cost producers keeping one another in check through threat of retaliation. It thus seems imperative that firms pursuing a fight strategy attempt to offer consumers more surplus than competitors through a value-creation strategy, such as by increasing quality and extracting only enough surplus from the customer via a price increase to cover the incremental cost of the quality improvement. Even though quality improvement may be as easily imitated as price cutting, the quality escalation may not be seen as a similar declaration of war.

Given highly competitive industry circumstances and the decay of knowledge barriers, the only way for incumbents to deter entry is to ensure that entrants will earn insufficient returns to justify necessary capital expenditure. This can be accomplished by limit pricing, which will also ensure that incumbent firms will not earn sufficient returns to pay for sunk capital expenditure, resulting in large-scale transfer from shareholders to consumers of any surplus created by lowering production costs.

How does a firm decide whether to adopt a new technology and develop a more efficient organizational structure? If product price is sufficiently high to cover variable costs of production, but low enough to deter entry, shareholders must not be deriving sufficient payment to justify their investment ex post, meaning that they are actually collecting negative surplus. The only way an incumbent firm can satisfy its capital stakeholders and simultaneously prevent entry is by continuous innovation. Incumbents choose levels of innovation that will allow them to capture enough rents to pay capital stakeholders, and yet produce a small enough share of rents available to potential entrants that entry is not justified.[20] Incumbents can thus persist indefinitely.

How might an incumbent defeat this seemingly inevitable decay of market position and wholesale transfer of surplus to consumers? By pairing differentiation with continuous adoption of technology, a firm can change its relationship with its rivals. When the firm differentiates itself and "locks the door" against direct imitation, it has entered a state of monopolistic competition.[21] Although the price path will decline as some of the surplus from technological advances is communicated to the consumer, the firm can appropriate a certain amount. Profitability may vary in the short run, as long as the firm's goal is to prevent entry. All that is necessary to preserve incumbency is to remove the incentive for entry, for which a profitability-based incentive should suffice. Such a "virtual barrier to entry" can be described as a combination of (1) defining the flavor of duopolistic competition and (2) readying a technological response to potential entrants, knowing that the only entrants that surface will quickly exit—a "locking" tactic.

What would the structure of this new entry barrier look like? To answer this question, we must look at the entry decision from the viewpoint of the potential entrant. An entrant will choose to challenge an incumbent in a static market if the potential challenger's share of the discounted duopoly profits expected when exactly two rivals compete exceeds the value of the investment that must be sunk in order to enter the market. In markets in which it is particularly expensive to compete (i.e., that require high market-specific investments to establish a competitive position or significant ongoing plowbacks to maintain an established position in the face of substitutes), entry will never occur. This creates an odd form of protection for the incumbent monopolist, which will continue to realize extraordinary profits without the slightest threat of entry. The difference between the monopoly profit and one competitor's share of the duopoly pie can be significant, allowing for profits above and beyond the plowback costs. In addition, it is possible that entry required the sinking of a large perpetual investment, whose capital costs were sufficient to dissuade entry but, given no entry, yields extraordinary revenues.

A virtual entry barrier must thus take the form of some combination of the following three market foreclosure techniques:

1. Large entry cost or continuous expenditure

2. Artificially low duopoly rents created by some structural market characteristic, such as a kinked demand curve or other sharp change in market elasticity past a certain critical quantity

3. Some form of credible incumbent threat that would make life miserable for a potential entrant (e.g., a threat to flood the market with large quantities of low-marginal-cost goods)

The first two are exogenous characteristics of production technology and demand structure, respectively. The third is under the control of the incumbent firm. By actively pursuing these market-foreclosure technologies, a firm can enter the state of grace that economists call monopolistic competition, as described earlier.

We submit that continuous adoption of customer-driven information technology fulfills this function in a positive way—by providing buyer value through continuous innovation. The price to play in most markets has fallen rapidly, but the price to keep playing remains high, as cutting-edge technology retains a substantial premium to year-old technology. An incumbent can, by sacrificing some of its own profits to an "irrational" technological choice, force potential rivals to adopt similar "bleeding-edge" technology in order to compete. In return, the incumbent receives consistently extraordinary margins in the product market.

The difference between product-market gains from a firm's unique position and the seemingly bizarre hemorrhage of profits into the "bottomless pit" of IT is the profit measure of interest. This measure must be compared to the alternative profits realized by foregoing continuous expenditure and thus tacitly allowing entry. If the product market is commodity-like, these alternative profits are likely to be very low due to cutthroat pricing. Thus, continuous innovation will likely be worthwhile, especially in highly commodity-like markets; the increased product profitability will more than compensate for the money thrown into the bottomless pit of continuous innovation.

In addition to putting the choice of method of competition in the incumbent's hands, information technology supports the creation of a credible threat of vigorous competition. The transactional and informational aspects of IT enable particularly efficient use of traditional productive assets by identifying and facilitating redeployment of slack resources. To the extent that the technology in place permits efficient use of existing productive capacity, the amount of excess capacity the incumbent must build to deter entry is minimized. Since less excess capacity must be built to deter a price war, the total carrying cost of unused capacity will be lower. This reduction in overhead cost improves the profitability of the continuous innovator by compressing the cost of the entire amount of excess capacity. By demonstrating that excess capacity can be used extremely efficiently in case of a price war, a firm can lower the required capacity needed to deter.

Incumbent first movers receive indirect benefit as well as direct benefit from the adoption of technology for cost compression purposes. Cost compression benefits the first mover more than entrants because a first mover by choice builds more capacity than potential entrants would build were they actually to enter.[22] This indirect benefit, denied to the first-mover's potential imitators, constitutes a powerful defensive technology. If entry occurs, of course, a portion of this strategically built excess capacity is suddenly employed, with the rest held in reserve to enforce at least a semi-profitable outcome rather than an all-out price war.

The critical lesson, then, is that technology that can change the mode of competition in an incumbent's market is technology the incumbent must adopt early to maintain the advantages of incumbency. Slow adoption of technologies that enable construction of virtual entry barriers almost guarantees the unhappy ending of entry, overcapacity, and vicious price competition. Because the same technology is also available to competitors, prompt adoption is thus vital to the survival of incumbents with entrants at their heels.

Notes

Chapter 1

1. Paul A. David, *Computer and Dynamo* (Stanford Center for Economic Policy Research, 1989).
2. The Hay Point system was developed by a consulting firm of the same name. The Hay Point system is a methodology for determining compensation based upon responsibility, which, in turn, is defined by both financial (budgets) and number and reporting relationship (number and type of employees reporting to a manager).
3. The planning factors generally categorized potential investments into types such as "essential," "cost-saving," or "revenue generation," and established hurdle rates for each type. The hurdle rates had to be met in respect to projected cash flows of the proposed investment in order to be approved.
4. The "northeastward march" is the phenomenon of opening an annual report and seeing on page 1 or 2 a striking bar graph of revenue, earnings-per-share, or other financial measure increasing steadily for a long series of years.
5. Richard L. Nolan, "Managing the Computer Resource: A Stage Hypothesis," *Communications of the ACM* 16, no.7 (July 1973): 99–104. See also Richard L. Nolan, "Managing the Crises in Data Processing." *Harvard Business Review* 57, no. 2 (March–April 1979): 115–126.
6. The term *informating* is from Shoshana Zuboff, *In the Age of the Smart Machine* (Basic Books, 1988). Automating focuses on using computers to replace people (labor-saving); informating focuses on using computers to enhance the activities of people in carrying out work (use of computer-aided design by an engineer in designing a new product).
7. See Stephen P. Bradley, Jerry A. Hausman, and Richard L. Nolan, eds., *Globalization, Technology, and Competition: The Fusion of Computers and Telecommunications in the 1990s* (Boston: Harvard Business School Press, 1993).
8. For a discussion of the problem of the lack of coherence in an organization's IT architecture see Stephen H. Haeckel and Richard L. Nolan, "Managing by Wire," *Harvard Business Review* 71, no. 5 (September–October 1993): 122–132.

9. See Gary Hamel and C. K. Prahalad, *Competing for the Future* (Boston: Harvard Business School Press, 1994). Hamel and Prahalad propose a new view of strategy oriented toward transforming a firm's industry from within. We concur with this approach to strategy (see Appendix) but focus on the tactics required of senior managers to successfully transform the firm from the generic form of the industrial economy to an equally successful form appropriate for the information economy using the types of strategies suggested by Hamel and Prahalad.

10. See Tom Peters, *The Tom Peters Seminar* (New York: Vintage Books, 1994). Peters advocates extremely radical change, and cites many examples of companies that have only successfully changed after implementing unconventional change approaches.

11. Joseph A. Schumpeter, *Die Theorie der wirtschaftlichen Entwicklung* (The Theory of Economic Development) (Cambridge: Harvard University Press, 1962).

12. Max Weber, *The Theory of Social and Economic Organization,* ed. T. Parsons, trans. A.M. Henderson and Talcott Parsons (New York: Oxford University Press, 1947).

13. Alfred D. Chandler, *Strategy and Structure* (Cambridge: MIT Press, 1962).

14. See Joseph L. Massie, "Management Theory," in *Handbook of Organizations,* ed. James G. March (Chicago: Rand McNally & Company, 1965), 401.

15. Peter F. Drucker, *The Practice of Management* (New York: Harper & Row, 1954). In the early 1930s two General Motors executives, James D. Mooney and Alan C. Reiley published *Onward Industry,* which reappeared in 1939 under the title *The Principles of Organization* (New York: Harper and Row, 1947). Also see Ernst Dale, "Contributions to Administration by Alfred P. Sloan, Jr., and General Motors," *Administrative Science Quarterly* 1 (June 1956): 30–62.

16. See William Travers Jerome III, *Executive Control: The Catalyst* (New York: John Wiley & Sons, 1961), ch. 13.

17. For a more complete treatment of the theory behind forming a complete and coherent set of management principles, see David C. Croson, "Towards a Set of Information-Economy Management Principles," manuscript, Cambridge, Mass., 1994.

18. See Frances J. Aguilar and R.G. Hamermesh, "General Electric: Strategic Positioning," (381–174) (Boston: Harvard Business School, 1991).

19. Walter Wriston, *Risk and Other Four-Letter Words* (New York: Harper & Row, 1986), 134–136.

20. For an in-depth look at the process of selecting a set of management principles to ensure both conceptual coherence and internal consistency, see David C. Croson, "Towards a Set of Information-Economy Management Principles," manuscript, Cambridge, Mass., 1994.

21. Compare, for example, the design principles in Gareth Morgan's *Images of Organization* (Beverly Hills: Sage Publications, 1986). See also Robert Boyer's

"New Directions in Management Practices and Work Organization: General Principles and National Trajectories," Working Paper 9130, Centre d'Etudes Prospectives D'Economie Mathematique Appliquees a la Planification (CEPREMAP), Paris, August 1991.

22. See Bruce McHenry, "Corporate Principles in the Information Age: A Survey and Analysis" (master's thesis, Massachusetts Institute of Technology, February, 1994). The survey experience with McHenry and Brynjolfsson was invaluable to our understanding of management principles and practice.

23. Joseph A. Schumpeter, *History of Economic Analysis* (New York: Oxford University Press, 1974). See also Schumpeter's *The Theory of Economic Development,* trans. Redvers Opie (Cambridge: Harvard University Press, 1934.); note that this book was originally published in 1911, about the same time as Frederick Winslow Taylor's *Principles of Scientific Management.*

24. Creative destruction differs from a traditional first-mover advantage in that first movers may find themselves overextended if they attempt too much at once. Although creative destruction guarantees that "slow followers" will suffer, it does not make any prediction about the relative success of leaders and fast followers in a constantly changing environment. See the Appendix for further detail.

25. John R. Hauser, "The House of Quality," *Harvard Business Review* 66, no. 3 (May–June 1988): 63–73 provides a conceptual map of coherence. See also Croson, "Towards a Set of Information-Economy Management Principles."

26. Although this stress is minimized, it is hardly minimal.

Chapter 2

1. "The New Enterprise" is the name of the initiative that Apple undertook to achieve business transformation.

2. Michael Hammer, "Reengineering Work: Don't Automate, Obliterate!" *Harvard Business Review* (July–August 1990): 104–112 and Michael Hammer and J. Champy, *Reengineering the Corporation* (New York: HarperBusiness, 1993).

3. Eric K. Clemons, "Managing the Risks of Large-Scale Systems Projects; or Why So Many Re-engineering Efforts Fail Unnecessarily," working paper, 94-03-09, Department of Operations and Information Management, Wharton School of Business, University of Pennsylvania, 1994.

4. A bug-ridden recent revision of a popular word-processing package, for example, sent thousands of previously loyal customers to less snazzy but more stable rivals.

5. Data from CIOs attending the Harvard Business School program "Managing the Information Systems Resource (MISR)" in 1991–1993.

6. Susan Webber, "On Wall Street, Masters of Innovation," *New York Times,* October 24, 1993, F-11.

7. For example, see William R. Synnott, *The Information Weapon: Winning Customers and Markets with Technology* (New York: Wiley, 1987) on the use of IT as an offensive weapon.

8. The shift to case leaders is explained in Thomas Davenport and Nitin Nohria, "Case Managers: The End of Division of Labor?" Harvard Business School Division of Research Working Paper 93-034, 1992. This process of reorientation is the subject of an area of research at the Harvard Business School called "Achieving Service Breakthroughs," key results of which are reported in James L. Heskett, W. Earl Sasser, Jr., and Christopher W. L. Hart, *Service Breakthroughs* (New York: The Free Press, 1990.)

9. Edward N. Luttwak, "With a Rare Opportunity, Ford Blew It," *New York Times,* October 24, 1993, F-11.

10. See, for example, Michael Porter's *Competitive Advantage* (New York: The Free Press, 1985); only 30 of 560 pages treat defensive strategies.

11. For a description of a robust IT-enabled network, see Hossam Galal, Donna Stoddard, Richard L. Nolan and John Kao, "VeriFone: The Transaction Automation Company." 195-088. Boston: Harvard Business School, 1994.

12. M. Scott Peck, in *The Road Less Traveled* (New York: Simon and Schuster, 1978) and Chris Argyris, in *Strategy, Change, and Defensive Routines* (Boston: Pitman, 1985) have explored this tendency, albeit in very different research styles.

13. The past five years' press releases of a number of other large companies (DEC, Sears, and IBM in particular) engaged in incremental downsizing vividly illustrates increasing confusion and the resulting challenges to top leadership.

14. Examples, including these, can be found in Thomas Davenport, *Process Innovation* (Boston: Harvard Business School Press, 1993.)

15. Benson P. Shapiro and John J. Sviokla, "Staple Yourself to an Order," *Harvard Business Review* (July–August 1992): 113–122.

16. These seven infrastructures stem from the framework developed in Robert G. Eccles and Richard L. Nolan, "A Framework for the Design of the Emerging Global Organization Structure," in *Globalization, Technology, and Competition: The Fusion of Computers and Telecommunications in the 1990s,* ed. Stephen P. Bradley, Jerry A. Hausman, and Richard L. Nolan (Boston: Harvard Business School Press, 1993.)

Chapter 3

1. See the survey in Erik Brynjolfsson, "The Productivity of Information Technology: Review and Assessment," MIT Center for Coordination Science Technical Report 130, 1991.

2. This observation draws upon Paul A. David, "Computer and Dynamo: The Modern Productivity Paradox in a Not-Too-Distant Mirror," in *Technology and Productivity: The Challenge for Economic Policy* (Paris: OECD, 1991) and Richard L. Nolan, "Managing the Computer Resource: A Stage Hypothesis," *Communications of the ACM* 16, no. 7 (July 1973): 99–104, describing experiential learning in organizations.

3. For an expanded taxonomy of strategic appearances, see Drew Fudenberg and Jean Tirole, "The Fat Cat Effect, the Puppy Dog Ploy, and the Lean-and-Hungry Look," *American Economic Review* 74 (May 1984): 361–366.

4. Nolan, Norton & Co. benchmarks indicate new levels of revenue per employee ranged from $100,000 to more than twice that amount. Richard L. Nolan, then Chairman of Nolan, Norton, and Co., presented this data at the 1980 Nolan, Norton Annual Research Symposium in Innsbrook, Florida, as described in the Proceedings, February 1980. Also see Robert G. Eccles and Richard L. Nolan, "A Framework for the Design of the Emerging Global Organization Structure," in *Globalization, Technology, and Competition: The Fusion of Computers and Telecommunications in the 1990s*, ed. Stephen P. Bradley, Jerry A. Hausman, and Richard L. Nolan (Boston: Harvard Business School Press, 1993.)

5. Richard L. Nolan, Alex J. Pollock, and James P. Ware, "Toward the Design of Network Organizations," *Stage by Stage* 9, no. 1 (1989) and "Creating the 21st Century Organization," *Stage by Stage* 8, no. 4 (1988).

6. See the Appendix for an expansion of this argument illustrated by simulation.

7. Harold J. Leavitt and Thomas L. Whisler, "Management in the 1980s," *Harvard Business Review* 36, no. 6 (November 1958): 41–48.

8. For perspective, this is essentially the same as the total number of manufacturing jobs in 1994's economy.

9. Smart cards are both technological and economic reality. See, for example, the article "AT&T Unveils Card for ATMs that Has Wider Range of Uses," *The Wall Street Journal*, December 8, 1992, A6.

10. For a history of IT implementation in the banking industry, see James L. McKenney, *Waves of Change* (Boston: Harvard Business School Press, 1995.)

11. See Theodore H. Clark, *Linking the Grocery Channel: Technology Innovation, Organizational Transformation, and Channel Performance* (Ph.D. dissertation, Harvard Business School, 1994).

12. This Nolan, Norton & Co. research study sponsored by Lotus Development is available through Lotus Corporation, Boston, Mass.

13. See the Appendix for more detail on this substitution process.

14. See Robert Hughes and William Strecker, "Digital Equipment Corporation: Case Study of the Emergent Network Organization, *Stage by Stage* 8, no. 4 (1988): 12–18.

15. "Digital Equipment to Slash 14,000 Jobs in Core Computer Lines by Restructuring," *The Wall Street Journal,* by William M. Bulkeley, July 19, 1994, B3.
16. Ibid.
17. Alfred Chandler, *Scale and Scope: The Dynamics of Industrial Capitalism* (Cambridge, Mass.: Belknap/Harvard, 1990).
18. Richard E. Caves and Matthew Krepps, "Fat," working paper, Harvard University Department of Economics, 1993. Forthcoming in *Brookings Papers on Economic Activity.*
19. Erik Brynjolfsson examines four hypotheses of why such poor showings occur in "The Productivity of Information Technology: Review and Assessment," MIT Center for Coordination Science Technical Report #130, December 1991.
20. Long-term shareholders might theoretically have forever to capture the benefits, but a high cost of equity means that earlier is much better from a value-creation standpoint.
21. See, for example, Weber's Theory of Bureaucracy, as excerpted in *Max Weber on Capitalism, Bureaucracy, and Religion: A Selection of Texts,* ed. Stanislav Andraski, (Boston: Allen & Unwin, 1983) and Chester Barnard's *Functions of the Executive* (Cambridge: Harvard University Press, 1968). For economic examples, see Oliver Williamson, "Hierarchical Control and Optimal Firm Size," *Journal of Political Economy* 75 (April 1967): 123–138 and Guillermo A. Calvo and Stanislaw Wellisz, "Supervision, Loss of Control, and Optimum Size of the Firm," *Journal of Political Economy* 86, no. 5 (1978): 943–952.
22. See, for example, William Meckling and Michael Jensen. "Knowledge, Control and Organization Structure; Parts I and II," in *Contract Economics,* ed. Lars Werin and Hans Hijkander (Cambridge, Mass: Basil Blackwell, 1992), 251–274.
23. This dynamic crisis-control thesis appears in a slightly different context in Ramchandran Jaikumar, "A Dynamic Approach to Operations Management: An Alternative to Static Maximization," *International Journal of Production Economics* 27, no. 3 (October 1992): 265–282.
24. If agency problems can be circumvented through continuous contracting, perhaps dynamic self-appraisal may turn out to be the best possible performance-measurement tool. See George Baker, Kevin Murphy, and Robert Gibbon, "Subjective Performance Measures," working paper, Harvard Business School, 1993.
25. See, for example, Robin Cooper and Robert Kaplan, "Profit Priorities from Activity Based Costing," *Harvard Business Review* 69, no. 3 (May–June 1991): 130–135.
26. As reported in "High-Performance Workplace Attracts Investor," *Maine Sunday Telegram,* July 10, 1994, p. 61.
27. Ibid.
28. A number of popular books have expanded on this management-in-chaos notion. See, for example, Tom Peters, *The Tom Peters Seminar: Crazy Times*

Call for Crazy Organizations (New York: Vintage Books/Random House, 1994); Tom Peters, *Thriving on Chaos* (New York: Knopf/Random House, 1987); and James Gleick, *Chaos: Making a New Science* (New York: Viking, 1987).

Chapter 4

1. See, for example, Richard Cyert and James March, *A Behavioral Theory of the Firm,* 2d ed. (Cambridge, Mass.: Blackwell Business, 1992).
2. Agents signing long-term contracts give up the potential for opportunism in the middle for some signing bonus and security at the beginning. With short-term contracts, however, contracting agents can take advantage of their bargaining position to appropriate some of the surplus from a favorable chance outcome even if they had nothing to do with causing its occurrence.
3. See, for example, Keith J. Crocker and Scott E. Masten, "Mitigating Contractual Hazards: Unilateral Options and Contract Length," working paper 449, Graduate School of Business Administration, University of Michigan, 1987.
4. Paul R. Milgrom and John Roberts' work *Economics, Organization, and Management* (New York: Prentice-Hall, 1992) addresses these and other theoretically motivated organizational-design issues at an accessible level. Ramchandran Jaikumar and David Upton, in "The Coordination of Global Manufacturing," in *Globalization, Technology, and Competition: The Fusion of Computers and TeleCommunications in the 1990s,* ed. Stephen P. Bradley, Jerry A. Hausman, and Richard L. Nolan (Boston: Harvard Business School Press, 1993) examine these issues in the context of textile manufacturing.
5. For some contracts, this method of commitment may be impractical. For example, investment banks often have difficulty obtaining adequate commitments from their couriers—who sometimes need to carry $100 million or more in bearer bonds—that they will not suddenly disappear with the funds. In this case, no commitment on the courier's part could be believable by the bank; investment banks accordingly employ and exercise strong controls over their couriers rather than contract delivery to the lowest-cost bicycle messenger service.
6. For more on the interaction between communications costs and the maintenance of reputation, see David C. Croson, "A New Role for Middlemen: Centralizing Reputation in Repeated Exchange," working paper, Cambridge, Mass., 1994.
7. In *Markets and Hierarchies* (New York: Free Press, 1975), Oliver Williamson calls this condition *information impactedness.* David Kreps' "Corporate Culture and Economic Theory" (in *Perspectives on Positive Political Economy,* ed. James E. Alt and Kenneth Shepsle [Cambridge: Cambridge University Press, 1990]) addresses this issue as well.

8. When we speak of distribution of surplus to shareholders, we mean direct distribution to shareholders (whether as dividends or merely accumulated book value) rather than indirect distribution through optimal deployment of assets and growth of earnings, the long-term capital gains that comprise the majority of gains from stock holdings. Accumulated even without a dividend policy, these gains represent the long-term earning power of the firm's assets. As a claim on future earnings, this valuable economic asset is not allocated to the pool of negotiable surplus, but accrues to the shareholders as part of the residual claim on equity as it "drops to the bottom line" and accumulates as book value on the balance sheet. Of course, employees, suppliers, and customers may also be shareholders as well; in fact, equity ownership by such constituents should improve the efficiency of cooperative arrangements.

9. If everything were perfectly certain in the sense that all possible outcomes were known and describable (which is still a long way from being predictable in the usual sense), a very long contract detailing exactly what would happen in which case would be sufficient to eliminate the core barriers to long-term cooperation. However, these "complete contingent contracts" are recognized not to exist except in certain limited areas in which the nature of uncertainty is clearly known, standardized option contracts covering stocks and commodities being an example. In most cases, to write a complete contingent contract would take more time and effort than the contract was worth.

10. The hierarchy's strength is also its weakness. Renegotiation is complex, generating problems with dealing with a veritable deluge of potentially critical information, whereas agreeing on policies which are negotiation-proof is often necessary to avoid opportunistic behavior by suppliers, employees, and customers.

11. Indeed, opportunism in long-term repeated settings may even act to improve the payoffs from cooperative outcomes, as making side deals to circumvent wholesale cooperation acts as a spur toward surplus creation by everyone working together.

12. This wealth is composed not only of direct dividend payments, but also of capital gains from the market's valuation of the discounted earnings potential of the enterprise.

13. Surplus, not revenues or cash flows, ought to be divided according to the distribution of power. Toyota's management and labor leaders seem to understand this, whereas General Motors' seem in the past to have focused on distributing gross benefits, some of which must be used to pay for previous investments rather than distributed as excess. Any real struggle for power can be played out as a virtual struggle for much less cost.

14. This point about the need for continuous real-time audits versus traditional post mortem audits should not go unnoticed by public auditing firms. We

expect that in the near future, in order to remain viable, public auditing firms will implement IT-enabled audits for their clients.

15. William H. Meckling and Michael C. Jensen, "Knowledge, Control and Organization Structure; Parts I and II," in *Contract Economics*, ed. Lars Werin, Hans Hijkander (Cambridge, Mass.: Basil Blackwell, 1992) 251–274. See also Stephen H. Haeckel and Richard L. Nolan, "Managing by Wire," *Harvard Business Review* 71, no. 5 (September–October 1993): 122–132 for ways that IT architectures are increasingly capturing and deploying knowledge in organizations.

16. This indirect invocation of Blackwell's theorem reinforces the importance of early work by managerial decision theorists.

17. We term this coercive monitoring to distinguish it from monitoring for self-improvement (professional athletes viewing videotapes of their performance, for example, even when accompanied by coaches' criticism).

18. For an accessible analysis of the responsibilities of managers in negotiations, see David A. Lax and James K. Sebenius, *The Manager as Negotiator: Bargaining for Cooperation and Competitive Gain* (New York: Free Press, 1986.)

19. The arguments from Sanford J. Grossman and Oliver D. Hart, "The Costs and Benefits of Ownership: A Theory of Lateral and Vertical Integration," *Journal of Political Economy* 94 (August 1986): 691–719, and Michael C. Jensen and William H. Meckling, "Theory of the Firm: Managerial Behavior, Agency Costs, and Capital Structure," *Journal of Financial Economics* 3, no. 1 (1976): 305–360, are neatly summarized in Paul R. Milgrom and John Roberts' *Economics, Organization, and Management* (New York: Prentice-Hall, 1992).

20. This road map, called a Hamiltonian path, is the general mathematical solution to such an intertemporal division problem. (For mathematical readers: this is the optimal-control Hamiltonian path, not the traveling-salesman Hamiltonian path.) See, for example, Avinash K. Dixit, *Optimization in Economic Theory* (Oxford: Oxford University Press, 1976.)

21. To keep the analysis simple, we have assumed the price path to be determined not by managerial decision, but by competition, and the actions of managers to not affect the prices of resources in the rest of the economy. Both of these assumptions are easy enough to relax, but would only obscure our point: either side of the line is worse.

22. A firm that paid out 100 percent of its net revenues as dividends would quickly fold, so shareholders cannot collect everything "up front."

23. Management knows that these contracts are not optimal, but is constrained by the contracting technology from doing better—foiled by barriers to action, not of comprehension.

24. "Free cash flow" in this sense is the difference between revenues and associated cash expenditures, rather than the implicit returns to capital. We argue that

some of this free cash flow, although it "belongs" to shareholders according to industrial-economy principles, should instead be distributed to other stake-holders in the short run.

25. Whether this excess capacity exacerbated or ameliorated the competitiveness of the industry is an open question.

26. This example is based on Karen Wruck, "Safeway, Inc.'s Leveraged Buyout (A)" (294–139) (Boston: Harvard Business School, 1994) and joint teaching thereof with Steve-Anna Stephens in the 1991 and 1992 Harvard Business School Executive Education courses "Information, Organization, and Control," and "Managing Business Transformation."

27. Chester I. Barnard, *The Functions of the Executive* (1938; reprint, Cambridge: Harvard University Press, 1968), 215.

28. Ibid., p. 217.

29. Ibid., p. 220.

39. For a description of this conflict, see Lester Thurow, *The Zero-Sum Society*. (Cambridge: MIT Press, 1980).

Chapter 5

1. Here again we broadly refer to "production processes" as including factory management practices of both manufacturing and service firms. As we pointed out earlier, service firms in the industrial economy employed mass production and mass distribution techniques to produce their services (e.g., insurance) in "back office" factories.

2. Thanks to Professor John King of the University of California, Irvine for this observation (private conversation with the authors, July 1992).

3. For example, U.S. consumers demonstrated that they were willing to pay more for cars with the nameplate "Toyota" rather than the nameplate "Chevrolet" even though these cars came off the same production line.

4. Not all U.S. firms required trade sanctions to regain competitiveness. Xerox, for example, is understandably proud that it has never stooped to this measure.

5. Strictly speaking, this equivalence requires that the process handle only one item at a time; otherwise, the relationship between cycle time and throughput depends upon process capacity.

6. For a more detailed discussion of direct and indirect effects of technical change, see N. Rosenberg, *Inside the Black Box* (Cambridge: Cambridge University Press, 1982).

7. Now we are examining the objective of minimizing time, not necessarily minimizing cost in the tradition of Michael C. Jensen and William H. Meckling, "Theory of the Firm: Managerial Behavior, Agency Costs, and Capital Structure," *Journal of Financial Economics* 3, no. 1 (1976): 305–360.

8. Viewing cross-functional communication as a byproduct (rather than as a coproduct) leads to less communication than optimal, but its status as a "free" byproduct has historically kept such shadow networking more or less invisible and thus immune to hierarchical opposition.

9. See, for example, Jeanne M. Pickering and John L. King, "Hardwiring Weak Ties: Individual and Institutional Issues in Computer-mediated Communication," working paper, CSCW, 1992. The term "weak ties" is attributed to Mark S. Granovetter's "The Strength of Weak Ties," *American Journal of Sociology* 78, no. 6 (1973): 1360–1380. See also David C. Croson, "A New Role for Middlemen: Centralizing Reputation in Repeated Exchange," working paper, Cambridge, Mass., 1993.

10. The term *intrapreneur,* describing an "internal entrepreneur" who aggressively organizes resources to take advantage of opportunities, was coined by Gifford Pinchot III in *Intrapreneuring* (New York: Harper & Row, 1985.)

11. This is the framework presented in William Meckling and Michael Jensen, "Knowledge, Control and Organization Structure; Parts I and II," in *Contract Economics,* ed. Lars Werin and Hans Hijkander (Cambridge, Mass.: Basil Blackwell, 1992), 251–274.

12. The Harvard Business School case "Blue Cross/Blue Shield of Massachusetts" (Leslie R. Porter and Janis L. Gogan, 9-184-018, 1984) shows that the direct monitoring approach is still being used and perfected in modern companies even though it has been made totally superfluous by information systems.

13. Alfred D. Chandler, Jr., *The Visible Hand: The Managerial Revolution in American Business* (Cambridge: Belknap/Harvard University Press, 1977).

14. See Robert L. Simon and Hilary A. Weston, "Nordstrom: Dissension in the Ranks?" (A) (9-191-002) and (B) (9-192-027) (Boston: Harvard Business School, 1991 and 1992).

Chapter 6

1. Nolan, Norton & Company benchmark studies.

2. Far too many customer-orientation benchmarks use flawed logic similar to the flawed logic of the inebriated man looking for his keys under the streetlight. When asked why he was looking there, his response was "because the light is good." It is important not to give up on true customer satisfaction due to measurement difficulties.

3. Disintermediation certainly does not necessarily follow from lower information transmission costs; see David C. Croson, "A New Role for Middlemen: Centralizing Reputation in Repeated Exchange," working paper, Cambridge, Mass., 1994.

4. This issue of appropriately compensating a function for data collected and used by another function was researched, and reported on by Richard L. Nolan in "Controlling the Cost of Data Services," *Harvard Business Review* 55, no. 4 (July–August 1977).

5. See, for example, Thomas Davenport, Robert G. Eccles, and Laurence Prusac, "Information Politics," *Sloan Management Review* (fall 1992): 53–65.

6. One would hope that providing firms would make a policy of self-regulating their access to customer information; by quelling their instinct to monitor activities at too detailed a level, they might avoid triggering an aggressive privacy-protection response.

7. Paul R. Milgrom and John Roberts, *Economics, Organization, and Management* (New York: Prentice-Hall, 1991), 4.

8. "Lean production" is a term coined in James P. Womack, David T. Jones, and Daniel Roos, *The Machine That Changed the World* (New York: Rawson MacMillan, 1990).

9. Kenneth Arrow, *The Limits of Organization,* Fels Lectures on Public Policy Analysis Series (New York: Norton, 1974).

10. A truly fascinating analysis of the psychological effects of the tournament-type promotion system can be found in Harry Levinson's *Executive* (Cambridge: Harvard University Press, 1981).

11. The term "rainmaker" is used as jargon in investment banks and management consulting firms to refer to professionals who are uniquely able to drum up business or influence favorable outcomes in client organizations.

Chapter 7

1. For other analogies, see Gareth Morgan, *Images of Organization* (Beverly Hills: Sage Publications, 1986). For organization as an information processor, see John R. Galbraith, "Organization Design: An Information Processing View," *Interfaces* 4, no. 3 (1974): 28–36.

2. Thanks to Harvard Business School doctoral candidate Christopher Marshall for conversations on tuning this framework.

3. This observation stems from Nimzowitsch, *The Blockade* (Berlin: Schachverlag B. Kagan) excerpted in Aron Nimzowitsch, *My System* (New York: Harcourt, Brace and Co., 1930). See also David C. Croson and Robert H. Mnookin, "Sapping the Stonewall: Using Compound Threats to Bolster the Effectiveness of Plaintiff's Threats to Sue," working paper, Harvard Program on Negotiation, Boston, 1994.

4. See, for example, Richard E. Caves and Matthew Krepps, "Fat," working paper, Harvard University Department of Economics, 1993. Forthcoming in *Brookings Papers on Economic Activity*.

5. See, for example, James P. Womack, David T. Jones, and Daniel Roos, *The Machine That Changed the World* (New York: Rawson MacMillan, 1990).

6. These and other Xerox facts are from the book by Gary Jacobson and John Hillkirk, *Xerox: American Samurai* (New York: MacMillan, 1986).

7. Jacobson and Hillkirk make this point, as does Thomas Davenport in *Process Innovation: Reengineering Work through Information Technology* (Boston: Harvard Business School Press, 1993).

8. These five types of competition are identified and discussed in Michael E. Porter, *Competitive Strategy* (New York: Free Press, 1980).

9. In keeping with our previous analogy, BPR "cracks the shell" to create a way out for the emerging network organization.

10. For an excellent discussion of strategic outsourcing see James Brian Quinn and Frederick G. Hilmer, "Strategic Outsourcing," *Sloan Management Review* (Summer 1994): 43–55.

11. See Robert Simon's cases "Asea Brown Boveri" (192-139), "ABB: Accountability Times Two (A)" (192-141), and "ABB: Accountability Times Two (B)" (192-142) (Boston: Harvard Business School, 1992).

12. There has been great progress made recently in extending simulation and operations research techniques to create enterprise models which can be directly used to execute decisions. See Stephen H. Haeckel and Richard L. Nolan, "Managing by Wire," *Harvard Business Review* 71, no. 5 (September–October 1993): 122–133.

13. The theory of incompatibility stems from Oliver E. Williamson, *Markets and Hierarchies* (New York: Free Press, 1975).

14. Although sure to cause theoretical controversy, this assertion is a simple "revealed preference" result if agency problems in the use of these real options can be solved.

15. Robert Kaplan and David P. Norton, "The Balanced Scorecard—Measures that Drive Performance," *Harvard Business Review* 70, no. 1 (January–February 1992): 71–79 provides a broad conceptual address to this monitoring problem in practice.

Chapter 8

1. This is an application of the asset-ownership framework described in Sanford A. Grossman and Oliver D. Hart, "The Costs and Benefits of Ownership: A Theory of Lateral and Vertical Integration," *Journal of Political Economy* 94 (August 1986): 691–719.

2. Both of these examples incorporate "take or pay" provisions, a desirable check on abuse. See Ramchandran Jaikumar and David M. Upton, "The Coordination of Global Manufacturing," and Janice H. Hammond, "Quick

Response in Retail/Manufacturing Channels," chapters 7 and 8 respectively in *Globalization, Technology, and Competition: The Fusion of Computers and Telecommunications in the 1990s,* ed. Stephen P. Bradley, Jerry A. Hausman, and Richard L. Nolan (Boston: Harvard Business School Press, 1993).

3. Economies of scale and scope interact in practice. Whether the advantage in producing copper along with gold (scope) outweighs the disadvantages of relatively small scale in producing copper in general depends crucially on the cost structure of the various technologies. Thus, we might expect scope to fluctuate back and forth as new technologies are introduced. This is exactly what we should observe as firms change their diversification strategies with changes in technology.

4. See, for example, Richard E. Caves, *Multinational Enterprise and Economic Analysis* (Cambridge: Cambridge University Press, 1982).

5. Christopher A. Bartlett and Sumatra Ghoshal, *Managing Across Borders: The Transnational Solution* (Boston: Harvard Business School Press, 1989).

6. In this respect, the organization behaves like a nation, attempting to maximize competition to drive prices down as much as possible. The national assets are most productive, and the nation the strongest, when such competition is allowed and encouraged. As a result of internal competition, allocation of the network's resources proceeds more efficiently; all available resources are mobilized to maximize the ability of the global organization to accomplish tasks.

7. We are constrained by the lack of a new vocabulary for management. This "effectively signing contracts" terminology is awkward, but it is difficult to suggest an alternative formulation. But the idea of retaining reputation-based agents is hardly new; see, for example, Avner Greif, "Reputation and Coalitions in Medieval Trade: Evidence on the Maghribi Traders," *Journal of Economic History* 69 (1989): 867–882 and Paul R. Milgrom, Douglas C. North, and Barry R. Weingast, "The Role of Institutions in the Revival of Trade: The Law Merchant, Private Judges, and the Champagne Fairs," *Economics and Politics* 2 (1990): 1–23.

8. A curious symbiosis in adoption prevails; since consumers do get the surplus, they are certain to adopt the new technology, in turn ensuring that the communication providers do achieve sufficient volume.

9. We are incapable of distinguishing between gross fuzziness and fuzziness after improvements have been made in clarification technology. Boundaries may indeed have become fuzzier, but not as fast as our eyes have become sharper, resulting in a net gain in boundary clarity. Conversely, the boundaries may have fuzzed much faster than we have had our management control glasses updated—our prescription may still say "accounting-based control" when we need "incentive-based control." When we scrutinize boundaries, we observe that they are indeed more fuzzy on an absolute scale, but not nearly as fuzzy

as they appear when we use old-fashioned examination tools. This two-way increase in parallel fuzziness reinforces the need for systems to examine the relative merits of internal and external contracting.

10. Like financial options, these real options carry option lives and strike prices.

11. Bartlett and Ghoshal credit Thomas J. Peters and Robert H. Waterman, *In Search of Excellence* (New York: Harper & Row, 1982) with the original discussion describing the "simultaneous loose-tight coupling" as the organization of contractual relations between firms.

12. In the contracting example, only one party has such an interest in full collaboration, not the party who controls the weak ties.

13. Sanford A. Grossman and Oliver D. Hart, "The Costs and Benefits of Ownership: A Theory of Lateral and Vertical Integration," *Journal of Political Economy* 94 (August 1986): 691–719.

14. This employment relationship usually prohibits hazardous or degrading activity. Of course, these activities can still be contracted on for a premium, as any nuclear power plant worker could attest.

15. See Pierre Hessler, "Being Global and the Global Opportunity," in *Globalization, Technology, and Competition: The Fusion of Computers and Telecommunication in the 1990s*, ed. Stephen P. Bradley, Jerry A. Hausman, and Richard L. Nolan (Boston: Harvard Business School Press, 1993): 243–255.

16. Although the study itself is confidential, the key issues to becoming global used in the study are described in John L. Daniels and N. Caroline Frost, "On Becoming a Global Corporation," *Stage by Stage* 8, no. 5 (1990): 1–14.

17. Howard V. Perlmutter, "The Tortuous Evolution of the Multinational Corporation," *Columbia Journal of World Business*, January 1969. See also Howard V. Perlmutter and David A. Heenan, "Cooperate to Compete Globally," *Harvard Business Review* 86, no. 2 (March–April 1986).

Chapter 9

1. Our framework is based on Robert G. Eccles and Richard L. Nolan, "A Framework for the Design of the Emerging Global Organization Structure," in *Globalization, Technology, and Competition: The Fusion of Computers and Telecommunications in the 1990s*, ed. Stephen P. Bradley, Jerry A. Hausman, and Richard L. Nolan (Boston: Harvard Business School Press, 1993).

2. The seven infrastructures were originally described in Eccles and Nolan, "A Framework."

3. "Core competencies," while rapidly becoming a standard term, first received attention in C. K. Prahalad and Gary Hamel, "The Core Competence of the Corporation," *Harvard Business Review* (May–June 1990): 79–91.

4. See, for example, Harry Lasker's "Continuous Learning Systems," *Stage by Stage* 10, no. 2 (1990): 19–22.

5. See, for example, Robert G. Eccles and Dwight B. Crane, "Managing through Networks in Investment Banking," *California Management Review* 30, no. 1 (fall 1987): 176–195. See also Robert G. Eccles and Dwight B. Crane, *Doing Deals: Investment Banks at Work* (Boston: Harvard Business School Press, 1988).

6. See, for example, Robert Axelrod's *The Evolution of Cooperation* (New York: Basic Books, 1984).

7. See, for example, Joseph Bower, *Managing the Resource Allocation Process* (Boston: Harvard Business School Press, 1986).

8. See, for example, Michael C. Jensen and William H. Meckling, "Specific and General Knowledge, and Organizational Structure," *Nobel Symposium No. 77* (Stockholm: August 1990).

9. For a description of an approach using leading indicator measurements for transformation, see Robert S. Kaplan and David P. Norton, "Putting the Balanced Scorecard to Work," *Harvard Business Review* 71, no. 5 (September–October 1993): 134–142.

Appendix A

1. Oliver E. Williamson, "Hierarchical Control and Optimal Firm Size," *Journal of Political Economy* 75 (April 1967): 123–138. See also Oliver E. Williamson, and Sidney G. Winter, *The Nature of the Firm: Origins, Evolution, and Development* (New York: Oxford University Press, 1991) for classic articles along with some new analysis.

2. See, for example, Robert G. Chambers, *Applied Production Analysis: A Dual Approach* (Cambridge: Cambridge University Press, 1988).

3. This is not to say that real firms will experience evolution, however. Policy preferences may discourage supervisors from dismissing subordinates even when obviated by technology. Unfortunately, the link between efficiency and incentive compatibility is too complex to address here.

4. Ironically, traditional performance measures which measure absolute or relative amounts of slack would indicate that downsized hierarchies may be less efficient, as demands on supervisors decreased faster than do their numbers.

5. In the spirit of intrapreneuring, it is natural that a level 3 intrapreneur might see a profitable opportunity to "cut out" level 2, make a side deal with level 1 employees (creating an intrapreneurial team), pay level 2 some amount to leave without a surplus-destroying fight, and split the generated cost savings with shareholders.

6. In this following graphical walk-through of the major phases of the simulation, hierarchical models are presented as triangles rather than stacks of squares for ease of exposition. This is not an assumption of continuity; the actual simulation addressed the problems generated by indivisibility and discrete change.

7. When future technology development cannot be reliably predicted, management will either forecast less progress than will actually occur—in which case barriers to action that seem important today will be alleviated—or forecast more progress than will be made—in which case barriers to comprehension will predominate, owing to the inability to formulate an optimal plan for the use of future technology.

8. For a more formal treatment, see Carliss Y. Baldwin and Kim B. Clark, "Modularity and Real Options," working paper, Division of Research, Graduate School of Business Administration, Harvard University, 1992.

9. In particular, Michael E. Porter, "The Contributions of Industrial Organization to Strategic Management," *Academy of Management Review* 6, no. 4 (October 1981): 609–620, as well as the better-known *Competitive Strategy* (New York: The Free Press, 1980) and *Competitive Advantage* (New York: The Free Press, 1985).

10. This is essentially the argument of Michael Keren and David Levhari, "The Internal Organization of the Firm and the Shape of Average Costs," *Bell Journal of Economics* 14 (autumn 1983): 474–486.

11. Technological advances that cannot be exploited without anticipatory investments in flexibility may generate regret, but they do not often generate organizational learning.

12. Carliss Y. Baldwin and Kim B. Clark, "Modularity and Real Options," working paper, Division of Research, Graduate School of Business Administration, Harvard University, 1992, explicitly considers option values in this context.

13. John Child's "Information Technology, Organization, and the Response to Strategic Challenges," *California Management Review* 30, no. 1 (fall 1987): 1–15 discusses such improved contract monitoring through IT. This parallels the problem of relationship-specific investment or asset specificity but the assets in question are difficult to quantify: reputation among customers, for example, or accumulated goodwill from brand definition stressing consistent performance.

14. Jacob A. Marshak and Roy Radner, *The Economic Theory of Teams* (New Haven: Yale University Press, 1972), among others.

15. In *The Economic Institutions of Capitalism* (New York: The Free Press, 1985) Oliver Williamson suggests that this redistribution problem can and should be considered separately from the surplus-creation problem. Whether management actually does voluntarily share the created surplus with the workers—who have, after all, performed an integral part in its creation and thus "deserve"

the surplus just as much as the managers do, if "deserving" matters—is important in the long run but not in the short run.

16. Technically, we are claiming that whether restructurings are strategic substitutes or complements is, in practice, irrelevant to real-world managers' decision making. "Conjectural variation" does not enter.

17. Armen Alchain and Harold Demsetz, "Production, Information Costs, and Economic Organization," *American Economic Review* 62, 2 (1972): 777–795.

18. Product differentiation under duress to escape competition can be considered flight, as differences in consumer tastes will separate the new market subspace occupied by the fleeing firm from the original site of competition just as surely as geographic distance for a cement manufacturer. See Kenneth Judd, "Credible Spatial Preemption," *Rand Journal of Economics* 16 (Summer 1985): 153–166.

19. Philip Morris or RJR/Nabisco and the changing composition of the tobacco/food balance in their business portfolios would be a good example here. See also Gordon Donaldson's "Voluntary Restructuring: The Case of General Mills," *Journal of Financial Economics* 27, no. 1 (September 1990): 117–141, as a "move on" strategy for continued growth.

20. This is a sort of limit pricing argument, but relies on speed of innovation rather than price as the incumbents' decision variable. Presumably, innovation is a strategic substitute ex ante entry and a strategic substitute ex post entry.

21. This differentiation exerts a positive externality on rivals, as these rivals are in effect passively differentiating themselves by not changing their strategy. The lessening of rivalry creates a positive spillover, however; large enough spillovers may induce a game of "Chicken," wherein firms try to get their rivals to incur the costs while everyone shares the benefits.

22. Specifically, this cost compression benefits the potential entrant only on the difference between the capacity necessary to enforce joint-monopoly and joint-competitive capacity, whereas the incumbent benefits from the monopoly capacity to the joint-competitive capacity. Since the joint-monopoly capacity is presumably lower than the monopoly capacity, the incumbent gains the compression benefit over more capacity and would thus be willing to pay a larger fixed fee to acquire such cost-compression ability. This conduct-based first-mover advantage may be the unstated theoretical foundation behind Richard Foster's thesis in *Innovation: The Attacker's Advantage* (New York: Summit Books, 1986).

Index

About the Authors

Richard L. Nolan, the Class of 1942 Professor of Business Administration at the Harvard Business School, teaches MBA courses on information strategy and management. Prior to returning to the Harvard Business School faculty in 1991, he served 14 years as chairman of Nolan, Norton & Co., a company that he co-founded in 1977 with David P. Norton. Nolan, Norton & Co. specializes in information technology management consulting and was merged into KPMG Peat Marwick in 1987. Nolan has published widely in the information technology and general management press, including the *Harvard Business Review* and *Sloan Management Review.* His most recent books are *Globalization, Technology and Competition,* with Stephen P. Bradley and Jerry A. Hausman, and *Building the Information-Age Organization,* with James Cash, Robert Eccles, and Nitin Nohria.

David C. Croson is a lecturer in operations and information management at the University of Pennsylvania's Wharton School of Business and a Ph.D. candidate in business economics at Harvard University. He conducts research in the areas of information technology's effects on corporate strategy and internal organization, the reputational role of intermediaries in the evolution of interorganizational alliances, and the strategic role of voluntary commitment in tort law.